BLUE MOON TURNED GOLD

The Rebirth of Manchester City

Graham Gordon

ISBN: 1500882178
ISBN 13: 9781500882174

TABLE OF CONTENTS

1

'BLUE MOON'-
THE STORY OF CITY TOLD
IN ONE SONG

Margo Timmins and the Birth of an Anthem

Margo Timmins had a beautiful voice, deep-set blue eyes, an incredible mane of hair and a brother who pestered her into becoming the lead singer of his band. After the Cowboy Junkies' first album bombed, she was ready to resume her career as a social worker rather than suffer the stage fright which troubled her in concert. Persuaded to give it one more go, the twenty-six -year-old Canadian chanteuse stood before the mic in Toronto's Church of the Holy Trinity, famed for its fantastic acoustics. The date was November 21 1987 and she prepared to sing a completely new version of Rodgers and Hart's classic 1934 ballad, ' Blue Moon'. She retained its famous first verse whose four lines are known off by heart by every Manchester City fan in the land. But Margo Timmins had no way of knowing she was about to match a great song with a great football club.

The first time Manchester City fans sang 'Blue Moon' was on August 19, 1989 at Anfield. Obliged by the Liverpool FC stewards to wait behind in the away supporters section, they were downcast after the defeat of newly promoted City. It was not that City had been humbled. The score was 3-1 and, after all, Liverpool were the reigning champions, playing on their own ground. But it was yet another in the seemingly endless series of reverses that had afflicted City throughout the Eighties. Long gone were the glory days, the League Cup win in 1976 being the last time the club had won a trophy.

As they belatedly filed out on to Walton Breck Road, a handful of City fans struck up 'Blue Moon'. It was sung in a sorrowful way but it caught on instantly. Soon it was heard at Maine Road and, by the end of the season, it was a club anthem.

Those City fans, some of them teenage lads, many in their twenties and early thirties, had heard various different versions of 'Blue Moon' over the years, all of which had impacted vaguely on their subconscious. But the difference with 'Blue Moon Revisited', released in the UK late in 1988 was that it came with a video which featured close-ups of Margo Timmins as she emoted her sad song. It was aimed to draw male attention and it certainly did.

Timmins wasn't scantily clad in the style of an R&B diva. Far from flaunting her bare midriff, her body was entirely covered by an ankle – length, loose-fitting blue dress and, rather than prancing about voluptuously, she sat still on a stool. Her sex appeal lay partly in her helplessly tousled hair, the sensual way she hugged herself, her luminous blue eyes and downcast gaze and, perhaps above all, in the knowing half smile which occasionally flitted across her lips, as if she knew a secret but wasn't going to reveal it.

Manchester City supporters had long stood alone, used to the negativity of certain journalists and broadcasters who could scarcely contain their excitement as they chronicled the erratic progress of United but scoffed at the loyalty of fans turning up religiously at Maine Road in the dark days of the Eighties. If a City supporter at that time had "a dream in my heart" it was merely of First Division survival and a decent run in the F.A Cup. Yet even that would fade in the Nineties when City were relegated to the third tier of English football and fans had to pin their hopes on a play-off with Gillingham.

Yet, counter to the third line of Hart's first verse, City fans did have "a love of my own", but it was an unrequited love. Those who held the reins of power at Maine Road seemed more interested in their own business dealings than in satisfying the fans' hopes for an attractive and successful football team.

Foremost among them was Chairman Peter Swales, ex-uniform presser and sheet music hawker, a man who'd struck it rich with rented tellies before he ousted the old-timey Alexanders from power. With his clownish combover, camel hair coat, England blazer and suede hush puppies, Swales was a figure of fun-at first ! Obsessed with charisma, his first question on interviewing a potential new manager was-" 'Ave yer gorrit? Charisma, I mean". Belatedly answering his own question he sacked eleven managers at an average of two year intervals.But the one coach deemed charismatic, Malcolm Allison, was permitted to purge the squad's best players with disastrous results.

When ' Blue Moon' established itself as City's anthem of the Nineties, Richard Rodgers' melody -melancholic but arresting, sad but defiant -struck a chord with Manchester City's supporters while Lorenz

Hart's words, beguilingly murmured by Margo Timmins, had a real resonance about them. The strange thing was that the original composition of this superb song had dated precisely from the first great era in Manchester City's history and its two most dramatic re-interpretations heralded two great periods in the annals of the club.

Rodgers and Hart and the Rise of Manchester City

'Blue Moon' was the product of two wealthy, well educated Jewish Americans, Richard Rodgers and Lorenz Hart. New York City born and raised, their songwriting partnership had begun when they were students at Columbia University. Rodgers, who majored in music, wrote the melodies and Hart, a journalism graduate, wrote the lyrics. In the Twenties, their shows were lauded on Broadway and, in the Thirties, they scarpered to Hollywood where the glitz was glossier and the pickings even richer.

Their musical partnership would be unsurpassed. This was what landed them an MGM contract in 1933 and a commission to write a song for the beautiful blonde movie star Jean Harlow the following year. Harlow's role was that of a naive but ambitious girl who longed to become a movie heroine and Hart's task was to find words which would fit the mindset of her character.

Consider Rodgers' melody for 'Blue Moon' - the striking chords it opens with, its pleading tone, murmuring yet insistent, then the gentle modulation in the bridge when the clouds seem to lift- and you can see at once why it's been recorded umpteen times by the biggest names in music, why it's featured in hit movies and, in its various versions, has sold millions of copies.

The first recording of 'Blue Moon' was made in January 1935 by Connie Boswell, a twenty-seven-year-old singer who, stricken with polio, had recorded it from a wheelchair. Her rendition, backed by the immaculate strings of the Victor Young Orchestra, is romantic, impeccable and utterly sad. No one would for one moment guess it could one day become a football anthem. Yet, in the first of a series of coincidences which would link Rodgers and Hart's song to Manchester City FC, the club's first great period coincided with the birth of ' Blue Moon '.

While things were looking up for Rodgers and Hart, so they were for Wilf Wild, secretary- manager of Manchester City from 1932 onwards. At a time when coaching was almost unheard of in the English game, Wild's main input was buying players and selecting the team. Not a footballer himself, he looked more like a bank manager of those days - hair brushed carefully back from his high forehead, a forbidding gaze, a tweed suit and waistcoat, above which his neck was half- throttled by a tight collar and tie.

Though there were already good players on City's books, Wild's signings were key: an extra goalscorer, Alec Herd, nabbed from obscure Scottish club Hamilton Academicals; Geordie full back Sam Barkas, from Bradford, a cultured distributor in an age when most in his position were puddings, a man who could translate defence into attack; and, above all, Peter Doherty, born in Ireland, bought from Blackpool, a superbly gifted artist.

With City at Wembley for the 1934 Cup Final, the match was preceded by the introduction of the team to the Duke of York, the future George VI, whose embarrassment over his stammering would form the basis of the film 'The King's Speech'. Sam Cowan, the City skipper and sterling centre half, whose easy, jovial manner meant that he was far more relaxed than the nervous prince, had the task of introducing his teammates. Careless of the exact form of royal address, he ventured "Your Majesty" and would later be told off by an FA official for not using the phrase "Your Royal Highness". He presented Fred

Tilson, the fiery centre forward never far from the heart of the action, a Yorkshireman with a cheery grin and a mouthful of bad teeth. Tilson had taken a right battering over the years and, though he was only thirty-one, he looked fifty. Cowan introduced him, putting the Duke's sense of humour to the test with the words "Tilson's playing today with two broken legs !".

While the City lads were struggling to contain their mirth, Cowan went on to present Eric Brook, left winger with a licence to roam and a shot on him so ferocious he could score from the touchline. Brook was a blunt Yorkshireman from a coalmining town, with greasy yellow hair, sunken- cheeked and lantern -jawed. When the Duke extended his hand, Brook took it but contented himself with a slight forward inclination of his napper. Then it came time to introduce Matt Busby, future manager of Manchester United. As Busby produced a deep formal, obeisant bow -on which the film footage would admiringly dwell- Brook was seen frowning, lips pursed, giving Busby a 'Give over, you daft sod!' look. The last to shake hands was Ernie Toseland, nicknamed ' Twinkle Toes Toseland', a fine, ballplaying winger but fast and strong with it, as befitted a converted Rugby Union three-quarter. Toseland looked away immediately after the handshake as if embarrassed by the pomp and ceremony of it all.

The Cup Final commentary was provided by Tom Webster, a smirking prat in a trilby hat, who reckoned his sarcastic remarks about Manchester were the height of humour. Whatever Webster thought, City prevailed 2-1 with Tilson's brace cancelling Portsmouth's early lead. This had stemmed from an error by nineteen -year-old Frank Swift, from Blackpool, who would go on to be one of England's greatest goalkeepers. As City strove to close out the game in the final minutes, Swift was maithered by a cameraman behind his goal taking snaps every single second regardless of whether there was any goalmouth action or not. Unable to tell the photographer exactly where to go,

Swift's nerves were cranked beyond the limit and he fainted in relief on his goal line as the final whistle sounded.

When City returned to Manchester to proudly display the hard-earned trophy, they were back in a world far different from what they'd encountered at Wembley. A crowd estimated at one million people turned out to welcome them home and to watch in delight as the heroes of the hour were driven through the City streets in a Fingland's bus. And where were United when all this was going on? Desperately staving off relegation-from the Second Division!

With Sam Cowan proudly displaying the trophy, Eric Brook grinned at Matt Busby hastily dousing a ciggy when he realised the cameras were on him. They proceeded to the Town Hall. Replying to the Mayor's welcome, Cowan expressed the hope that they'd soon be back at Wembley to defend their trophy. After all, they'd already been there two seasons on the run, having lost to Everton in 1933 when Tilson was out injured and Swift's predecessor, the hapless Les Langford, had been unnerved by Everton's burly, bustling centre forward Dixie Dean and ended up, like the ball, in the back of his own net.

Though there was no swift return to Wembley, Wilf Wild would construct an even finer team though he'd shocked many by offloading Matt Busby, still only twenty-seven, to Liverpool. But Wild had a new playmaker in his sights, Peter Doherty, and Doherty would be the fulcrum of City's great 1936-7 season when the League title was first won-even as United were being relegated! Doherty would score 30 of the 107 goals and Brook, Herd and Tilson weighed in with 20, 17 and 15 respectively.

Sadly, no archive footage remains of this achievement. In an era when 74,000 packed Maine Road for a game with West Brom -just as 84,000 had witnessed the Cup tie with Stoke three years earlier- no film crew could be found to travel north and record the scintillating attacking play of a team which was carrying all before it. As for Doherty, peer of Tom Finney and Stanley Matthews, but unlike them not eligible for selection by England, not a trace of him would remain on celluloid.

Elvis, The Revie Plan and Bert Trautmann

A decade and a half later, in July 1954 the first radical reinterpretation of ' Blue Moon' was waxed. Sam Phillips, producer of Sun Records in Memphis, Tennessee cut a two and a half minute version of Rodgers and Hart's song which took it right out of the musical museum dubbed 'standards'.

Elvis Presley, aged nineteen, who knew the song by heart, took the mic. Guitarist Scotty Moore's simple clip -clop rhythm substituted for the lavish orchestration of previous versions while Phillips enhanced the oddness of the take by running the tape through a second recorder head to create a startling echo effect.

'Blue Moon' as sung by Elvis is haunting, ethereal at times, very different to his rock'n' roll songs, true to Rodgers' melody but sung far more powerfully than ever before. He makes the song young, modern and personal.

Six weeks earlier than Presley's ' Blue Moon' makeover, Hungary's football team had humiliated England 7-1 in Budapest, a result which confirmed that the famous 6-3 victory at Wembley in November 1953 was no one off. England had been undone by the Hungarian coach Gusztav Sebes who devised the deep -lying centre forward plan and used the great Nandor Hidegkuti to implement it.

Among the crowd watching at Wembley was Les McDowall, then in his fourth year as manager of Manchester City. An Indian- born son of Scottish missionaries, he 'd turned to football after losing his job as a draughtsman during the Thirties and had played for City before the war.

In the early Fifties, United were the dominant force in Manchester football. Long- serving manager Matt Busby established an excellent nationwide scouting system and kept faith with the lads it found. Busby was rewarded with the FA Cup in 1948 and the First Division title in 1952. In contrast to this, City had been relegated in 1949, just before McDowall took over.

Les McDowall took City out of the Second Division and made several crucial signings. Welshman Roy Paul was a rugged defender, a hard drinking ex-coal miner from the Rhondda Valley with wavy, jet black hair and a fierce gaze. A man who both urged his teammates on and threatened to thump them if they lost, he was an inspirational skipper. Ken Barnes was a creative wing half, an ex-postie from Brum, thin, dark- haired and nicknamed ' Beaky' for his long nose.

But the one who was McDowall's key signing was Don Revie, ex-brickie from Middlesbrough, with a big shock of hair and a long, gaunt face which made him look like a butch version of The Smiths' frontman, Morrissey. He was serious, intense and opinionated. But he was also a player of exceptional skill with a keen football brain. If McDowell was following in the footsteps of Wilf Wild, Revie would be his Doherty, except that Revie was not so prolific a scorer as the great Irishman.

McDowall was fortunate to inherit the outstanding German- born goalkeeper, Bert Trautmann. His signing, in 1949 had triggered mass protests in Manchester, disturbing many Citizens, especially Jewish ones, in the immediate aftermath of World War II. Given a chance to prove that he might be a Jerry but was certainly no Nazi, Trautmann's spectacular shot- stopping and above all, his exceptional bravery, soon endeared him to City fans.

Coming away from Wembley, Les McDowall began to cast his key players in the role of the great Hungarians. Bert Trautmann would be Gyula Grosics, a keeper who initiated attacks by precise throws rather than the time-dishonoured English tradition of booting it out long and hard -no matter where it ended up. Barnes became Joszef Bozsik, able to tackle powerfully but also a classy midfield passer. And Don Revie became Nandor Hidegkuti, the deep lying centre forward personified.

City's League positions, once back in Division One, were far from good - 15th, 20th and 17th in successive seasons. And McDowall, even as he revolved the Hungarian style in his mind's eye, was cautious about implementing it. Only after a long and highly successful run for City's reserves did he agree, at the start of the 1954-5 season, to transfer it to the first team. When City lost the opening match of the season 5-0, many supporters, strongly influenced by English football pundits' scorn for anything which savoured of the modern, the innovative and - God forbid !- the theoretical, derided the so-called 'Revie Plan'.

But a successful run in the FA Cup converted most of the sceptical supporters. What's more, by the time City reached Wembley, McDowall had added another outstanding player. Bobby Johnstone was Scottish, signed from Hibs, a diminutive but highly skilful forward and a goal-scorer as well with a ratio of 1 to 3.

At Wembley, the Sky Blues faced Newcastle United whose style was conventional. Their star performer was Jackie Milburn. Milburn wasn't a deep lying centre forward - he was a direct, bustling, traditionally English leader of the line - a hero figure for the media as well as the Magpie fans. Still, there was also their dribbling wizard, the little Scotsman Bobby Mitchell, known as 'Dazzler' at St. James Park

Pundit hostility to City's modern methods was there for all to see on the eve of the Final. With City's sensible tracksuits, not usually worn in the English game, being dismissed as "a flashy gimmick", they were dubbed 'The Gaudies' in chortling contrast to the Geordies.

To the delight of all who cleaved to the traditional English way of doing things and were suspicious of anything which smacked of 'Johnny Foreigner', nothing went right that day for City. They were caught cold by Milburn's crunching header after only forty-five seconds. Recovering from that setback, they then lost full-back Jimmy Meadows with eighteen minutes gone. He was forced off with a ruptured cruciate ligament, a dangerous injury in the twenty-first-century and a career -ending one in the fifties. Substitutes were not then allowed, injuries being considered a hazard of manly sport.

Going down to ten men altered City's game plan. Trautmann began kicking out from hand as it was feared that throws into the wide open spaces would expose City to danger. As for the notion of the deep lying centre forward, that went right out of the window. Even so, City played some good football and equalised just before half time with a wonderfully acrobatic flying header from Johnstone. Sadly, it didn't last and, early in the second half, with Mitchell weaving his magic against tiring defenders, Newcastle scored twice more. The final result was 3-1 and it would've been more had it not been for Trautmann's bravery in diving at the feet of Newcastle's marauding forwards.

Next year, City returned to Wembley and, in their change strip of maroon and white stripes, beat Birmingham City 3-1, upsetting pundits who'd praised Birmingham's "open, direct and honest approach". Once again City had a man injured but this time it was in the closing stages. Bert Trautmann took an accidental knee in the neck from Peter Murphy, Birmingham's rampaging centre forward. This should've led to his immediate withdrawal but he insisted on playing on though clearly in great pain. Though his teammates had to resort to ' kick it anywhere ' clearances to stop Birmingham getting near him, City saw out the remaining seventeen minutes and emerged victorious. In actual fact, Trautmann had sustained a broken neck and was at risk of fatal injury throughout that time. His exceptional bravery would become the story of the 1956 Cup Final and, from a human point of view, rightly so.

But, in strict football terms, the story was that Manchester City had outclassed Birmingham. The Brummies' solitary goal came from a moment of City defensive hesitation whereas City would've scored more had it not been for Birmingham's fine keeper, Gil Merrick. City's opener was an absolute gem. Revie picked the ball up deep in his own half, ran with it, delivered a pinpoint pass to Roy Clarke on the wing, pointed to the exact spot where he wanted it returned and, when he got it back, executed the most delicate back flick to play in Joe Hayes –who struck it home. So far from City being a man down as they'd actually been the previous year, it seemed to many observers that they were playing with an extra man due to the strategic superiority of the system they used.

At the post-match banquet, there was a glimpse of Trautmann's appeal to women when twenty-three year old pop singer Alma Cogan giggled as she serenaded the wounded hero. Sadly, her repertoire didn't stretch to ' Blue Moon' and she contented herself with the novelty song ' Where Will The Dimple Be? ' Next day, when City returned to Manchester for a civic parade, they made an open bus tour through the streets of the city and were rapturously acclaimed in scenes which reminded some observers of VE Day. In Bert Trautmann they had perhaps the first superstar of the modern game. The Lord Mayor's speech was drowned out by shrill cries of "we want Bert, we want Bert !!" and only when Trautmann himself asked for hush did it finally descend.

Trautmann was tall, blond, athletic and brave-and had a cute foreign accent. Most of the girls who attended Maine Road or had gone up to London for the Cup -and screamed their feelings for Trautmann in the city centre- couldn't have cared less about deep- lying centre forwards, the Revie Plan and suchlike concepts.Any more than Elvis' adoring teenage girl fans concerned themselves with whether or not he'd sold out rock 'n' roll when he went to Hollywood. Football had become an extension of show business, not the prerogative of all-male crowds. Though Bert Trautmann was a dignified man who shunned the opportunity for cashing in showbiz-style on his heroism and sex appeal, he was, a decade before George Best's name would be linked with The Beatles, a kind of footballing Elvis.

The Marcels and Malcolm Allison

Five years later, in February 1961 a doo-wop vocal group from Pittsburgh named The Marcels came to New York, at the suggestion of Columbia A and R man Stu Phillips to record 'Blue Moon'. When Richard Rodgers heard the record being played repeatedly on the radio he figured it was a total assassination of his song. Unable to enlist Lorenz Hart's support - the lyricist had drunk himself to death nearly twenty years earlier- he had to campaign against The Marcels on his own. Regardless of the royalties he stood to lose, he took out ads in the papers urging people not to buy. Rodgers was wasting his time. 'Blue Moon' by The Marcels soared to the # 1 slot on the Billboard Hot 100 and did exactly the same on the UK charts.

The Marcels, all five of them, could certainly sing. Their voices were a sweet blend of two tenors and a baritone and, on ' Blue Moon' the close harmonies are perfectly meshed. The only trouble with The Marcels' version is Fred Johnson's bass. With a mischievous sense of humour, he introduces the track with nonsense syllables and keeps repeating them during the full two and a half minutes.At the end, he utters the very words "blue moon" in a deep, slow, 'fool' voice.

You could hear Johnson's scat -singing extravaganza more than one way - either as an inspired piece of comic malarkey or, as Rodgers obviously thought, an insult - or simply as inappropriate dumbass humour verging on piss-take. But the enormous chart success of 'Blue Moon' as rendered by The Marcels took the Rodgers and Hart ballad into totally new territory. Hastily cooked up when everyone wanted to get home quick in a New York snowstorm, it made 'Blue Moon' pop - brash, more than a touch vulgar, brimming with chutzpah, entirely novel and a total breach with the past.

Round about the time The Marcels' 'Blue Moon' was making an impact on Britain's airwaves, Malcolm Alexander Allison, possibly the most gifted and certainly the most controversial manager in Manchester City's history, was at Cambridge University. He wasn't studying anything there but, had there been a degree in football, Allison would've been a cert for a First. Ever since he deliberately failed his eleven plus exam as a boy in Bexleyheath, he'd been obsessed with the game. Clever enough to have benefited from grammar school, the young Malcolm had junked an academic education to avoid going to a rugby -playing school.

On Charlton Athletic's books at eighteen, he'd been kept out of the first-team after loudly criticising the club coach. During his six years with West Ham, he'd taken coaching sessions while still a player but his promising career as a centre half had been wrecked by a bout of TB and the removal of one lung.

Distraught at the premature ending of his playing days while still on the right side of thirty, Allison became a car salesman then a professional gambler before opening a nightclub. When his briefly disrupted yearning for the game returned, he hove to at Cambridge. Dismissive of the undergraduates' football skills, Allison was impressed by the way they hung on his every word when he strove to impart his coaching drills.

Like Les McDowall before him, Allison had been at Wembley when the Hungarians demolished England 6-3 and certain ideas which had already been forming in his mind were crystallised by the Magical Magyars. He would eventually write a coaching manual entitled 'Soccer For Thinkers'. As Allison saw it, English football was predicated on stupidity -with the same old routines boringly worked

through time and time again. He ridiculed everything the establish-
ment coaches held dear: training without the ball; training in the
mornings only; tucking into bangers and mash with chips; baggy
shorts and heavy boots; fullbacks hanging back and never overlapping; forwards remaining static rather than a front line which would
switch positions. In short, the whole hidebound works!

The person responsible for Allison's appointment to City was Joe
Mercer, ex-Everton, ex-Arsenal, and former England stalwart, newly
appointed to manage at Maine Road. Mercer was jovial, decent and
popular but he had relatively little interest in coaching and modest
tactical acumen. His important achievement was to recognise Allison's
potential - having met him on an F. A.course - and to recommend the
City board to appoint him.

Finding a team stuck in the Second Division and attracting crowds
barely into five figures, Allison took City to the Second Division championship, the Division One title, the F. A. Cup, the League Cup and
the European Cup Winners Cup in the years up to 1970. He identified
players with high potential, often at lower division clubs, and brought
them to Maine Road. There he transformed them into great players - Colin Bell from Bury, Mike Summerbee from Swindon, Francis
Lee from Bolton. He fostered the development of the brilliant young
players already on City's books - Neil Young and Mike Doyle among
them- and he combined these diverse talents in a side which played
sparkling attacking football with tremendous team spirit.

The zenith of Allison's City was the home game where Tottenham
Hotspur, a good side in its own right, was crushed 4-1 on December 9,
1967. After a snowfall, the pitch had been inspected more than once
before it was deemed playable and the markings were only just visible.

But so agile, graceful and self assured were the City players that the match was dubbed ' The Ballet on Ice '.

Despite conceding an early goal from a set piece scored by Spurs' expensive star striker, Jimmy Greaves, City never looked back. In an astonishing display of attacking football played on a surface where the man in the street might well've been slipping perilously about, they interpassed sublimely, danced nimbly round their markers, intercepted with ease and shot powerfully and accurately. Everything they did seemed effortless but it was in fact the product of Allison's gruelling training regime, so intense that actual matchplay conditions seemed relaxing in comparison. Looking like Lowry's matchstick men suddenly animated as gliding cartoon characters, they turned the Maine Road turf into a magic carpet. Nonchalant in the face of the early setback, they flitted shadowless across the frozen surface, some tall, lean and dark like Summerbee, Young and Doyle, others blond like Bell and Lee. Spurs were outclassed and reprieved from massive defeat only by the width of the goalposts. As for City keeper, Ken Mulhearn, presciently clad in a tracksuit, he was little more than a spectator desperately trying to keep warm by slapping his gloved hands against his body.

The 'Ballet on Ice' elicited constant roars and gasps from the enthralled crowd as incident- packed football unfolded with scarcely an interruption. A fortnight before Christmas, it relieved the drudgery of Yuletide shopping for City's most loyal fans who trudged to Maine Road on a desperately bleak afternoon. What's more, Malcolm Allison's entire team, and indeed his whole squad, was English to a man with the sole exception of Scotsman Bobby Kennedy. But what a contrast they provided with the English National team, led as it was by grim- faced, humourless manager Sir Alf Ramsey !

The years 1965-70 were the greatest thus far in City's history. They needed to catch up fast on a Manchester United reaping the benefits of a long- established scouting network which had found the likes of Bobby Charlton and George Best and with a budget far in excess of City's - one which had brought Denis Law to Old Trafford for a six-figure sum. But, while journalists lavished praise on United's individual stars, it was Malcolm Allison's City whose display of collective football was perhaps the finest the English game had seen.

Sadly, it didn't last. Allison's weakness for rash boasts and bold strokes got the better of him. These tendencies had already surfaced when, having won the First Division title, he bragged that City would "terrify the cowards of Europe". In fact, the Sky Blues were knocked out of the European Cup in the first round by Turkish club Fenerhbace. Ambitious for total control at Maine Road, Allison got it by siding with the faction which was trying to oust the Alexander family from the chairmanship. Joe Mercer was kicked upstairs as general manager and, though City looked set to win the First Division crown once again, in 1972, Allison's purchase of the Cockney showboater Rodney Marsh disrupted the balance of the side and they finished fourth. Mercer was humiliated by the removal of his office and personal parking space and he left. With the soon -to- be- notorious Peter Swales installed as Chairman, City flirted with relegation in 1972-3 and Allison resigned.

As the sparkling Sixties gave way to the stale Seventies a different man emerged from the person who'd impressed the Cambridge undergraduates, the directors of Bath City and Plymouth Argyle and won the trust of Joe Mercer. The intelligent, articulate, witty football analyst Malcolm Alexander Allison gave way to 'Big Mal', favourite of ITV pundit panels: a cigar -chomping, gold medallion -sporting dice-rolling, hard -boozing, free- shagging reckless rapscallion.

Like The Marcels, Malcolm Allison had been pop, innovative and stylish. But, just as Fred Johnson had been unable to resist the pull of the scat -singing riff and the nonsense syllables and had ended up by parodying Rodgers and Hart's creation, so Allison's foolhardy recklessness undermined his own best work and damaged the very Manchester City he himself had elevated.

Graham Gordon

Liam Gallagher, Beady Eye and the Premiership Title

When Margo Timmins recorded her version of the Rodgers and Hart classic in November 1987, she asked RCA to issue it as ' Blue Moon Revisited ' with the subtitle ' Song for Elvis'. But the new lyric doesn't reference the deceased ' King of Rock 'n' Roll'. With extra words added by Timmins herself, It's a lament for the singer's lost lover, someone whom she'd adored but who "one sad day, went away and died".

The Manchester City of the Nineties was cherished by the fans even as it tottered and fell, division by division And ' Blue Moon' was sung even as they trudged to Macclesfield and York. This was the actual City, unlovely and unsuccessful. But it was scarcely the real City, the teams their dads told them about and over whom their grandads reminisced, a City bold, brave and beautiful - as bold as the Revie Plan which had opposing centre halves wringing their hands in despair, as brave as Bert Trautmann putting his life on the line for the Sky Blues and as beautiful as 'The Ballet on Ice'. That City had, it seemed, vanished for ever, departed and dead.

These new fans, girls as well as lads, Natalie Pike just as much as Noel and Liam Gallagher and Ricky Hatton were given tantalising glimpses of what might once again be when the drab curtains of Maine Road were briefly drawn aside to reveal a second German hero, Uwe Rosler, or an icon from an exotic location such as Georgia's Georgi Kinkladze or Bermuda's ace marksman Shaun Goater with his better than one in two strike rate.

In the new century, City would escape from their Nineties trough, sporadically flourish and move to a bright new home in the City of

Manchester Stadium. But, until the takeover by the Abu Dhabi United Group in 2008, it would fail to establish any coherent plan to recover its status as one of England's foremost clubs.

In July 2011, Cheadle-based sportswear firm Umbro, a subsidiary of Nike and supplier of uniforms to Manchester City, asked rock band Beady Eye to promote the new season's kit by recording ' Blue Moon'.

Beady Eye formed two years earlier, after the dissolution of Oasis following the Gallagher brothers' ultimate quarrel. Like his brother Noel, Liam Gallagher, Burnage born and Levenshulme raised, had been a Manchester City fan since early childhood. Not all his new bandmates shared that enthusiasm but they'd all absorbed Gallagher / Manc style.

Though Liam Gallagher's City credentials were beyond dispute, Beady Eye's 'Blue Moon' had strictly commercial origins and many fans cringed at the start of the video, which saw Gallagher reverently approaching a mannequin, stooping to kiss the badge on the sky blue shirt before turning and solemnly uttering the words "come on City". To keep things pop-friendly, guitarist Andy Bell wore a space helmet and the set was lit from below with a misty pale blue glow !

The video apart, Beady Eye's version is a significant reinterpretation. Liam Gallagher's crooning delivery is the polar opposite of his snarled rock vocals and his whistling break is a fine touch while Andy Bell's slide guitar harmonies add another sonic layer to the overall effect, bringing out the beauty of Rodgers' melody in the way the orchestral strings first did.

Connie Boswell had pioneered 'Blue Moon', Elvis had modernised it, The Marcels had popified it and Margo Timmins had turned it sexy.

But it was Beady Eye who made it Manc. The song which had lived a life in parallel to that of Manchester City and had become an unofficial fan anthem in 1989 was now, in 2011, formally wedded to the club. Liam Gallagher sang the famous first verse and the little- heard second but he shyed away from the third verse and the fourth, doubtless fearing Lorenz Hart's genteel lines wouldn't suit him. The lyric cannot be quoted here for legal reasons but it can be read in full on the club's official website.

The first three lines of the third verse teeter on the brink of bathos and both Elvis Presley and Margo Timmins had also taken care to avoid them. But, in junking that verse, the full meaning of the song is lost. 'Blue Moon' is a confession of loneliness and an admission of failure, yes, but it's also a longing for redemption, a prayer which is answered when that same baleful blue moon which has mirrored the singer's desolation is suddenly suffused with a beautiful glow - and, when he looks up , he finds the blue moon has turned to gold!.

When Beady Eye recorded their version of the song, City had already taken the first step on the road to redemption.The F.A Cup was won in May 2011, the club's first trophy for thirty-five years and its first success in that competition since 1969. Hopes were high for Premiership success in 2011-12 and soon City were at the top of the Premiership table, beating United 6-1 at Old Trafford.

City still stood alone but UEFA vitriol had superseded the old media mockery. Michel Platini, president of UEFA and advocate of Financial Fair Play, seemed fearful that the old order would be undone by Abu Dhabi treasure. His pronouncements dwelt on the precise sums which Sheikh Mansour was stated to have spent in bringing in world-class players. He blithely ignored the expenditure incurred, albeit over many years, by Real Madrid and Milan in carving up the Champions League and of Manchester United in establishing their national hegemony. He bizarrely compared City to the likes of Paris St.Germain and Anzhi Makhachkala, the former founded eighty years after City, the latter almost a hundred. And he effectively brushed aside the contribution of the Abu Dhabi Group- as part of the Etihad Complex development- to the revitalization of East Manchester.

Throughout 2011-12, City supporters' hopes were raised only, as it seemed, to be dashed once again as the campaign neared its close. United seemed to have one hand on the Premiership trophy. But a series of six straight wins by City, including the defeat of Sir Alex Ferguson's men at the Etihad, redressed the balance. Yet, as City faltered in the final game against Queens Park Rangers, the old cries of 'Typical City ' and 'Cityitis', often uttered by City supporters known for their scepticism and gallows humour, were on the tip of commentators' tongues.

Only a few minutes of stoppage time stood between United and what would've been their twentieth title and, as it seemed to more than one smirking pundit, the established order would be confirmed yet again. These were the men who'd forgotten, if they ever knew, the glorious history of Manchester City going back beyond the Sixties, to the Fifties and Thirties and even a hundred years distant when Billy Meredith was acclaimed the finest footballer in the land. Well versed in the dreary calculus of Etihad expenditure, they cared little for the unparalleled loyalty of City fans demonstrated when, at the nadir of the club's fortunes in the late Nineties, average attendances of 28,000 were recorded. They had ridiculed Sheikh Mansour's Project which he'd explained to the supporters in his Open Letter of September 2008. And, in one case, had snickered on hearing how lads adorned their grandfather's graves with blue and white scarves after the Cup Final victory.

But one last twist of fate remained to confound all who were poised to write off City's title hopes.Edin Dzeko and Sergio Aguero, heirs to Doherty and Brook, to Revie and Johnstone, to Colin Bell and Mike Summerbee, struck twice in 'Fergie Time'. As Vincent Kompany displayed the Barclay's Premiership Trophy to 45,000 overjoyed fans, ' Blue Moon' resounded in the Etihad. No strange celestial events were noted that night in the skies over Manchester but, for those who'd stayed true to Manchester City for so long without a dream in their hearts, the blue moon had turned to gold.

2

MANSOUR AND MUBARAK -
THE TEN KEY DECISIONS

S heikh Mansour bin Zayed Al Nahyan , City's owner, is storied in banner and song and there's a unique and revealing document, his open letter to Manchester City fans, published when the Abu Dhabi United Group takeover was finalised on September 27 2008.

The very fact of issuing that letter marked Sheikh Mansour, thirty-seven year old royal , as very different from his peers among those major European clubs which were not publicly owned. Would such a statement have escaped the pen of criminally -indicted politician Silvio Berlusconi, ex-nightclub crooner, purveyor of dumbass TV and owner of Milan ? Or Tom Hicks and George Gillette, 'the Toxic Twins', the leveraged buyout specialists whose inglorious co-ownership of Liverpool was ended only after a bitter court battle? Or United's Malcolm Glazer or Chelsea's Roman Abramovich?

In the open letter, Mansour paid tribute to "the greatest fans in the world", confessed that he'd been "deeply touched" by "many expressions of goodwill and joy"and acknowledged "the heritage and potential of Manchester City". "We are very aware that without you there would be no club to buy" he continued, assuring supporters "you will be heard by the organisation at the highest level".

Predictably there were many in the media who scoffed at Mansour's letter even though it contained no glib assertions or crass boasts. "We are ambitious for the club, like you, but not unreasonably so and we understand it takes time to build a team capable of sustaining a presence in the top four of the Premier League and winning European honours". While open about the fact that "Premiership football is one of the best entertainment products in the world and we see it as a sound business venture", Mansour stressed that " we will absolutely spend time listening to you the fans about what you think about the future of the club".

Though other important decisions would be taken later- one in regard to football philosophy and another concerning the ideal manager to implement this- the key decisions were taken between 2008 and 2012. There were ten :

1. First, Sheikh Mansour resolved to buy the club. In doing so, he rescued City from the clutches of Thaksin Shinawatra, sometime Prime Minister of Thailand, a man accused of human rights abuses and convicted of corruption. Mansour had let it be known to Sulaiman Al Fahim, Dubai- born, American -trained real estate tycoon and reality TV host, that he was interested in acquiring a Premiership club. A keen footballer himself, the Sheikh already owned the Al Jazeera club in Abu Dhabi and followed the English game with increasing interest.

Fahim knew Amanda Staveley, young blonde British businesswoman, daughter of a Yorkshire rollercoaster operator and ex-girlfriend of Prince Andrew. Staveley knew Shinawatra was desperate to sell and the deal was soon concluded. Shinawatra was permitted to remain as honorary president but, within six months, he was dismissed.

Despite frequent media claims that Mansour "could just as easily have bought Spurs, Everton or Newcastle United", the fact remains that he chose City not on a whim but as a rational business decision based principally on its ready-made stadium, only five years old and leased from Manchester City Council. City now had at the helm a man who, unlike the owners of most rival clubs, hadn't needed to claw his way to the top in the cutthroat world of big business but was a patrician, a man whose family, yes, had inherited colossal wealth but had already shown how to use those riches wisely.

2. At the same time as his Open Letter was published, Mansour's second key decision came into effect. This was the appointment of Khaldoun Al Mubarak as club Chairman. Taken aback by the enormous worldwide media interest in the City takeover, the Sheikh had been dismayed by the brash talk of al Fahim who bragged that City would sign the best players in the world in short order, cost what it might. Fahim had never been more than a point man but now he was discreetly sidelined.

Khaldoun Al Mubarak, aged only thirty-three, was a scion of the Emirati officer class. Tall, burly and athletic, he'd been a keen footballer himself. A man who combined intellect with inexhaustible energy, he was an Economics and Finance graduate of the prestigious Tufts University in Boston. For all that he absorbed American get up and go in business and sported Californian -style designer stubble, his sporting culture was strictly European. He'd followed Serie A keenly for many years before increasingly turning his attention to the Premiership.

On his return to Abu Dhabi, Mubarak was immediately identified as a highflyer and he rose like a meteor, first in the oil business then in construction. Appointed CEO of government investment company Mubadala, his breakthrough came with the government restructuring after Sheikh Khalifa succeeded to the presidency. Khaldoun became chairman of the Emirati Executive Affairs Authority. Both in industry and in sport, he rapidly became a stellar figure. One minute he was inspecting the world's largest aluminium smelting plant, the next he was checking out the construction of a mighty gas pipeline and it wasn't long before he was smiling with satisfaction as he watched the Formula One Ferraris and Maclarens roar round the new Abu Dhabi circuit. In short, it was a key adviser to the Nahyan dynasty, a cabinet minister in all but name, who was now assigned to Manchester City.

Just as the Viceroys of British India had represented the far distant monarch Victoria, so Khaldoun was man on the spot for Sheikh Mansour. Unlike the Viceroys, Khaldoun didn't have to take up residence. The realities of intercontinental air travel meant he could continue in all his other posts yet be in Manchester within hours to implement key decisions. If anyone thought he would be some kind of absentee landlord, they would be swiftly disillusioned.

Though Shinawatra was gone, two of his most important appointments remained in post. One was Brummie-born CEO Garry Cook. Cook had been Stateside for over twenty years. Charged by Nike with marketing basketball megastar Michael Jordan, he'd implemented Brand Jordan and shifted shoes by the shedload not only for aspiring Jordans but also as a cool fashion item in the youth market. Cook's understanding of soccer was decidedly open to question but this didn't stop him making motormouth pronouncements about Brazilian superstars and their capacity to generate shirt sales. Mansour and Mubarak had been expected to get rid of him but were principled and loyal operators who would not lightly cast a man aside.

3. When Garry Cook showed Mubarak round club premises, the new Chairman ordered the instant refurbishment of Carrington and Platt Lane. The training pitches, the gyms and the medical facilities were barely up to scratch for the useful players already on City's books but they'd be hopelessly inadequate for the stellar footballers the club now aimed to sign. Critics sneered that the £ 2.7 million outlay was chicken feed for Sheikh Mansour but that was not the point. The new owner meant business, he had a clear plan for the transformation of Manchester City, a four-year project, which, despite supercilious media scoffing, he intended to realise.

4. Sheikh Mansour resolved to implement squad investment. In his Open Letter, he'd noted the acquisition of Brazilian legend Robinho from Real Madrid (for a fee of £32 million) and described it as "a signal of our very real intent". For the time being, Mansour and Mubarak were content to rely on the footballing judgement of Shinawatra's other main man, Welsh manager Mark Hughes, grizzled and grim-faced . Described in the Open Letter as "the best young British manager"- the very words Garry Cook had used about him when he was appointed!- Cook's confidence wasn't shared by most Citizens.

Mark Hughes had been 'Sparky' at Old Trafford but was merely 'Leslie' at Eastlands. As boss of Blackburn Rovers, over a period of four years, his achievements had been modest and his style so relentlessly physical that his team were nicknamed 'Black Eye Rovers' - in distinct contrast to the sparkling attacking play encouraged at City by Sven-Goran Eriksson. But Hughes, like Cook, was the man in post and Abu Dhabi were keen to signal their preference for continuity and their refusal to rush to judgement.

Sheikh Mansour bankrolled Mark Hughes' first signings in the window of January 2009 to the tune of £50 million. It was spent on British Isles players - whizzbang winger Craig Bellamy, honest Wayne Bridge and impulsive keeper Shay Given plus Dutch enforcer Nigel de Jong. In comparison with Fahim's boast that he'd sign Cristiano Ronaldo for over £100 million and Cook's all- too -real but unsuccessful pursuit of the Brazilian Kaka from AC Milan, it seemed modesty personified in contrast to the Galactico-style bragging of men who were not footballing insiders.

In the Summer of 2009, expenditure was doubled as another round of players was recruited. But once again the narrowness of Hughes' outlook was clear. Gareth Barry and Joleon Lescott were solid British professionals who would do much sterling work for City, Barry in particular. And the foreign players had "already proved themselves in the Premiership"- an old shibboleth invariably trotted out by track-suit managers. Emmanuel Adebayor and Kolo Toure had starred for Arsenal and Carlos Tevez for United. But, for all Tevez' undoubted Latin skills, he was ruggedly English in his direct and forceful approach. As for Paraguayan centre forward Roque Santa Cruz, who'd been with Hughes at Blackburn, he was no more than an old-style targetman.

5. Khaldoun's next decision showed a determination to avoid the kind of signings which had tempted both Fahim and Cook. Robinho had not fully adjusted to the Premiership, despite moments of inspiration, and never seemed fully committed to the cause. Thus the post of Football Administrator was created with a view to finalising signings only after a meticulous dossier had been compiled on the player, not only his onfield skills but factors such as real intelligence, language abilities, family background and general lifestyle factors. The Administrator was also to oversee the recruitment of youngsters to the Academy and similarly strict requirements were laid down. These developments had been foreseen in the Open Letter when Mansour

stressed that "we also want to see the Academy continue to develop talent and ... bring home grown players into the team". "We are building a structure for the future and not a team of all stars", he emphasised.

It was clear that, while Hughes was still in post, he was no longer the fulcrum of football decisions. Brian Marwood, ex-Arsenal player, former chairman of the PFA and Cook's colleague at Nike was brought in. So as not to hurt Hughes' feelings, Marwood wasn't given the controversial title of Director of Football - known to arouse the resentment of British managers! But It would be Marwood who would be charged with preparing dossiers - a far cry from the situation which Mubarak had found a year earlier when there wasn't even a personnel department!

One sentence in the Open Letter had foreseen the very real possibility that the new City would be a victim of media misrepresentation. "Despite what you may have read" it ran " I have bought the club in a private capacity and as part of my personal business strategy to hold a portfolio of business investments". "I am a long-term investor" it continued, assuring City supporters "we are here for the long haul" Needless to say, British tabloid hacks didn't read the Open Letter if they were even aware of its existence. But within twelve months, a more serious threat to City's development would rear its head.

6. In September 2009, UEFA issued its sanctimoniously -named Football Fair Play Regulations announced by its President, Michel Platini. Former captain of France and a wonderfully gifted player who'd lit up Euro 84 with his artistry, Platini had degenerated into a pompous, corporate bureaucrat. Speaking in Monte Carlo before the Champions League draw, he prissily laid down the law as decreed by UEFA. Clubs who wanted to be in that competition, or in the Europa League, would have to balance their football -related spending on a

three-year basis leading up to 2014-15. Starting in 2011-12, the greatest annual loss permissible would be €45 million. If they did not comply, they would be punished, not only by fines and transfer bans but by exclusion from the main competitions. Platini pontificated about the alleged evils of "sugar daddies" and smirked as he singled out City for criticism. "Manchester City can spend £300 million if they want to" he said, pausing ominously before delivering his threat "but if they are not breaking even in three years they cannot play in European competition!"

Michel Platini would soon get his answer. Interviewed by The Guardian, Khaldoun demolished the UEFA President's spurious claim that Abu Dhabi's ownership was a danger to football. "I could accept the argument if we were artificially building up the club through debt" he said." But, in our case, the club will be in the healthiest position because there is no debt. We have funded it through equity including the signing of the players".

Khaldoun subtly turned the tables on Platini when he countered "I believe what we're doing is a fair way to inject competition into football without debt". Seeing right through the UEFA smokescreen, the Manchester City Chairman characterised the UEFA directive as a means to perpetuate a closed shop in football, one which would provide a monopoly on European success to the historically richest clubs. "The argument (that City are unhealthy suggests that the big clubs which make the most money must remain the big clubs, that the status quo must remain" he continued, adding "is Mr Platini saying that only Real Madrid and Barcelona have the right to be competitive in La Liga?"

Beyond the hypocritical pretence of concern for lower -tier clubs, UEFA was acting in the interests of a cabal of powerful clubs with wealthy backers such as Real Madrid and AC Milan (and even supporter-backed clubs such as Bayern Munich) who had a stack of Champions League and European Cup trophies in their cabinets. Bayern Munich Chairman Karl-Heinz Rummenigge had been among those openly hostile to City.

Mubarak pointed out that in the United States there were salary caps and there was a franchise system designed to ensure financial and sporting equality between clubs but that no such provisions existed in Europe. He went on to address the issue of Abu Dhabi investment in Manchester City. "I appreciate the argument about having so much money" he calmly responded. "The way I answer it is: yes, this is a club, but it is a business too, and in business you are there to compete. And we are striving to build the club the right way, with a respect for its heritage and the fans".

Khaldoun Al Mubarak had outwitted Michel Platini in debate. But, to combat FFP, more than words would be needed. After careful legal consultation, in September 2011, City announced a sponsoring deal with Etihad Airways. In return for naming rights over the City of Manchester Stadium, City would receive £350 million in sponsorship over a ten-year period. It remained to be seen how effective this would be in outmanoeuvring UEFA.

7. As season 2009-10 began to unfold, so Sheikh Mansour and Chairman Mubarak began seriously to doubt the managerial ability of Mark Hughes. Clearly Hughes had made a good initial impression on Mubarak. He didn't yell, bawl and bluster in traditional British style. He didn't dress like a tracksuit manager. Indeed his sombre suits, coupled with his habitual frown and pursed lips, his reluctance to give his face a holiday, made him come across more like an undertaker. At least he was a serious-minded man and popular with his players.

Hughes may or or may not have been "the best young British man-ager" as Garry Cook had originally introduced him. But what did that really signify? All the leading English clubs, except only for United, were obtaining success with European managers: Arsene Wenger had been in post for twelve years at Arsenal and had developed ' The Invincibles', Rafael Benitez had won the Champions League for Liverpool in his first year while Jose Mourinho had instantly delivered the Premiership title to Chelsea. Unlike the less successful Premiership clubs which love to appoint high-profile British ex-players, top foreign coaches imported into England were dedicated students of the game with hard-won coaching certificates in their homelands and high win percentages in their statistical records. Mark Hughes, by contrast, was a long-time associate of Sir Alex Ferguson and was well thought of by the League Managers Association.

One year into his tenure at Eastlands, Hughes had enjoyed a budget far beyond what he could have dreamt of when he first took over. He'd acquired the likes of Shaun Wright -Phillips, Bellamy and Bridge for a total of £35 million. His better signings from abroad, Pablo Zabaleta and, above all, Vincent Kompany, came about as a result of Mike Riggs' scouting. Now he'd splurged somewhere between £118 and £137 mil-lion either on Premiership stalwarts or on "foreigners if they've previ-ously proved themselves in the Premiership". Gareth Barry was a solid and reliable player but Joleon Lescott, prised away from Everton after protracted negotiations, had a dangerous mistake in him at the best of times. Santa Cruz was an outmoded targetman, Sylvinho was well past his best when he was signed and Adebayor, though gifted, was tempera-mental and erratic. Only Carlos Tevez matched the profile of a world-class player. What's more, Hughes' defensive organisation was suspect and his lack of tactical acumen had been embarrassingly demonstrated in a match at White Hart Lane when City's left flank comprising the veteran Sylvinho and the reluctantly backtracking Robinho was repeat-edly exposed by Aaron Lennon before Hughes belatedly substituted.

When Hughes was finally fired, in December 2009, there was a predictable outburst of pundit rage against the sacking of a brave British battler. But Hughes' spending spree had not lifted City higher than a temporary eighth place after an initial end of season tenth whereas Sven- Goran Eriksson, with far less funds at his disposal, had finished ninth - and played attractive football whilst doing so. Hughes' return to full-time management six months after he was ousted from Eastlands was anything but impressive, a mediocre 32% win percentage at Fulham, a dreadful 27% at Queens Park Rangers and at Stoke City (at the time of writing) an unconvincing 36%. Those figures spoke for themselves.

8. Hughes was immediately succeeded by Roberto Mancini, former manager of Inter-Milan who, until six weeks earlier, had been unavailable to any club for legal reasons. Khaldoun Al Mubarak, who'd become a Commander of the Star of the Order of Italian Solidarity for his work in promoting trade between Italy and the UAE, had followed Italian football for many years. He was fully familiar with Mancini's managerial record. He knew not just that Mancini had guided Inter to three successive scudetti but also that it was his team which, in 2006-7, had established a Serie A record of seventeen victories on the run. They finished with a total of 97 points for the season, unprecedented in any European country. Over the four years of his managerial tenure at the San Siro, Mancini's win percentage was 61.67. What's more, Inter had previously been without a league title for seventeen years until Mancini won it again for them.

Khaldoun had, of course, to consider whether success in one national competition would translate into another. But the example of Carlo Ancelotti, Mancini's great rival at AC Milan strongly suggested that it would. Ancelotti had been appointed manager of Chelsea six months earlier and was well on his way to the Premiership title. The decision to give Mancini the helm at Eastlands was thus made on strictly logical grounds far removed from the ludicrous "ave yer got charisma?" criteria of Peter Swales or whoever it was that gave Hughes' name to Shinawatra.

By the autumn of 2011, Garry Cook had fallen after a spectacular email own goal. Gaffe-prone though he was, he knew his stuff as an adman. His 'My First City Game' campaign and his relocation of the ticket office so Citizens didn't have to queue in the rain had gone down a treat and many were sorry to see him go.

9. In September of that year, Sheikh Mansour and Khaldoun Al Mubarak had to deal with hitherto unheard -of acts of insubordination by Carlos Tevez. Fined just short of £400,000 for his apparent reluctance to take the field as a substitute in Munich, he beat a hasty retreat to Buenos Aires and, to all intents and purposes, went on strike. Having moved swiftly to ensure that Roberto Mancini's authority was not compromised, the club took no further action and there was speculation they might be prepared to let Tevez go in the next transfer window.

But, in January 2012, Kia Joorabchan, Tevez' Iranian-born adviser- a man who was a high-profile visitor to Eastlands in the Shinawatra era- tried to strike a cut-price deal which would transfer Tevez to Silvio Berlusconi 's AC Milan. On the 25th, Tevez and Joorabchan got their answer. Tevez' self-imposed exile would be construed as gross misconduct, he would be fined £1.2 million and have his wages stopped.

Mubarak followed up with a statement in the Abu Dhabi English-language newspaper, 'The National '. If Tevez, Joorabchan and AC vice -president Adriano Galliani reckoned they could pull off a transfer for less than €30 million, then, he implied, they had another think coming. Mubarak 's unshakeable self-assurance and biting wit was displayed in the pithy comment - "Mr.Galliani and his advisers have developed a misplaced sense of confidence from their premature discussions with Carlos and his advisers. If they want to be a consideration in this transfer window they would do better to stop congratulating one another and begin to look at how they would begin to meet our terms".

Milan didn't meet City's terms and a couple of weeks later Tevez was back in Manchester and had apologised to Roberto Mancini. He would contribute significantly to City's title- winning run-in both with the winning goal he laid on for Samir Nasri against Chelsea and in his performance against Norwich.

Sheikh Mansour and Khaldoun Al Mubarak's pragmatic stance had been vindicated. They knew full well what Tevez had done for City in previous seasons and Khaldoun had once expressed his belief that the Argentinian would become "the finest player in the world". They'd never shut the door on Tevez' rehabilitation whilst at the same time upholding Mancini's authority. Such were City's financial resources that they could afford to take a firm line with a mutinous footballer but, in acting as they did, Mansour and Mubarak had laid down a vital marker. Manchester City might be the world's wealthiest football club but it would never compromise with player power nor be held to ransom by shadowy advisers.

10. The last of the big decisions was taken on April 8, 2012, in London, this time by Khaldoun Al Mubarak together with Roberto Mancini. City had just been defeated by Arsenal and television cameras captured the Chairman in the Emirates' directors box with a face like thunder. City had led the Premiership table for most of the season but now, with only six games left, were eight points behind United.

Media speculation was rife that Sheikh Mansour and Mubarak were infuriated with underachievement and intended to sack Mancini at the end of the season. His replacement, so pundits figured, would be none other than Jose Mourinho, his successor at Inter Milan, now close to winning La Liga with Real Madrid. Mourinho's track record at Porto, Chelsea, Inter and Real was unsurpassed and, though many Citizens thought of him as typically United and indeed bound for Old Trafford after Ferguson's retirement, there were those who craved his arrival at the Etihad. But, happily, Mubarak did not share their views.

His body language might have suggested anger to many observers but in fact Mubarak was stunned. On his way down to the away dressing room, however, his resolve intensified. As he would reveal to the official City website a few weeks later, his thoughts were that "we are not giving up". He had no intention to "raise the white flag and sulk" but was determined to "fight until the very last second of this Championship". He knew intuitively that Mancini would share his resolve. "We have got very close over the years and I know how he works" he said, going on to explain "he is a very strong character who wants to win more than anyone I have ever seen". Within seconds, Chairman and manager rapidly agreed that "if we could win all our games and have a bit of luck we could still pull it off !".

But Mubarak and Mancini would not leave matters at heroic resolve and instant pep talks to a hurting squad. They " looked at each other and decided to take the pressure off the team". From then on, Mancini, in interview, with the confidence born of knowing he had the full support of his Chairman (and, crucially, of the owner himself), repeatedly took the blame for City's wobble and suggested that United were already as good as champions. Talking to his players, however, both at Carrington and pre-match, he took a very different line, insisting that City must fight to the last second of the last game, that United were vulnerable and that the title could still come to the Etihad. As indeed it did!

Such were the ten key decisions, made by Sheikh Mansour and on his behalf which transformed Manchester City: he bought the club, he brought in Khaldoun Al Mubarak to run it, he revitalised Carrington and Platt Lane, he bankrolled player purchases, he insisted those purchases should be made on the basis of dossiers not hunches or videos, he availed himself of Etihad Airways' sponsorship to counter UEFA's attempt to clip City's wings, he sacked Mark Hughes, he hired Roberto Mancini, he faced down player power in the Tevezgate affair and he backed Mancini when all seemed lost only five weeks before City won the title. No wonder a banner was draped at Eastlands stating 'Manchester Thanks You Sheikh Mansour'!

A minority of Citizens have found it difficult to accept the renaissance of Manchester City, hankering after the homeliness of Maine Road, the absence of massive investment, the heroic loyalty of the dark nineties. Colin Shindler has renounced his football faith and even the estimable David Conn has anxiously pondered the transformation in depth even though he would be overcome with emotion on May 13th, 2012.

But for the younger generation of City supporters, born like Ricky Hatton in the early years of City's tragic decline, starved of success and dismissed as mere 'noisy neighbours', thrilled by City's defeat of United in the Demolition Derby which paved the way for ultimate triumph, there would be no doubt. Some were youngsters brought to the new stadium by their dads, others had marched to Macclesfield and York, still more could speak, as did Noel Gallagher, in tears as he watched the overthrow of United from his hotel room on tour, of " forty years of loyalty rewarded". And as the stalwarts of the Joe Mercer era, Mike Summerbee, now a club ambassador, Tony Book and Francis Lee took pride of place when the first Premiership trophy was first paraded round the Etihad, there was a symbolic union of the icons of the sixties with the heroes of a new century.

3

THE RISE AND FALL OF A MAESTRO: ROBERTO MANCINI

Roberto Mancini could name that tune, of course. Indeed he knew it well. Composed six years before he was born in a small town near the Adriatic coast, he'd heard it many times as a boy on his parents' radio. The son of a Marchese joiner, he'd grown up in the mountains of Campania, not far from Naples where his mother came from. But he'd never expected to hear it sung in English, still less by thousands of people using his own name and extending him a warm welcome to their city. That was before he took the helm at Eastlands at the end of 2009.

Against all the crap spawned by the Eurovision Song Contest, 'Nel Blu Dipinto Di Blu', sung by its co-writer Domenico Modugno, stands out. It didn't win the contest but, marketed in the United States under the title of its chorus, 'Volare', it topped the Billboard Hot 100. Its popularity endures and, uploaded on You Tube not long before Mancini was made manager of Manchester City, it's had over four million views. City fans' adaptation was simple, direct and effective:

Mancini, oh-oh
Mancini, oh-oh-oh
He came from Italy
To manage Man City
MANCINI-OH-OH-OH!

But why did Manchester Cty supporters, certainly the bulk of them, feel an instant affinity for an Italian football coach whose only experience of English football was a few weeks on the books of Leicester City? While some were intrigued that his surname so closely resembled the name of his new club, City's more knowledgeable supporters knew Mancini's record, not merely at Inter- Milan but at Lazio where, operating under severe financial constraints and with players whose wages had been slashed by 80%, he kept the club within range of the Top Three and won the Coppa Italia.They also knew about his successful career playing for ex-City boss Sven- Goran Eriksson both at Sampdoria and, before the club became cash-strapped, at Lazio, where they won Serie A. City fans valued Eriksson's judgement. He'd been sacked against their wishes to make way for Mark Hughes and they'd soon hear his glowing reference for Mancini - "he was always like a coach when he was a player. He was a coach, he was the kit man, he was the bus driver, he was everything".

Mancini had long been interested in coming to England. At Sampdoria, he'd listened to Graeme Souness' tales of rugged tackling barely restrained by referees and he'd palled up with David Platt. Later his buddy Gian-Luca Vialli had managed Chelsea and his mentor Eriksson had become English national team coach. He himself had almost been lured to Blackburn and he'd only quit Leicester when an unexpected offer of management at Fiorentina had cropped up. Now he eagerly welcomed the chance of marrying Italian tactical know-how with English competitiveness.

But it wouldn't t be long before British pundits would make negative comments about Roberto Mancini. Mark Hughes would describe his predecessor as "an autocrat" and John Barnes would put him down as "a martinet". But Mancini's determination to win and his intolerance of player power sat well with most Citizens. Colin Schindler might romanticise the era of 'Typical City' and 'Cityitis' but the bulk of the fans were sick to the back teeth of the long years of stagnation, of retardation by rented telly merchants, of the bogroll blues and, above all, of the taunts of the Rags and the disdain of their manager. If ' Bobby Manc', as he was soon admiringly dubbed, aimed to crack the whip with the lazybones, good on him!

For all Mancini's emphasis on discipline, both personal and tactical, he was not an exponent of "winning ugly" or a ruthlessly pragmatic coach like Jose Mourinho, furthering his career by carefully calculated moves and never staying too long at any one club. Indeed Mancini had been on Sampdoria's books for fully fifteen years and he'd deliberately chosen to play for an unfashionable club at a time when Italy's Top Three were falling over themselves trying to sign him. Inter was of course one of the Three, but it was a club in decline without a Serie A title to its name for seventeen years. What motivated Mancini was the challenge of transforming an underachieving club not hitching his waggon to institutions such as AC Milan, Real Madrid or Barcelona where success is regarded as the norm.

Right from the off, Roberto Mancini cut a distinctive figure in the City technical zone. Immaculately dressed, he demonstrated his commitment to the City cause with an elegant blue and white scarf. But, as his long hair, dark but greying, flapped about this way and that while he gesticulated his exasperation with the side he inherited, he resembled nothing so much as a demanding maestro of the Italian Opera.

He was the football equivalent of a virtuoso conductor such as Arturo Toscanini or Giuseppe Sinopoli.

Mancini demanded the highest standards and had exemplified them himself in the Golden Nineties of Serie A when the world's finest players flocked to Italy. His swerving dribbles, his audacious volleys- and the astounding backheel from eight metres with which he scored for Lazio against Parma- would be immortalised on You Tube. Still, the stylist could be a hard knock himself if he chose to be, red -carded - and banned for six weeks - for a brutal foul on Paul Ince. Friend and colleague of Sven-Goran Eriksson he might be, but this was a man of a very different stripe to the mild-mannered Swede.

In his life outside football, Mancini was devoted to his family. Strictly brought up by his stern but loving father Aldo, he was happily married to Federica and a good father to his sons Filippo and Andrea. A devout Roman Catholic, he'd been an altar boy in Jesi and Ancona and had long aspired to make a pilgrimage to the Bosnian town of Mejugorje where apparitions of the Virgin Mary had been reported since 1981. Aesthete and athlete, Mancini's interests were fashion, cuisine, and wine, on the one hand, and tennis, cycling and golf on the other.

The first thing Mancini did as City boss was to order training in the afternoons as well as the mornings. This startled the British members of Mark Hughes' squad. "When we get home after the afternoon session we're getting caught up in the rush-hour traffic jams", they tweeted. 'Tough shit!', was the reaction of City supporters, 'welcome to the working week!' The only thing was that the malcontents had the support of Raymond Verheijen, Hughes' fitness coach and Craig Bellamy's personal trainer. Now Bellamy might've been with his eighth club, he might've had previous for abusive texts, golf club wielding and allegations of off- field assault and he'd been once described by the avuncular Sir Bobby Robson as "an unusual and volatile character". But the whizzbang winger from Wales was a wholehearted and spectacular player and many Citizens had taken him to their hearts. So, when he complained that two sessions a day was knackering his kneecaps, Mancini had to tread carefully.

Undeterred by the opposition of certain squad members, Mancini set about tightening the City defence. His methods soon bore dividends. Whereas twenty-seven goals had been conceded in the half season under Hughes, only sixteen were conceded under Mancini. There would be seven clean sheets under the new boss but there'd been only four under Hughes. These figures spoke for themselves.And, though Carlos Tevez would criticise Mancini's defensive tactics, his goalscoring was even more prolific under his new manager than it had been under Hughes.

There was also the problem of Robinho. The Brazilian superstar had been foisted on Hughes but, where the old boss had learned to live with him, Mancini was soon impatient. Robinho's skill was there for all to see but the Italian's exacting eye soon noted his reluctance to track back and his general indolence. Substituted as a substitute in a sad performance against Everton, he was soon back in Brazil, slung out on loan to Santos.

Mancini believed a strictly professional ethos should be cultivated to fulfil Sheikh Mansour's project. He could often be seen in the technical zone urging his players not to relax after scoring. What's more, the show business style goal celebrations which flourished in Hughes' days were moderated under Mancini. Skysters might lament the departure of Robinho and his dumbass thumbsucking and the toning down of Emmanuel Adebayor's asinine antics but Mancini had no use for frivolity.

At the end of Mancini's first half season in charge, City only narrowly lost out, in the last game of the season, on a Champions League place when they were defeated by rivals Tottenham. Chairman Khaldoun spoke of "a major achievement" but stressed the need "to build a mindset" - a probable reference to the cavalier attitude of certain prominent players whom Mancini had inherited.

The one aspect of Mancini's CV which was open to criticism on rational grounds was language skills. Far from the effectiveness of Rafael Benitez, still less the total fluency of Arsene Wenger, Mancini's English was limited. Sure, it was far better than his fellow –countryman, Fabio Capello, the manager of England, a man who deplorably claimed he could get by with only a hundred words. But it wasn't good enough to interact with his players still less to cope with the media. Mancini promptly set about correcting the weakness by taking private lessons with a tutor and, though his English would remain without nuance, it improved significantly. In interviews, he dispensed with an interpreter but continue to think in Italian and mentally translate, needing a little time to answer questions. But some of those he faced were so crass that he would merely smile broadly before replying!

Within three weeks of becoming manager, Mancini made a very significant signing. Patrick Vieira, the former Arsenal star, storied in the Gooners' song ("born in Senegal, plays for Arsenal"), the man who brought 'Volare', to Highbury and whom Mancini had himself taken to Inter, committed himself to Manchester City. Possibly the finest tackler in the history of the game, Vieira was now thirty-three and there were those who criticised Mancini for hiring the veteran. But the manager's reasoning was sound. A member of France's 1998 World Cup winning squad and captain of the Invincibles, Vieira had also been one of Mancini's own Italian title-winners.

If ever a man had acquired the confidence born of success, it was Patrick Vieira. 6'4" tall, a dignified and imposing presence, he was no longer the young firebrand of his Arsenal debut. Vieira exhibited a self- belief which soon transferred itself to his new teammates. Re-adjusting to the pace of the Premiership, he was soon making key assists. He would not become known for his goals but he never had been. His career club average was one in ten and he slightly bettered that for City. His second season at Eastlands, when he acted as a kind of unofficial team leader, would be more significant.

On the eve of the Wembley Derby Semi, Vieira made an inspi-rational speech to the squad. Acknowledging United's history, he stressed that this was a new era. His English teammates, in particular, embarrassed at first by this distinctly non-laddish episode, and unac-customed to footballer eloquence, were rapidly convinced. United were overthrown and Napoleon's dictum that, in conflict, " morale is to the material in the ratio of two to one" was borne out on the football field. Vieira's appearance as a substitute in the Cup Final was in fact his swansong. He would announce his retirement and become in effect an ambassador for the club before taking over as manager of the Elite Development Squad.

In the summer of 2010, Roberto Mancini started to send the Hughesite doubters packing. Stephen Ireland- who'd wangled his way out of the Republic of Ireland squad with sussed- out ruses - was offloaded to Aston Villa in part exchange for the brainy teetotaller James Milner. Ireland 's skill had not been in doubt but his mentality - a word Mancini used time and time again when discussing footballers - certainly was. Soon Ireland, who'd stalled on the deal by demanding a couple of million quid from City for his consent, was claiming that young City players were "money -obsessed"!

It would take Mancini a further year to seal Craig Bellamy's permanent departure but, in the meantime, he got rid of him on loan to Cardiff. As for Robinho, he'd suddenly found his old Sao Paolo stomping ground less restful than he thought. But scarcely had the staff at Carrington time to say "eh up, he's back!" than Mancio was on the phone to Milan, flogging him to Berlusconi for €18 million - a nifty piece of business if ever there was one!

It would take longer to dispose of Emmanuel Adebayor. The Togolese striker was a player of high technical skill, no doubt about it and an intelligent man who spoke English at machine gun speed. It was a pity that he never learned to curb his celebrations. Leaving aside the irresponsible cavorting in front of Arsenal fans which might well have led to a riot, his hat-trick against the mediocre Poles of Poznan did not merit an exaggerated choreography. Bandanna-sporting and beaming, Adebayor came on like a latter-day Lionel Ritchie. It was the kind of thing which might've had Richard Keys chortling but it was scarcely the mark of a mature man setting about the task in hand in a restrained and professional manner.

James Milner was not Mancini's first English signing. In the initial transfer window Adam Johnson had arrived from Middlesbrough. Mancini had been impressed by his display in the FA Cup tie between the two clubs but he'd accepted the recommendation of others. Eager to recruit promising young English players who could be moulded before bad habits became ingrained, he took a chance on the twenty-two -year-old Johnson, a player with unusual technical skill for an Englishman and with a powerful shot to boot.

The summer of 2010 saw heavy expenditure. There would be two key acquisitions. The first was the Valencia playmaker, twenty-four-year-old David Silva. Mancini had hoped to sign Silva to Inter, so deeply impressed was he by the little Spaniard's performance when Valencia knocked Inter out of the Champions League. Silva had gone on to be part of Spain's World Cup winning squad in the summer of 2010 and thus had experience of winning at the highest level.

The next was Yaya Toure from Cote d'Ivoire, who, with Barcelona, had won both La Liga and the Champions League. Normally employed defensively by Barca, his combination of physical power with high skill was something Mancini was determined to use in an attacking way.

In signing his compatriot Mario Balotelli, barely twenty, Mancini was taking a considerable risk with a player who'd been in trouble with his previous club, Inter. But when Mancini had been in charge of him, there'd been little bother, a situation which changed dramatically when Mourinho took over. Still, Balotelli had been a member of a squad which had triumphed both domestically and in the Champions League. Key to the signing was Mancini's belief that this son of Ghanaian immigrants was an unusually gifted player, potentially one of the best in the world, whose talents he wished to lock in to Manchester City before one of the European giants pounced.

Two other players completed Mancini's summer signings. Both were full backs- Jerome Boateng, Berlin-born with a West African father, signed for £10 million from Hamburg and Aleksandar Kolarov, a Serb, who arrived from Lazio for 16 million.

It was at this time that Mancini added David Platt to his staff - officially as first-team coach. The pair had been pals since playing in the same Sampdoria team in the nineties and, having spent seven years in Serie A, Platt could converse in his boss' native language. More importantly, he was a conduit between Mancini and the English players, able to translate the manager's thoughts into footballspeak if need be. Relaxed and approachable, Platt's personality contrasted with the intense and sometimes aloof Mancini. But the appointment did not go down well with most Citizens. Though he was an articulate man, his previous punditry had been seen as negative towards City and it would take him some time to live this reputation down. What turned things around was Platt's ability, in press conferences, to deal with often hostile journalists and take the wind out of their sails. This relieved the pressure on Mancini.

Brian Kidd had been Technical Development Manager at Eastlands for three months before Mancini's arrival and he was then appointed assistant manager. Though Kidd had starred for United in his youth, he was Collyhurst through and through and had been on City's books for three years in the seventies. What's more he'd been on the wrong end of rude remarks in Sir Alex Ferguson's autobiography. An assistant manager at United, Leeds, Sheffield United and Portsmouth, not to mention the English national team, Kidd knew English football from ground level up.

Manchester City's progress in 2010-11 was marred by some bad moments - the ugly defensive blunders at Molineux, the humiliation at home by Arsenal and the three defeats in a row in late October and early November when the media pounced. But they'd stopped Chelsea after the Londoners' run of five straight wins and got back on track at the turn of the year. They were, albeit briefly, title contenders and they embarked on a strong run in the FA Cup despite making heavy weather of defeating teams from lower divisions.

Mancini continued to fine -tune and tighten the defence and ten clean sheets were achieved. But, slowly and surely, a more expansive and expressive team began to emerge. Partly it was a question of class and partly of confidence. As Yaya's staggering, surging runs became increasingly effective, as David Silva's brilliant footwork began to open up defences, as Mario Balotelli caused gasps with cameos of audacious trickery and as Carlos Tevez joined the three of them in memorable moves, so Citizens became convinced that a great side was in the making.

Team confidence was crucial and it spread from the key players to the others. Yaya prowled Eastlands like a Barcelona baron, Silva - who many pundits had reckoned would be too slight to cope with the Premiership hurly-burly - became hardened to rugged tackling and delighted in evading it, Tevez carried all before him and Balotelli responded to the mentorship of Patrick Vieira.

Three players from the pre-Abu Dhabi era emerged as men who believed in the project and enjoyed great rapport with the Citizens. Joe Hart, having been on loan at Birmingham City. was unknown to Mancini at the start of the season.Given his chance, he soon showed himself to be a fine shot-stopper, remarkably confident for his age and boldly urging his teammates on. Pablo Zabaleta was a cult hero, a rugged and wholehearted player who thoroughly adjusted to Manchester life. Allowed indefinite compassionate leave to visit his comatose father after a motorbike crash in Argentina, he enjoyed mass tweets of support. He returned to play a key role in the Cup Derby Semi, despite suffering a brutal Paul Scholes foul. Vincent Kompany was a captain in fact before he was in name and helped to keep the team focused after the November tabloid attack. He encouraged his teammates, he defused incidents and he intelligently analysed matches.

Over it all presided Roberto Mancini, providing many an iconic image: his short hair at the start of the season when he briefly trusted the Manchester climate; wearing both the sky blue and the red and

32a2actt22

white striped scarf on one bitterly cold day ; urging calm after the equaliser against Blackburn; tense and frowning, tightlipped in the technical zone as he played every kick of every game; the touchline incidents with British managers, Mark Hughes and, before that, Everton's David Moyes; saluting the Citizens at Craven Cottage when the Mancini Song reverberated round the ground as City hammered Hughes' Fulham 4-1.

While Mancini himself did not go in for disrespect towards opponents and unhesitatingly admired Rooney's wonder goal in the Old Trafford Derby, he had to contend with continuing media hostility. There were accusations that he was "whingeing nonsensically " and that his "foreigners" were "in dilettante mode ... taking one look at the Britannia tundra and emerging with their gloves on". He could be a hard taskmaster, no doubt about it but he would not be the inflexible authoritarian the tabloids painted, accepting the team's wish for loud music in the dressing room.

Mancini led City to a fine end of season run with seven successive wins- broken only by a defeat at Goodison- which saw them clinch third place and qualify outright for the Champions League. They overcame United in the Cup Derby Semi. And he had the last laugh on the scribes who'd relished the comment of Stoke's Tony Pulis, their "no-nonsense Welshman" when he remarked that "you can have all the money in the world and the top players but a team playing against you as a team takes a lot of beating". Stoke's rugged tackling was of no avail to them in the Cup Final where they were outclassed by City and would've been defeated by a far bigger margin if it hadn't been for goalkeeper Sorensen.

With no World Cups or Euros, Roberto Mancini could plan for season 2011-12 with even more care than before. His two major signings,

Silva and Yaya, had been superbly successful. Balotelli, bought for the future, remained a fine prospect despite copping persistent tabloid attention for his off- field eccentricities, some real, many invented or grossly exaggerated. Milner had brought the English virtues of workrate and determination but with more tactical savvy than most English players and with no chav-type vices. Mancini had been unlucky with his fullbacks. Both Boateng and Kolarov had been injured early in the campaign. But whereas Kolarov recovered both his ankle and his appetite for the game, Boateng would not be content without a guaranteed start and was sold to Bayern Munich.

By August 2011 Mancini had weeded out most of the remaining Hughesian signings, retaining only the estimable Gareth Barry, the resolute Nigel de Jong and, of course, Tevez. Dalglish's Liverpool took Bellamy, Villa got redundant keeper Shay Given and Shaun Wright-Phillips hove to at Queens Park Rangers. But Adebayor was still on loan and buyers couldn't be found for the plodding Paraguayan centre forward Roque Santa Cruz and the gormless Brazilian Jo, rivals in ineptitude with strike rates each of one in seven!

With the stables cleared, Mancini brought in a Rumanian backup keeper, Pantilimon, a Montenegrin centre back Savic and gave Owen Hargreaves a chance to revive his career. Hargreaves, cut loose by United, British by nationality but brought up in Canada, a reliable guy in the manner of Barry and Milner, had much to offer if his injury-plagued career could be revived. In signing Gael Clichy from Arsenal, the manager acquired a replacement full-back and a member of Wenger's Invincibles. But it was Clichy's clubmate, Samir Nasri, whose signing showed most clearly the new path Mancini intended to tread.

Samir Nasri was a player of high technical skill and intelligence, often imaginative and unorthodox, able to conjure goals right out of the blue. Though he preferred the role of playmaker, that was denied him at the Emirates where Cesc Fabregas ruled -and so he was often deployed on the wing. The capture of Nasri, for £22 million, provided Mancini with insurance in the event of injury to David Silva. But it was also a vote for fantasy. With a defence far more secure than what he'd inherited, Mancini could afford to develop a more expansive style. Pigeonholed as a defensive manager by pundits whose notion of Serie A was usually about twenty-five years out of date, Mancini had exemplified surprise and panache in his own playing days and admired it himself in such colleagues as Ruud Gullit.

With David Silva, Yaya Toure and now Nasri, City were well-equipped to become an attacking team. But Mancini felt that they were over -dependent on Tevez for goals. Already, in the January 2011 transfer window, he'd brought in the Bosnia-Herzegovina striker Edin Dzeko, acquired from Wolfsburg for £27 million but Dzeko was taking his time to adjust to the Premiership rough-and-tumble.

A new striker was needed, someone of power and class, able to join the interplay of Silva and Yaya, prolific and physically hard. This led Manchester City to pay Atletico Madrid a club record of £38 million for the Argentinian centre forward Sergio Aguero. The son-in-law of Diego Maradona, Aguero was only 5'8" tall but he was a powerhouse of determined running, and highly skilful. His strike rate, both in La Liga and in the blue and white stripes of Argentina, was one in 2.5!

For six weeks City rode the crest of a wave, beginning with the 4-0 defeat of a skilful Swansea City in a match notable not only for Sergio Aguero's wonderful debut but for sparkling attacking Interplay. City went on to win five of the next six games, scoring nineteen goals while conceding only five and leaping to the top of the table. The outstanding single display was the 5-1 crushing of Spurs at White Hart Lane.

Dzeko scored four in that match and looked a fine centre forward, excellent in the air and fast but intelligent too and, despite an uncertain first touch, an accurate passer. Samir Nasri also had an excellent game against Tottenham. Three of the key assists came from him and his defensive backtracking stood out in contrast to the blind racing of the Spurs wingers, Bale and Lennon.

But David Silva was City's kingpin as City carried all before them in game after game. He was the fountainhead of the team's attack, his ball control instantaneous and his left foot passing forensic. He it was who initiated changes in the angle of attack, even while nimbly hurdling many a ruthless boot intended to halt him in his tracks. Silva was the living incarnation of Mancini's 2001 pamphlet ' Il Trequartista,' published by the Italian FA.

On September 27, however, in the Allianz Arena, City came unstuck against Bayern Munich. Edin Dzeko had reacted badly to being substituted even before Carlos Tevez appeared to refuse a summons from the bench. It was an unprecedented act of insubordination in the world of football and it was used in certain quarters to imply that Mancini lacked people skills and was secretly detested by his players. Indeed City's indifferent form in the Champions League, where they'd been placed in the so-called 'Group of Death' with Bayern and Napoli was used as a stick with which to beat the manager.

City would not emerge from this group and there were many media references to Mancini's unimpressive record in the Champions League while with Inter. But he was not the only outstanding manager to struggle in Europe's top club competition. Arsene Wenger had never won the trophy in fifteen years with Arsenal and Sir Alex Ferguson only twice in his twenty-five year reign at Old Trafford. Yet Wenger's failure was rarely mentioned and Ferguson's relative lack of success never. On the other hand, Rafael Benitez- like Mancini a foreigner who didn't court the media or provide a ready source of quotes- achievement in winning the crown with a distinctly ordinary Liverpool team wasn't saluted as it should have been.

If Mancini had a case to answer in Europe, it lay not in his tactical approach but in his unbridled will to win. He could hardly be blamed for the abandonment of the Champions League Quarter-Final Derby against A.C. Milan when Inter's fans went crazy and launched flares onto the pitch.But Inter's 2007 knockout by Valencia had ended in a mass brawl between the two teams. And when Inter succumbed to Benitez' Liverpool the following year, they had a man sent off in each leg. In his playing days, Mancini's hot temper had been notorious -punching Trevor Francis in the Sampdoria dressing-room, slugging it out with Paul Ince on the pitch and having to be restained by his teammates when he threatened the blundering ref after Sampdoria lost to Barcelona at Wembley in the 1992 European Cup Final. But, in England, an older and wiser Mancini, subdued by his own halting English, seemed, in comparison to his youthful self, like the quintessence of cool.

In the immediate aftermath of the Tevez Incident, it was crucial that Roberto Mancini's authority should be seen to prevail. He himself had said Tevez would never play for him again and, if certain elements in the media thought that Citizens might have divided loyalties between their manager and their onfield hero, they were soon disillusioned. 'Tevez out' banners began to appear and the Argentinian received a ferocious kicking all over City fansites. Before long, Tevez beat a retreat to Buenos Aires and City pressed on without him, sustaining their assault on United's Premiership crown.

In the 'Demolition Derby', on October 23, City destroyed Manchester United 6-1 at Old Trafford, a result which stunned the football world. Tabloid hacks had made hay with an incident a couple of days earlier when the Fire Brigade had been called to Mario Balotelli's home. But Mancini ignored the furore, selected Balotelli and saw him score twice in a display which suggested that he'd come of age. There were those United supporters who tried to excuse their own team's display by pointing to the sending off of Jonny Evans -a dismissal which Sir Alex Ferguson had not challenged. But City were one nil up at that time and, if Evans had not, as last man, restrained Balotelli as he was surging on goal, would've almost certainly doubled their lead. What's more, attempts to scapegoat David de Gea, United's youthful keeper were beside the point. De Gea was to blame for only one goal, the fourth.There was of course far more to City's triumph than a dismissed centre back and a single goalkeeping error. United's off-the-cuff approach and the wayward positioning, at key times, of Young, Smalling, Anderson and Nani contrasted with City's impeccable discipline and constant varying of the angles of attack

Roberto Mancini had shown himself a master coach in selection, deployment and substitution. He brushed aside the redtop claptrap about Balotelli and had seen his protégé dramatically come good. He'd unleashed his attacking fullbacks, one of whom, Richards, provided a key assist for the third goal. He curbed City's eagerness to attack following Evans' dismissal, instructing them, from the technical area, to play wide and slow so as to tire United out and, by the last ten minutes, some of the men in red shirts were plainly knackered. His introduction of Dzeko, fast, fresh and direct, produced two more goals and a key assist, transforming a victory into a humiliation. City had upstaged their rivals, inflicted a severe psychological blow and gained a lead in terms of goal difference which would prove crucial at the end of the season.

Though Manchester City took ten points from the 'Group of Death', they were eliminated, in third place behind Napoli. But, in the Premiership, they continued to ride high, playing scintillating football and not sustaining their first defeat till December 12 at Stamford Bridge. A silly intervention by Joleon Lescott stopped City holding on for a draw just as, at Anfield a fortnight before, his gaffe had let Liverpool back into a match when they were being outplayed. City got back to winning ways six days after the Chelsea defeat when they hung on to their lead against Arsenal, a side who'd recovered excellently after a poor start of the season. In this game Mancini's inventive substitutions contrasted with Arsenal Wenger's simple like for like swaps.

2012 started on an unhappy note for City when, in the Third Round of the FA Cup, they yielded their hard-won trophy to United. Once again there'd been a man sent off yet this time the dismissal was not of a stand-in defender like Evans but of Vincent Kompany, top-class centre back and inspirational skipper. Chris Foy produced the red card for what he claimed was a two footed tackle -in fact Kompany's challenge was grounded and immaculately targeted. The result was that City played for eighty-five minutes with only ten men - unlike United at Old Trafford, who went down to ten only at the start of the second-half. To compound the problem, David Silva was injured early and had to go off at half time.

Roberto Mancini's half-time redeployment was masterly. Switching to three centre backs provided vital defensive security and, at worst, damage limitation whilst allowing one of these, the highly mobile Richards, to roam upfield sporadically. He was the one who won the free kick from which City's first goal was scored. Bringing on an additional full-back, Zabaleta, took the psychological and positional pressure off Kolarov who'd suffered a nightmare against Antonio Valencia. Kolarov's wonderful freekick strike opened the scoring for City and his low cross would've led to to an equalising goal had it not been for a further blunder from Foy. Mancini also deputed James Milner to take over playmaking duties in the second half and he went on to provide a key assist for City's second goal. He disconcerted Ferdinand throughout, thus sowing confusion in the United ranks. And he initiated the move which ought to have led to a penalty- for blatant handball by Big Jones.

Though a dreadful refereeing display had put City at a disadvantage barely five minutes after kick-off and had denied them the chance to level the scores and force a replay, the heroic fightback against United was both a moral victory and a great achievement by Mancini. It served to strengthen the squad's belief in itself, having done so well against its foremost rivals in such dire circumstances.

There was a six-week spell at the beginning of the year when City appeared to be faltering. They were eliminated from the Carling Cup in the semi-final by Liverpool and they were beaten twice away in the Premiership. This was not due to any loss of morale but to the absence of Yaya Toure, away at the African Nations Cup, and David Silva out injured. The extent of City's reliance on these two great players was thus exposed.

Though City revived as an effective force when Yaya and Silva returned, their displays lacked the verve of the first half- season. Two consecutive defeats in March, one at the Liberty Stadium and the other to Sporting Lisbon in the Europa League (compounded by aggregate defeat to the Portuguese a week later) brought a bout of media scepticism and even doom -mongering. City had blown their chances in the League, it was suggested, and United would take the title once again. In fact the remaining three months of the season saw City gradually climb back into contention and it was during this time that Roberto

Mancini, both off -field and on, made his most vital contributions to winning the title.

The first was the rehabilitation of Carlos Tevez. Mancini had expressed to Abu Dhabi his willingness to welcome Tevez back, provided that the AWOL striker would apologise for his action in Munich. Taken to task by questioning pundits about having "softened your stance on Tevez" Mancini replied "if I am soft, it is because I am a good man". His lack of nuanced English didn't provide a satisfactory reply and even made him seem self-righteous. But Mancini had been guided by his Roman Catholic faith and his belief in forgiveness - provided, of course, the sinner had repented. What's more, when Mancini conferred with Khaldoun Al Mubarak and Sheikh Mansour, it was agreed that, from a pragmatic point of view, the return of Tevez would reintroduce a player of unquestionable skill and, once he was over the white lines, commitment. By now, Tevez, chastened- and bored by his life of luxury and idleness in Buenos Aires- both needed and wanted to reassert himself as a footballer.

Tevez was reintroduced in the closing stages of the home game against Chelsea, after the Londoners had taken the lead. City equalised via the penalty spot but, with the Citizens beside themselves with anxiety and many urging players to shoot from impossible situations, Mancini insisted on a probing attack, even as he urged his defenders forward. It was then that Tevez and Nasri worked a brilliant one-two from which Nasri scored. City had thus established a new Premiership record of ten home wins on the run and, more important, revived their challenge to United.

After the Chelsea game, City relapsed, drawing at the Britannia Stadium, being held to a home draw by Sunderland and suffering defeat at the Emirates. The match against Arsenal saw much heroic defending, notably from Kompany, but City were badly let down by Mario Balotelli. Seeming completely unfocused, he contributed virtually nothing, complained persistently with little justification, should've been sent off early for a dreadful foul and was ultimately dismissed in stoppage time.

Balotelli had not kicked on from his fine performance at Old Trafford. He contributed occasional goals and was an impeccable penalty taker but there were times when he seemed like an adjunct to the team rather than an integral part of it. Too often he appeared to lack the stomach for genuine football combat, tending to substitute petulance for determination. True, he was being vilified in the media for what were no more than boyish indiscretions but this was beside the point. His onfield displays had scarcely justified his selection even before the debacle of the Emirates.

Though Roberto Mancini could often be seen remonstrating with Balotelli, he was reluctant to discipline him. In many ways Mancini saw himself in the young man from Brescia. In his own youth, Mancini had been brought to heel by Italian national team coach Enzo Bearzot for an unauthorised night out in New York. Labelled a 'bad boy' by the media, he never held down a regular place in the Italian national team despite the brilliance of his club performances. He did not want Balotelli's career to be similarly blighted. But, in his continual indulgence of the wayward Mario, Mancini had sometimes seemed unable to see the wood for the trees. Now the three game ban imposed by the FA would render Balotelli unavailable and pave the way for Carlos Tevez' selection. The young Italian returned to the fray as a substitute in the final game against QPR and Mancini could point to his assist which set up Aguero for the title-clinching goal. But Balotelli had not been pulling his weight in the weeks when City's title challenge faltered and, if the FA had not resolved Mancini's dilemma for him, the results in the final run-in might well have been different.

It was after City's defeat at the Emirates, which left them eight points behind United with only six games remaining, that Mancini, having received assurances from Khaldoun Al Mubarak, devised a crucial strategy. He insisted to journalists that the title was as good as in United's hands. But he sang a very different tune at Carrington and in the dressing room, insisting that all was not lost and that the team must fight to the very end. Mancini was quite prepared to accept the blame for allowing United to overhaul City 's lead and to fuel speculation as to his own future. He knew that he retained the confidence of Abu Dhabi and was thus free to soak up the pressure and take his players out of the spotlight.

Carlos Tevez and Sergio Aguero put Norwich City to the sword at Carrow Road, combining in devastating fashion to rout the East Anglian side. Though the final score was 5-1, the match had been in the balance for a while and it needed Mancini's introduction of a not -fully -fit Yaya to stem the tide. Later he would send on the speedy Adam Johnson to race past the exhausted Norwich defenders and add to the goal tally which he was convinced would prove significant in the race against United.

By the time United arrived at the Etihad on April 30, the situation was critical with Ferguson's team needing only a draw while City had to win to go level on points and thus lead on goal difference. Mancini would make three vital contributions to City's crucial one- nil victory. First, he soon spotted that Patrice Evra at left back- a man psychologically drained by being embroiled in the Suarez- Evra episode-was a weakness and he directed Pablo Zabaleta and Samir Nasri to combine and repeatedly attack the French left back.

Second, while Sir Alex Ferguson remained static on the bench for much of the match, monitoring his decision to seek a draw, Mancini was active throughout, shouting volubly, not in wild tracksuit manager style but with clear- cut instructions.

Finally, in the seventy-fifth minute, he turned the tables on Fergie when the United boss leapt from his seat to protest a foul on Welbeck. Shedding his earlier cool, Ferguson confronted Mancini and let fly with four letter words and a 'shut your trap' hand gesture. This was the man who'd brought Kevin Keegan to the brink of tears in 96 and left Rafael Benitez taut with anger in 09. Few men had faced Sir Alex without flinching from his steely blue gaze. But this time Mancini stood up to him eyeball to eyeball, snarling "you can fackeen talk, huh! ". The United boss fired only one more volley before returning to his seat, rattled by Mancini's nerve. Far from being a sideshow, the fact that their boss had not prevailed would transmit uncertainty to his players whilst Mancini's boldness had a positive effect on his men and they ran out the winners 1-0.

The title race went down to the wire and, in the closing stages of the vital final match against Queens Park Rangers, City had gone behind 1-2 after a blunder by Lescott and Nasri's failure to track back with Mackie. With disbelief turning to agitation among the Citizens, Mancini tuned his voice to full volume. Gaunt, dehydrated, licking his parched lips, ageing a year every minute, he wasn't just urging Silva not to dawdle at corners but was shouting instructions on the precise angle of delivery. Once Dzeko had capitalised on Silva's high dropping ball, heading it in after a clever corkscrew run, Mancini's fierce, heavily accented voice scoured the Eastlands air, roaring, imploring, beseeching, commanding – "you gotta getta theez gol! You GOTTA getta theez GOL !!!"

Oblivious to his lieutenants beside him, David Platt and Brian Kidd, blowing hot and cold, regardless of the alternating currents of hope and despair which surged through the crowd, Mancini's sheer belief, not merely in the possibility of victory but in its certainty, did not waver for one moment. His devout Catholicism, reinvigorated by his long- prepared- for -pilgrimage to Mejugortje, was the touchstone of his faith and, whilst the entirety of the Etihad longed for victory with every fibre of their being, Mancini was probably the only person in the stadium who counted on a miracle. As Sergio Aguero, the last of his key signings, delivered the coup de grace with an instinctive but ruthless strike, his thirtieth of the season, the crowd erupted and Roberto Mancini embraced Kidd and Platt in an outburst of collective joy.

The victory presentation followed, all the more ecstatic for the forty-seven thousand Citizens because of the seeming destruction of their hopes which had proceeded it. But now ' Blue Moon' resounded,' Hey Jude' resonated and, as Roberto Mancini, draped in the Italian tricolour, strode to the podium so ' Volare', recast as ' The Mancini Song' rang round the Etihad to acclaim the maestro of Manchester City.

***

Manchester City supporters looked forward to the start of the 2012-13 season with high hopes. The Premiership title would be a stepping stone to even greater accomplishments. Deadwood would be pruned, stellar players signed and City would move on to great things in the Champions League.

But little of this happened. True, City sold Adebayor to Spurs for £5 million and Adam Johnson to Sunderland for twice that amount. Bridge and Santa Cruz were loaned out and, against the wishes of many supporters, Nigel De Jong was sold to A C Milan. But the incoming transfers were distinctly underwhelming. Two were English, Jack Rodwell from Everton and Scott Sinclair from Swansea City. Roberto Mancini put a brave face on it when he said they would be "ones for the future". As for Maicon, the thirty-one-year-old Brazilian right back signed from Inter Milan, he was more likely one from the past, his defensive frailty ruthlessly exposed by Spurs' Gareth Bale nearly two years earlier. And, at centre back, the inexperienced Serbian Matija Nastasic replaced Montenegrin flop Stefan Savic. Javi Garcia, a Spanish defensive midfielder, signed from Benfica, was scarcely a name to wow the fans.

Four of the five newcomers – plus stand-in goalkeeper Richard Wright – arrived on the final day of the transfer window, suggesting frantically concluded business as well as lacklustre purchases. It would not be long before Roberto Mancini began to impute blame to Brian Marwood, City's football administrator. He charged that Marwood had been dilatory in pursuing transfer targets. As a result, Mancini implied, the brilliant Belgian winger Eden Hazard, had signed for Chelsea instead while ace Dutch striker, Robin van Persie, had thrown in his lot with Manchester United.

Frustration in the transfer market would be followed by disappointment in the Premiership. City would before long be overtaken by United and could never make up lost ground. The Champions League performance was worse. Though admittedly placed in a difficult group which contained Real Madrid, Borussia Dortmund and Ajax, City finished last, failing to win a single game. In the F A Cup, the club reached the Final only to be defeated by Wigan Athletic, who were about to be relegated from the Premiership.

But off -field events would be even more significant. After a hiatus of twelve months following the departure of Garry Cook, Ferran Soriano was appointed CEO. And the keynote of Soriano's CV was five successful years as Finance Vice President of F C Barcelona from 2003. A multilingual Catalan with a degree in Business Administration from prestigious RPI in upstate New York, he'd previously been a highflyer with multi-national Reckitt Benckiser, producers of bestselling products such as Dettol, Strepsils and Air Wick.

During his five years with Barcelona, Soriano presided over an increase in revenue from €123 million to €308 million and turned a €73 million loss into a €88 million profit. But he fell from power when his backer, Joan Laporta, was ousted from the club presidency.

Soriano's three-year tenure as Chairman of Catalonia-based airline Spanair was less than fully successful but, within the world of football, his reputation remained high and that commended him to Sheikh Mansour and Chairman Mubarak. The importance of business acumen had become higher than ever before due to the threat from FFP and dealing with this would clearly be a major part of Soriano's brief.

Within two months of Ferran Soriano's appointment, a former colleague of his at the Camp Nou had rejoined him at the Etihad. This was Aitor Begiristain, a forty-eight-year-old Basque, usually known as Txiki. He'd held the post of Sporting Director at FC Barcelona, arriving with Soriano in 2003 as part of the Laporta ticket but surviving two years longer. The post of Director of Football was created at Manchester City in October 2012 and Txiki was duly appointed.

Txiki became famous as a member of Johan Cruyff's 'Dream Team' which, in the early nineties, won four successive La Liga titles and triumphed in the last European Cup Final. He was a goalscoring winger, a notably confident and decisive player.

When he hung up his boots, Txiki, an unusually articulate footballer and a man of distinctive appearance with a prominent nose and piercing stare, worked for four years as a respected football analyst at Televisio de Catalunya. His sharp and measured observations were the credentials for his appointment at the Camp Nou.

Txiki's brief as Sporting Director had been player recruitment. And, while Barcelona concentrated on enlisting promising boys and instilling a football ideology based on skill and patience, it was important to sign players who already exemplified those virtues on the world stage. They would be the models for Barcelona's exceptionally skilful young cohort – Xavi, Iniesta, Fabregas and above all, Lionel Messi – to emulate.

During his tenure, Txiki recruited such outstanding players as the Brazilians Ronaldinho, Deco and Dani Alves, the Frenchman Thierry Henry, the Cameroonian Samuel Etoo and the Swede Zlatan Ibrahimovich.

In most cases, Txiki was able to secure his transfer targets for relatively modest fees. He disliked the Real Madrid 'Galactico' policy favoured by President Florentino Perez. Txiki criticised the arrogance and prima donna mentality associated with certain Real players. Indeed when Ronaldinho and Deco began to exhibit show business attitudes, he sold them. But he faltered with the signing of Ibrahimovic from Inter Milan for no less than €70 million. Not only was the Swede an exorbitant buy but his egoism made it difficult for him to blend with Barcelona's established stars. Though he was got rid of, after only one season, to AC Milan, the club lost a fortune on the deal and the whole affair was widely considered a blot on Txiki's otherwise astute record.

While he was Sporting Director at Barcelona, the club was coached first by Dutchman Frank Rijkaard and later by Catalan Pep Guardiola, a fabulous era during which fourteen trophies were won, five La Liga titles and two Champions Leagues included. What's more, Txiki was the prime mover in the appointment of Guardiola, at that time the B team coach, whom some Barcelona directors gravely underestimated. There were those wished to appoint Jose Mourinho –so Txiki duly went with Soriano to interview the Portuguese. But, for all Mourinho's successes in Portugal, England and Italy, Txiki considered him too confrontational to work happily at the Camp Nou. He unhesitatingly recommended Guardiola and was vindicated by the trophies Pep won. Without doubt, President Laporta considered Txiki a prime component of the club's success, describing his appointment as "the best decision I ever made".

***

Armed with a new five year contract, Roberto Mancini seemed relaxed, at first, about the arrival of Txiki. With Brian Marwood redeployed as Academy Director, player recruitment would be entrusted to the man from Barcelona, known throughout football as someone who acted with great despatch to achieve his ends.

Mancini seems not to have feared for his own position even though Pep Guardiola had left Barcelona and was taking a sabbatical in New York. Guardiola's decision to coach Bayern Munich, announced in January 2013, may have fortified Mancini's confidence and, in any case, he enjoyed a good professional relationship with Khaldoun Al Mubarak. Whilst the majority of Manchester City fans still held him in high regard, there were media reports of dressing room mutiny. While this was exaggerated, significant dissent did exist.

Following the incident in Munich in the title -winning year, it seems clear that a number of players had sympathised with Carlos Tevez. Certainly there was little problem in reintegrating Tevez in the squad after his return from Argentina. If Mancini had been relaxed in taking the AWOL Argentinian back, he must have felt his position strengthened after the Premiership title was clinched in May 2012. It would scarcely be surprising if an already outspoken man had become more volatile afterwards. Without doubt Mancini engaged in public criticism of his players, notably Joe Hart whom he blamed for conceding a last-minute goal which gave United a 3-2 derby victory at the Etihad in December 2012. And there were clearly visible verbal exchanges on the touchline between Mancini and both Samir Nasri and James Milner.

During 2012-13, Vincent Kompany's form, supreme during the title -winning season, declined markedly and it was reported that he'd become disenchanted with his manager, a man he'd earlier recognised as an outstanding tactician. Though Mancini had his supporters in the dressing room, the growing distance between manager and club captain was a significant development.

Throughout his managership, Roberto Mancini had left himself open to charges of favouritism over his indulgent attitude towards Mario Balotelli. His view that Balotelli was a football genius not bound by ordinary rules was one not shared in the City dressing room! And Mancini's faith in his wayward compatriot had been made to look publicly foolish when paparazzi snapped them violently arguing at Carrington. Balotelli's return to Italy in January 2013, when he signed for AC Milan, must have been sanctioned by Soriano and Txiki and, though Mancini acquiesced, his position was scarcely strengthened.

City's elimination from the Champions League and their failure to make inroads into United's Premiership lead counted against Mancini and, even before the embarrassing Cup Final defeat to Wigan in May 2013, the decision had been taken in Abu Dhabi to dismiss him at the end of the season. And, on May 13th, twelve months to the day since City clinched the Premiership title, his departure was announced. It was lamented by the majority of City fans, several of whom combined to take out a prominent ad in La Gazzetta dello Sport thanking Mancini in Italian for all he'd done for the club.

Without doubt, Roberto Mancini had been a major factor in the rebirth of Manchester City. He'd purchased great players such as Yaya Toure, David Silva and Sergio Aguero, he'd made the side hard to beat and his incredible will to win, was seen at its most incandescent in the climactic title -clinching game against Queen's Park Rangers.

These were the factors which had pulverised the antique notion of 'Cityitis' and won him a permanent place in the supporters' hearts.

But Mancini stood heir to the long -established Italian tradition of victorious football emanating from structured defence. It was established in the 1930s by the outstanding coach Vittorio Pozzo, the man behind Italy's two pre-war World Cup successes. Though Serie A in the 90s, the era of Mancini's personal stardom, had moved far away from the stifling catenaccio of earlier decades, Italian football would continue to prize victory regardless of how it was achieved and would value tactical intelligence over beautiful play. This ran clean counter to the football ideology enshrined in Barcelona and cherished by Ferran Soriano and Txiki Begiristain.

That football philosophy originated with one man, Laszlo Kubala, who played for over a decade in the blaugrana strip. Kubala was a self-declared 'citizen of the world ', a ginger -haired Hungarian-Slovak-Polish footballer who fled Communist Budapest lying low in the back of a truck, having refused call-up for military service. He ended up in Barcelona, signing for the club in 1950.

At that time the Catalans were seeking to reassert themselves after defeat in the Spanish Civil War and they took to Kubala precisely because of his mixed background and international outlook – he represented three different countries. Where the Italian school of football had taken root during Mussolini's Fascist dictatorship, the Catalans revered boldness and elegance and this was what Kubala provided.

Kubala was a brawny cove with legs like tree trunks but he played with a balletic grace, defying opponents to dispossess him as he stood with one foot on the ball or, at other times, dangling a boot in the air. Once they'd taken the bait, he'd dodge them with a swerve or a drag- back and surge menacingly away. His extraordinary sense of balance enabled him to recover from the most bruising challenge and, as a playmaker, he was supreme, finding teammates either with an impudent backheel or a gliding pass on the run. A powerful dead ball kicker, he was also a prolific goalscorer, holding the record for Barcelona strikes until Lionel Messi exceeded it.

The football fans of Barcelona were gripped with 'Kubalamania' and they packed out the existing stadium, Las Corts, paving the way for a move to the Camp Nou in 1957. It was then that Kubala roped in two other great Hungarian players who'd gone into exile after the failure of the Hungarian Uprising the year before. Sandor 'Golden Head ' Kocsis, possibly the finest header of a ball the game had seen, and Zoltan Czibor, a brilliant goalscoring winger, had both starred in 'The Magical Magyars' famous 6-3 victory over England at Wembley in 1953.

The Barcelona team in which Kubala, Kocsis and Czibor starred, together with the first great Spanish player, Luis Suarez I, defeated the hitherto all -conquering Real Madrid in the European Cup, First Round in 1960-1 but were never crowned champions, losing to Benfica in the Final through a combination of goalkeeping blunders and sheer bad luck.

Barcelona returned to the forefront of progressive football with the appointment of Dutch coach Rinus Michels in 1971. Michels had won three successive European Cups with Ajax Amsterdam and was also the prime mover in the introduction of 'Total Football ', a system which went further than mere reliance on skilful and intelligent players to emphasise spatial awareness and introduce constant positional interchange.

It was no coincidence that Hungary and Holland should both be prominent in the development of beautiful football. The advance of the game in both countries owed much to two two English coaches who were derided at home because they emphasised skill and intelligence rather than strength and 'getting stuck in'.

Both these coaches had links with Manchester. Jack Reynolds was born there and played for City. But he relocated to the Netherlands and coached Ajax for nearly thirty years before mentoring the young Rinus Michels. Jimmy Hogan studied for the priesthood at St Bede's College in Salford but, against his parents' wishes, became a professional footballer. Interned in Austria-Hungary during the First World War, he went on to coach a number of clubs in both Austria and Hungary as well as co- managing, with Hugo Meisl, the Austrian Wunderteam.

Rinus Michels' star player at both Ajax and Barcelona was Johan Cruyff. Cruyff 's phenomenal skill was exemplified in the famous 'Cruyff Turn' where, on the left wing, he would drag the ball behind him with his right boot, swivel through 180 degrees and leave the defender for dead. Even more astonishing was the 'Phantom Goal ' where, facing away from goal, against Atletico Madrid, he scored with a neck-high backheel volley. Feats such as that wowed the blaugrana fans while his command of the Catalan language endeared him to the community. Five years as star player would be followed, starting ten years later, by eight years as coach and among the outstanding players of Cruyff's 'Dream Team 'was Txiki Begiristain.

This then was the Barcelona lineage, Kubala-Michels -Cruyff, which Txiki inherited, first as a player then as Sporting Director, inherited – as did Ferran Soriano as club administrator. It was best exemplified by Cruyff's dictum - "it is not enough to win, you must play beautiful football!" It was a football ideology to which none of the great Italian coaches, not Vittorio Pozzo, not Marcello Lippi and certainly not Roberto Mancini, had ever subscribed.

In his first press conference since Mancini's sacking, given on May 23, 2013, Ferran Soriano virtually reiterated Cruyff's words. "We are looking to play good football and to win and I said that in the right order" he remarked. Soriano praised Mancini for his contribution to City's development. "He is a champion, a winner" Soriano said - "to change the mentality of the club was great and we thank him". But he indicated what he saw as Mancini's main weakness and, in doing so, confirmed what the chief objective of Sheikh Mansour was. "We want a manager who knows about man -management" he affirmed and continued "it is impossible for us to win – to win the Champions League in the end – if we don't have a group that behaves like a family. We want a family where there are no (unjustified) criticisms and where everybody respects everybody and, to do this, you need a senior coach".

Soriano's words were effectively an epitaph on Roberto Mancini's three and a half years as manager of Manchester City. Mancini had indeed been a maestro, the man who had done most to eradicate the lamentable notions of 'Typical City' and 'Cityitis 'and who had dedicated himself to achieving City's first Premiership title. Yet Mancini had a track record of conflict with players, most spectacularly Carlos Tevez, but also Edin Dzeko, Samir Nasri, James Milner, Joe Hart and, critically, Vincent Kompany. Though Mancini despised the English long ball tradition and casual mentality, his football ideology depended first and foremost on relentless commitment and sharp intelligence. It did not, as did the Barcelona tradition of Kubala, Michels and Johan Cruyff, uphold the primacy of beautiful football in its own right.

4

THE LIBERATOR,
MANUEL PELLEGRINI

On Sunday, May 11, 2014, he stood before the microphone at the Etihad Stadium in East Manchester, his words resounding to the Citizens, 47,000 supporters of Manchester City.

His grey hair, albeit long even luxuriant, confirmed his sixty years. But his broad shouldered, six foot one inch frame, was a reminder of his days as an international centre back. Still, he looked anything but the stereotypical British manager, tracksuited, barking orders, bellowing and dog whistling on a touchline rampage.

Had you come across Manuel Luis Pellegrini Ripamonti in Lancaster Castle – visiting to pursue his keen interest in history – and heard him speaking fluent if heavily accented English, you would likely have taken him for perhaps a South American consular official. But, on May 11, the Chilean's suit, though elegant, was far from immaculate. It was saturated with champagne, fired at him by his players as they celebrated winning the Barclays' Premiership trophy.

And soon Pellegrini would be seized bodily by a posse of his brawniest stars and tossed high into the air six times. He reacted with typical calm, a broad smile lighting up his normally serious and sometimes lugubrious features.

Banners at the Etihad that day had already displayed his image on a sky blue ground with the words ' This Charming Man ', an allusion to the eighties song by Manchester band, The Smiths, inscribed. And the stadium had resonated to a fans' song its surreal lyric, referencing the owner as well as the Chilean coach. Reportedly dreamed up by two young Manc brothers, bored and bladdered at a funeral, and set to the tune of 'Yankee Doodle', it goes like this:

Sheikh Mansour went to Spain
In a Lamborghini
He brought us back a manager,
Manuel Pellegrini!

The players' posse which threw Pellegrini into the air was cosmopolitan, new MCFC : skipper and central defender Vincent Kompany, Brussels- born son of a Congolese political exile, as intelligent as he is athletic, studying for a Masters degree in Business Administration at Manchester Business School; goalkeeper Joe Hart, blond and British, his trimly waved hair famed in anti- dandruff ads but just now roughed up by the fans who'd cornered him in a scrum ; Yaya Toure, Ivorian midfield colossus, sporting his country's orange, white and green tricolour and with an ice pack strapped to his hamstrung leg ; Edin Dzeko, Bosnian striker and mighty header of a ball, born and brought up in a Sarajevo ravaged by civil war; and Pablo Zabaleta, Argentinian right back, and fans' favourite, seen as the embodiment of rugged resolve and hailed in a song, rehearsed time and again over the season and prophesying the recapture of the Premiership title.

After the medal ceremony and the triumphant raising of the Premiership trophy by Vincent Kompany, plus the flares and the fireworks, the party gradually wound down with the players' girlfriends, wives and small kids attracting Sky's cameras. When Pellegrini was spotted with one of his toddler granddaughters in his arms, the photographers homed in. But his wife, the former, Carmen Gloria Pucci, a civil engineer still practising her profession in Chile, remained in the background as did their three sons.

On the following day, in an inversion of typical weather – bright sunshine over Manchester, bucketing down with rain everywhere else – an estimated 100,000 City supporters lined the Civic Parade route from Albert Square via Deansgate to Exchange Square as Pellegrini and the players paraded the beribboned trophy and its companion, the Capital One Cup, in an open- topped bus. Sky blue favours were everywhere, scarves brandished by gap-toothed old geezers who remembered the triumphs of the sixties and thought they'd never come again, pullovers adorning plump matrons and shapely girls alike, a gang of lads standing perilously on a narrow concrete ledge thirty feet above the pavement, all linked 'Together' (the very word proclaimed in banners) in an explosion of joy.

With the squad were the backroom staff, men as homespun Manc as 'Kiddo ', Brian Kidd, Collyhurst born and bred, once of United, but at Eastlands since 09 plus soon-to-retire head kit man Les Chapman. 'Chappy ', from Royton, had been an invaluable behind-the-scenes joker, a comic manque, adept at lessening pre-match tension with his mimicry and gurning, eyeball -swivelling antics. Then there was cult hero, Ruben Cousillas, Argentinian assistant manager, dubiously welcomed on mancityfans.net as "looking like a cross between Marco Materazzi and Oliver Cromwell's death mask", a man of grim visage who'd in fact endeared himself to Citizens with his manic celebrations of memorable goals rending the air with screams of " GO-O-O-O-LAZO-OOOOOOO!!!!!! "

These were the Citizens, many of them ageing veterans of the last days of Maine Road, Kippax stalwarts who, among ultra-loyal crowds averaging 28,000, had kept the faith in the dark days of the nineties as City tumbled through the divisions and prepared to meet lowly York and Gillingham. And, back at the Etihad, there'd been the forty- something veterans of the Madchester music scene, such as Noel Gallagher and Johnny Marr, both City fans from boyhood, who, back in the years when only Georgi Kinkladze's wizardry lit up the gloom, would've asked you what you'd been smoking if you'd told them that City would ever entertain Barcelona and Real Madrid.

On the thirteenth of May, the second anniversary of the club's first Premiership triumph, under Roberto Mancini, the squad jetted to Abu Dhabi to open the new Hazza bin Zayed Stadium. They'd already been congratulated by the triumvirate, Emirati chairman Khaldoun Al Mubarak, Catalan CEO Ferran Soriano and Basque Director of Football, Txiki Begiristain. With Pellegrini, these men would soon be in the presence of Sheikh Mansour bin Zayed Al Nahyan, the forty-three year old football-loving prince whose munificence had made this possible, photographed on the 11th in palatial celebration cutting a giant cake in the shape of the BPL Trophy. Now, in the luxurious St. Regis Hotel on Saadiyat Island, each member of the squad shook hands with Sheikh Mansour.

But the immediate focus was on Manuel Pellegrini. Fans, players and pundits concurred that his calmness had brought a harmony – dubbed both by friends and scoffing outsiders as 'holistic ' -to a previously strife-torn dressing room. His experience, seniority and football record in Spain had led Soriano and Txiki to recommend him to Khaldoun.

But, in truth, Pellegrini's greatest achievement was to liberate an immensely talented but sporadically dysfunctional squad – who'd lost the 2013 Cup Final to Wigan Athletic – from the restraints imposed by Mancini, the manager who'd been unable to follow up his 2012 success and who'd failed totally in the Champions League, unable to win a single game.

In doing so, Pellegrini had liberated the Citizens from the hoary old jibes about 'Typical City' and ' Cityitis' . These were the supporters who'd suffered until the very last minute of the last day against Queens Park Rangers, to see their team come back, by the skin of its teeth, from 2-1 down to snatch a 3-2 win. This time there'd been no tension-filled escape. Instead, West Ham United had been almost brushed aside in a comfortable 2-0 victory.Where, the last time, Sir Alex Ferguson's United had been stunned to learn, in Sunderland, that City had pipped them at the post, this time Brendan Rodgers' Liverpool, struggling to beat Newcastle United at Anfield and reliant on a City defeat, seemed almost to have given up hope that the Hammers could somehow bail them out.

Not all Citizens had welcomed Pellegrini's arrival in 2013. Whatever the players thought about him, Roberto Mancini, the dapper, volatile, Sky Blue scarf- wearing showman had won a place in the hearts of many fans. And, at Wembley, the most resentful of them, furious at reports of Mancini's impending dismissal, had spat out chants of "stick your Pellegrini up your arse, you can stick your Pellegrini up your arse, you can stick your Pellegrini, he'll never be Mancini, stick your Pellegrini up your arse!".

On Ric Turner' s Blue Moon, leading City fansite, posters had clashed from the opening weeks of the season onwards. Much of the scepticism about the new South American coach was about his record- "he's never won owt in Europe, has he ?" Some of it was image -oriented. He was variously said to be too old, too downbeat, the 'holistic 'puppet of Txiki and Soriano and just a harmless 'nice guy '. Then there was the small matter of his nickname – imported from Spain, 'The Engineer '. To some it suggested a personality similar to Arsenal's professorial Arsene Wenger, eight years without a trophy to his name, the man written off by Jose Mourinho as " a specialist in failure". Indeed a substantial number of posters would've far preferred it if Mourinho had come to the Etihad instead of returning to Chelsea.

What's more, there were openly lookist jibes about his hairstyle (said to resemble veteran Coronation Street character Audrey Roberts), his wrinkles and bloodshot eyes. While some of this could be written off as banter, one high-profile poster went so far as to call Pellegrini "a fucking clown".

Soon Blue Moon's heavy hitters, articulate men who knew their football, were elevating the debate to a new level. Some kept an open mind. Others supported Pellegrini, pointing to his record in Spain and the endorsements of his former players, the likes of Diego Forlan, Pepe Reina and Ruud van Nistelrooy, all of whom had painted a picture of a deeply thoughtful coach and a humane and understanding man. As the wiser posters pointed out, the term 'engineer' was in fact a compliment, indicating a man of strategic savvy and tactical nous not merely a Wenger-style connoisseur.

***

Vitally important to Manchester City as Manuel Pellegrini would become, his career has a significance beyond City and indeed any of the nine other clubs which he previously managed. Indeed his life in football is a paradigm of the game's history and of the besetting arguments about 'the beautiful game 'and winning football.

To see where Manuel Pellegrini came from and what shaped his football philosophy, let's turn the clock back fifty years. He first fell in love with the game as a boy of eight when the finals of the World Cup were held in Chile. The year was 1962 and, for three weeks, Manuel sat glued to the TV set in his parents' home. Chile had a good team, a clever coach, Fernando Riera, and, in Jorge Toro and Leonel Sanchez, two very good players.

But they were not on the map with the reigning champions, Brazil, who had Pele, at twenty-one widely hailed as the greatest player in the world. He claimed that distinction from Alfredo Di Stefano who, at thirty-five, was no longer at his best. Di Stefano, Argentinian by birth and upbringing, had been the orchestrator of Real Madrid's five consecutive European Cup victories. He went to Chile as a naturalised Spaniard, looking to play the same role for his adopted country.

Neither Pele nor di Stefano lasted the tournament. Di Stefano arrived with an injury from which he never recovered while Pele tore a muscle in the group stages. But, while Spain were useless without their Argentinian maestro, Brazil had other great players – Didi, Vava and, above all, the fantastic dribbling, goalscoring winger Garrincha.

Chile reached the semifinals, beating Italy and the Soviet Union on the way before being well beaten by Brazil, who went on to overcome Czechoslovakia in the final. The point was that the best teams and the best players were South American and this was not lost on young Manuel.

As Pellegrini matured, he had little opportunity to cheer on his own country since Chile declined heavily from their peak in 62. But, as a connoisseur of classy football, he remain convinced that the Latin American game was inherently the most skillful, with qualities of verve and flair rarely matched by Europeans – with the notable exception of Holland.

Events were to back Pellegrini up in that belief. Even though the 66 World Cup saw England beating West Germany in the final, the level of skill had been well below that shown in the Intercontinental Club Championship - held later in the same year -when the Uruguayan team, Penarol, spearheaded by the gifted Ecuadorian Alberto Spencer, defeated the all -Spanish Real Madrid by an aggregate score of 4-0 in the two-legged final.

If Penarol's triumph was sadly overlooked by European journalists, the reverse was the case with Brazil's 1970 team -featuring Gerson, Tostao, Jairzinho, Rivelino and, above all, Pele - which won the World Cup in superb style in Mexico that year.

Pellegrini's parents had smiled benevolently at his boyish fascination with the 62 tournament. But, by now, he was sixteen and they believed he should be focusing on preparation for University. Emilio and Silvia Pellegrini were one of the wealthiest couples in Chile and had sent their son, to an exclusive private school in Santiago. By dint of hard work, Emilio, the son of an Italian immigrant from Tuscany, had built up a lucrative business in architecture and construction. His sports were tennis and golf, not football which was, so he thought, the preserve of the working class. Three years later, Emilio and Silvia were pleased that Manuel was beginning a course in Civil Engineering at the University of Chile but far less so that he was playing semipro football for the University team.

In the world of World Cup football, Argentina were victorious on home soil in 1978 but, in Spain in 82, another great Brazilian side, starring Zico, Socrates and Falcao unravelled as a result of a careless defensive error in the second round. In 86, again in Mexico, Argentina won- largely due to Diego Maradona -but the Brazilian team, eliminated on penalties in the quarter-final, was widely considered the best.

It was in that year,1986, that Manuel Pellegrini, now aged thirty-three, hung up his boots. Seven years before, he'd gained his degree in Civil Engineering and had came under immediate pressure from his parents to quit football and embark on a professional career like his brothers Pedro and Pablo, one a lawyer, the other an architect -and sister Silvia, a lecturer in journalism. He was, after all, a cultured man, a frequent visitor to art galleries with a keen interest in the history of Rome and in archaeology.

For a short while, Pellegrini worked as a civil engineer, being part of the team which rebuilt the Valparaiso region after the devastating earthquake of 1985 left one million people homeless. But after that work was completed, Pellegrini was contacted by Fernando Riera, now finishing his own coaching career, and urged to go into management.

Manuel Pellegrini had to face the fact that the South American style of football, the beautiful game of di Stefano, Pele, Garrincha, Spencer, Zico and Socrates was no longer dominant. Uruguayan football had descended into brutality, the Argentinian game sporadically lapsed into violence while Brazil, after 86, changed to a defensive orientation, a functional game which would win tournaments but was distinctly lacking in magic. If he wanted to enter management it would only be if he could find a way of reconciling the traditional South American game with the European, of wedding European stability to Latin flair.

In 1989 Pellegrini was galvanised by the emphatic European Cup triumph of AC Milan. Team coach Arrigo Sacchi had shocked Italian football by taking Parma from Serie C almost to the Serie A title and he'd done so with attacking football. Italy was the bastion of defensive football, of catenaccio, but Sacchi denounced the culture of fear and insisted that victory must be won with style. Moving to Milan, he benefited from mogul Silvio Berlusconi's funding and soon won the scudetto.

Sacchi had greatly admired Dutch coach Rinus Michels' Total Football and intended to adapt it to the Italian situation. His so-called 'pressing game' used a high defensive line where Milan set the tempo and attacked their opponents from the off. Short, quick passes would drag defenders out of position. But, if possession was lost, the whole team pressed high to deny their opponents the time to regroup and aimed to seize back possession at the earliest opportunity.

It was significant that, though the key defenders, Franco Baresi and Paolo Maldini, were Italians, the chief attackers, Marco van Basten, Ruud Gullit and Frank Rijkaard were Dutch, the last two being of South American descent, their fathers hailing from Surinam.

Pellegrini determined to implement, as far as possible, Sacchi's methods during his career in coaching in Chile. He moved promptly from club to club- Palestino, O' Higgins and Universidad de Chile, always handicapped by modest funds -as he would be during his successful three-year stint in Ecuador where he managed LDU Quito. It was only when he reached Argentina that he began to enjoy significant funding. He won the Argentinian championship first at San Lorenzo then at River Plate. And it was his record of success in Argentina which led small-town Spanish club Villareal, in 2004, to offer him a contract.

In his first season he took Villareal to third place in La Liga and, the following year, narrowly failed to reach the Champions League Final, losing to Arsenal in the semis thanks to a late penalty miss. In 2007-8 Pellegrini led Villareal to second place, finishing above the mighty Barcelona. And, in the following year, still operating on limited financial resources, he took his team to the Champions League quarter-finals, again losing to Arsenal.

Pellegrini's achievements with Villareal caught the attention of Real Madrid whose director- general, Jorge Valdano, appointed him as coach in June 2009. But the incoming president, billionaire Florentino Perez, had hoped for Jose Mourinho and he spent in excess of £200 million bringing in megastars such as Cristiano Ronaldo whilst offloading, against Pellegrini's wishes, proven performers such as the Dutchmen Arjen Robben and Wesley Snyder.

Pellegrini, in his sole season at Madrid, achieved a win percentage, at 75.00, higher than any of his predecessors, and Real finished with a club record of 96 points. But they'd been knocked out of the Champions League in the round of the last sixteen and, in La Liga, they finished second to Barcelona. He was then sacked and replaced by Mourinho. Pellegrini's response to his dismissal, in July 2010, was pithy. "I didn't have a voice or a vote" he said, adding "it's no good having an orchestra with the ten best guitarists if you don't have a pianist!".

Within months, Pellegrini was appointed coach by hitherto unsuccessful FC Malaga, now funded by new owner, the Sheikh of Quatar. At the time of Pellegrini's arrival, the club was struggling in eighteenth position and was rife with dissension. Pellegrini restored calm and raised the club to eleventh in the table. The following year they rose to an unprecedented fourth place and, in 2012-13, Malaga reached the quarter-final of the Champions League.

When Pellegrini first became aware, in the spring of 2013, of Manchester Ciy's interest in him, he realised at once that it would provide him with a unique opportunity. He would be generously funded, as he hadn't been at Villareal and only briefly at Malaga and he'd be able to work out a recruitment policy with Txiki, City's Director of Football, a man he held in high esteem. And, so far from contending with the constant interference of a self-made business-man like Real's Perez, he would be answerable to a far-distant Emirati prince who'd shown considerable patience with City's unsuccessful manager, Mark Hughes.

While managerial appointments at other English clubs were made sometimes on grounds of sentiment and with pundits preoccupied with trumpeting the virtues of quotable personalities such as Jose Mourinho and Jurgen Klopp, decisions at Manchester City were made on rational grounds alone. Manuel Pellegrini, unique among coaches, had demonstrated during the course of a twenty-five year career on two continents, his capacity for man- management and for getting the best out of modestly funded squads. This was what had led Ferran Soriano and Txiki to recommend him to Sheikh Mansour. His appointment, on a three-year contract, was announced on June 14, 2013. Eleven months later, he held up the Barclay's Premiership trophy before a packed out and delighted Etihad.

5

LAMBORGHINI FOOTBALL :
STYLE, POWER AND SUCCESS

Manuel Pellegrini's intentions were made crystal clear right from the 2013-14 pre-season friendlies, notably the Audi Cup, held in Munich. In the semi-final, City played AC Milan and, despite being without the injured Sergio Aguero, had raced into a startling 5-0 lead in little more than half an hour. All-out attacking play, with new signing Jesus Navas (from Seville) and Micah Richards prominent, delighted the many City fans who followed the game on TV, savouring goals by Silva, Richards, Kolarov and a brace by Dzeko. Then the game swung the other way with Milan profiting from defensive errors to pull three goals back. Some supporters were shocked by the ease with which these goals had been conceded and pointed with alarm to the high defensive line which Pellegrini had deployed.

The final, played against the European champions Bayern Munich, fielding a full strength team in their own Allianz Arena saw City take the lead when Alvaro Negredo (ex-Seville) burst past Javi Martinez and scored on the run. Bayern were gifted an equaliser through referee Wolfgang Stark's deplorable decision to penalise Zabaleta when the ball rebounded off his trailing arm as he jumped. They then took the lead when Mandzukic punished Boyatta's poor positioning. Even then, City had an excellent chance to draw level when Dzeko, cleverly played through by James Milner, scuffed his shot when one-on-one with keeper Neuer.

City's performance in the Audi Cup had a crucial effect on the season which lay ahead. It convinced Manuel Pellegrini that he had a squad capable of taking on the best in Europe and emboldened him in his commitment to attacking football.

The high hopes aroused by the Audi Cup were translated into Premiership proof when City took on Newcastle United at the Etihad on August 19. The Magpies' strong running and rugged tackling was no match for City's fluid and relaxed football which mirrored Pellegrini's stance on the touchline, hands in pockets, instructing, in contrast to Mancini's exhortation.

After David Silva opened the scoring with an early header, City never looked back. The second goal was fantastic. Vincent Kompany contemptuously robbed Papiss Cisse and surged into attack. He found Dzeko whose little backheel flick sent Aguero away to fend off Taylor and crack the ball home. Pellegrini was jubilant, pumping his arms in delight and shouting "bravo, boys!".

With Steven Taylor sent off just before half-time, City continued to press forward, as Pellegrini had promised they would, regardless of the number of goals they'd scored. Yaya added one with a free kick and Nasri another while Negredo, on as a substitute in the last ten minutes, had a perfectly good goal disallowed.

The Citizens has been royally entertained by City's high speed interpassing and, though Newcastle were a man short for the entire second half, they'd already been outclassed. In the midst of all this, however, came a bad blow. Vincent Kompany was injured. The skipper had been back to his best, giving a superb demonstration of central defensive play – one which recalled Johan Cruyff's paradox that what you need for bold, attacking football is a strong, convincing centre back.

It was a very different story away to Cardiff City on Bank Holiday Monday. With Nastasic now injured as well as Kompany, Garcia was sent into central defence where he would be badly exposed for pace.

With Clichy ill at ease, newly signed Brazilian midfielder Fernandinho failing to adjust to the Premiership and Yaya saunter-ing, City couldn't get going. Though they took the lead, it was soon undone by errors from Zabaleta and Hart, resulting in a 2-3 loss on their first road trip. Pundits would round on Pellegrini, accusing him of ingenuous tactics and absurdly claiming he'd been outwitted by Cardiff manager, Malky McKay.

The home game against Hull City could've been lost within the first twenty minutes, Hull having missed two good chances and hav-ing a goal disallowed. Though Nastasic had returned, he looked half asleep and with Yaya not an impressive captain, it was left to Zabaleta to try to spark the team into life.

Citizens were restive, unhappy with Fernandinho -who'd replaced the popular Gareth Barry – and particularly critical of Dzeko who was substituted at half time. There was a general perception of a lacklustre approach which Negredo did much to assuage by his bold attitude and a headed goal. After Yaya scored with a free kick, the points were safe but many supporters remained unconvinced.

On transfer deadline day, Txiki signed Martin Demichelis, a thirty-three year old Argentinian centre back. He'd played under Pellegrini both at River Plate and Malaga but he was crocked in training the day after he signed.

At the Britannia Stadium, City had to manage without David Silva, who'd done his hamstring playing for Spain. Once again Negredo impressed, his ball skill giving the lie to his reputation as merely a rugged battler. But Stevan Jovetic, the Montenegrin striker newly signed from Fiorentina, could make little impact. City got a point from Stoke in a goalless draw yet there was a lot of sniping at Pellegrini, especially from fans who resented Mancini's sacking.

In the Champions League, City had been drawn in the same group as Bayern Munich, CSKA Moscow and relative minnows, Viktoria Plzen from the Czech Republic. Sky televised the match in Pilsen and, in the early stages, radiated negativity over City's failure to score. Yet, with Kompany back, the defence was far more secure and soon Sky had to moderate their tone as Aguero scored twice and Yaya delivered a fantastic strike, as precise as a free kick yet delivered on the run.

The match which truly transformed perceptions of Pellegrini's City was the Manchester derby, which took place at the Etihad on September 22 with United now under the managership of ex- Everton boss David Moyes.

Though Citizens, initially, were nervous about the absence of David Silva and, even more so, about the appointment of Howard Webb as referee, they would soon be roaring with delight over City's fabulous interpassing which left United initially perplexed and ultimately outclassed.

What was notably impressive was the Pellegrini effect on two players in particular, Samir Nasri and Aleksandar Kolarov. Nasri stepped up to the plate in Silva's absence and put in a tremendous stint to match his undoubted high skill. And Kolarov, considered by many a defensively dubious full-back, was transformed into a dynamic wing back, spreading alarm in the United ranks with his low, whipped crosses.

With Fernandinho getting the hang of Premiership pace and Negredo powerful, even indomitable, United's belated free kick goal from Rooney was their sole response to a dynamic finish by Aguero plus goals by Nasri, Yaya and Negredo.

The performance was an absolute triumph, which would be celebrated on the MCFC official site with slow motion montages, showing the fans' delight at City's triumphant artistry-replete with music by Vivaldi no less!

The humiliation of United, more emphatic even than in Mancini's 6-1, was what swayed the majority in favour of Pellegrini. He would be increasingly seen as dignified and classy, a man who'd restored team spirit and provided beautiful, successful, attacking football.

Yet City came unstuck once again away from home in the Premiership. After taking the lead at Villa Park, they saw Villa revive and notch the winner from a Route One move as a result of a bad mixup involving Kompany, Nastasic and Hart.

Pellegrini's post -match comment- "in five minutes we threw into the dustbin all we achieved in the match" perfectly summed up a game which City should've won but had lost solely due to individual errors.

October 2, when Bayern Munich arrived for their Champions League match with City, was an evening to stun the Etihad into silence. Joe Hart' s goalkeeping error, after only nine minutes, allowed Ribery to score and the Sky Blues were so shaken by this that it would be a full twenty minutes before they even mounted an attack. Bayern's zealous, intelligent midfield men, Lahm, Schweinsteiger and Kroos were prominent in winning two thirds of the possession and only a last-ditch tackle by Nastasic on Muller prevented them adding to the score.

For ten minutes after half-time, City got into the game yet when Bayern varied their tactics and delivered a sudden long ball, Clichy was caught failing to play offside. A few minutes later, another error by Hart permitted Robben to score.

It was only when Pellegrini sent on David Silva, returning after a long layoff, together with James Milner, on seventy minutes, that City looked like stemming the tide. Guardiola prematurely withdrew his three key players and finished the match looking very agitated that City might, after all, snatch a draw.

Only a world-class save from Neuer prevented Milner from scoring and, with ten minutes left, Silva gave a nutmeg pass to Negredo whose swivel and strike, in off the far post, left Neuer helpless. With five minutes left, City nearly scored again and Bayern were reduced to ten men with Silva sending Yaya clean through only for Boateng to bring him down and be sent off. Silva's freekick beat Neuer to the wide but cannoned off the bar.

After the match, the pundits had their knives out against Pellegrini. Jamie Redknapp blurted that "he should've played five in midfield. He sat there watching them being outplayed and never did anything to change it". And Gary Neville smirked as he quipped "if he was English, we'd have said he was naive".

These comments ignored the fact that Pellegrini, as a result of City's performance in the Audi Cup in Munich, had good reason for being confident he could achieve victory with two strikers. What's more, he did in fact switch to a five-man midfield- with Aguero dropping back - at half-time, when City were only one goal down. In fact, Bayern's goals resulted from individual mistakes by Hart and Clichy before the two substitutes, Silva and Milner, reversed the flow.

Pellegrini's real errors came in selection not in tactics. He'd chosen Richards and Clichy as full backs, doubtless with the aim of nullifying

Bayern's world-class wingers Robben and Ribery. But Richards was a total failure, positionally naive, getting in the way of others and seeking to counter it with reckless challenges. He and Navas, who looked forlorn in the absence of his Spanish-speaking buddy Zabaleta, proved quite incapable of containing Ribery. On the other flank, Clichy had been tormented not only by Robben but by Brazilian full-back Rafinha.

Pellegrini was also let down by key players such as Aguero, who seemed strangely hesitant, Yaya, who was nonplussed by tight marking and Nasri, who became stroppy and started to mouth off. The Chilean would tacitly acknowledge this by his comment " the image (he clearly meant "mindset" or "attitude") must be changed".

When Everton arrived at the Etihad three days after City's Champions League setback, the Sky Blues were expected to face a stern test. The Toffees were riding high under their new manager, Roberto Martinez, a media favourite. Unbeaten, on a roll, well -drilled, spirited and with some skilful players, they presented two principal threats, the Belgian Lukaku, on loan from Chelsea, a big, strong, fast centre forward and Leighton Baines, more than just a left back, a man who started many moves and was a formidable free kick exponent.

In the aftermath of the Bayern defeat, Pellegrini dropped several players – Richards, Clichy, Nasri, Navas and Dzeko and brought in Zabaleta, Kolarov, Milner and Negredo while David Silva was in the team from the start.

Pellegrini thus surprised those who'd written him off as a 'nice guy ' and went on to confound those who doubted his tactical nous. Joleon Lescott was brought in ahead of Nastasic, clearly with the aim of utilising his strength against the burly Lukaku while James Milner was detailed to close mark Baines.

Despite this, Everton grabbed an early goal. Not a jot flustered, City hit back within a few minutes, working an opening for Negredo to strike. Not only Lescott but also Kompany and even Silva were tackling Lukaku firmly while Milner was doing a good job on Baines.

The nonsensical claim that Pellegrini was "cavalier" even "gung ho" was shown up by a precise triangular freekick routine from which Aguero narrowly failed to score. Revealing how much work was being done on set pieces at Carrington, it also laid down a marker – 'we're different class '.

In the midst of this, however, Vincent Kompany was forced to go off with a hip strain and was replaced by Nastasic. Still, City refused to be cowed by Everton's aggressiveness. Milner was tackling like a tank and his doughty spirit was echoed by Kolarov who very reluctantantly left the field after a sly foul by Naismith had left him with blood streaming from a cut above the eye. As for Zabaleta, his heroism was a byword among the Citizens and, following treatment for a profuse nosebleed, he returned to win a penalty which Aguero converted. The Everton game was a vitally important one in restoring the team's morale after the Bayern defeat.

It was at Upton Park that City gained their first away victory in the Pellegrini era with Negredo's insouciant dummy setting up Aguero for a brilliant goal. Key to the victory was Fernandinho's greatly improved form.

City's next Champions League match was a dismal affair in Moscow's notorious Arena Khimki, home of CSKA. Going a goal down due to a defensive mixup, they had to contend with foul racist abuse of Yaya but fought back with a brace from Aguero. An excellent point-blank save from Joe Hart clinched three points.

Sadly, Hart turned from hero to villain at Stamford Bridge. Here, on October 27, facing League leaders Chelsea, Pellegrini had departed for the first time from his two striker deployment. Due to inept defending by Clichy, Chelsea took the lead. But, in the second half, Aguero scored a brilliant goal and City's skill began to turn the game around. Yet Howard Webb failed to punish Chelsea's skullduggery even as he awarded them unmerited free kicks.

Just as City were closing in on a well-deserved point, there was a gross mixup in the last minute between Nastasic and Joe Hart with Hart the main culprit, needlessly dashing out of his goal. Torres duly took advantage and scored.

This was a dreadful blow for Pellegrini and he had to suffer the spectacle of Jose Mourinho's classless triumphalism in front of the City bench. It was not surprising that he refused to shake hands with the Chelsea manager.

After the Stamford Bridge fiasco, Joe Hart would be benched for ten weeks with his Romanian deputy, Costel Pantilimon- at over two metres tall gigantic even for a goalkeeper- taking his place. At St James's Park, in the next round of the Capital One Cup, Pantilimon made an excellent point blank save to deny Newcastle in extra time with the scores level.

City took the lead after a fine move in which Dzeko and Negredo combined well, despite assertions to the contrary by pundits. Dzeko had started the season well and was clearly benefiting from Pellegrini's vote of confidence - only to be eclipsed by Negredo's outstanding form ! City won the match with a brilliant strike from the Bosnian when he turned and slotted the ball home at speed following a lovely move involving Milner and Silva. Though Jovetic's season would be riddled with injuries, City could now call on three highly effective strikers.

It was against Norwich City, on November 2, that the Sky Blues achieved their first tennis scoreline – 7-0. It was really money for jam and, into the bargain, two goals were lucky. Still, Norwich were utterly dominated.

The return of CSKSA saw City win 5-2 with Clichy conceding a crazy penalty and Nastasic and Demichelis on different wavelengths. Yet it made no difference to the outcome. By this time the Citizens had completed the coronation of hattrick hero Alvaro Negredo, chanting 'Beast, Beast, Beast, Beast!' as they acclaimed his every touch. Nasri, seen as a man transformed, was also lustily cheered and Silva departed to a rapturous standing ovation.

When City went up to Sunderland, however, there was bad news. Silva would be out for four weeks with a calf injury and Fernandinho was also hurt. It seemed clear that Pellegrini was operating rotation at full-back, given the strong physical demands on that position in his all -out attacking system. Yet, while Clichy and Kolarov could and did rotate, Richards was injured too frequently to deputise for Zabaleta on a recurring basis -though he did so at the Stadium of Light.

A below standard display from normally excellent referee Mike Dean allowed Larsson's potential leg breaker tackle on Garcia- from which the Spanish midfielder bravely recovered - to go unpunished. It was regrettable that Pellegrini did not protest this and shortly afterwards Bardsley wasn't called for a foul on James Milner and went on to score. This followed the manager's silence at Stamford Bridge in the face of Webb's peculiar decisions. It was a rare weakness, one of which he would soon correct.

Following this 0-1 defeat, on November 10, there would be much discontent from the Citizens who'd gone up to Sunderland. Fernandinho had been badly missed, Richards had been all over the place and Demichelis, though he looked good on the ball, found it hard to cope with the pace of the Premiership. The fact remained that City stood only seventh in the Premiership table, six points adrift of the leaders, Arsenal, and hindered by their three away defeats. Match of the Day pundit Alan Shearer doubted their fighting spirit but Manuel Pellegrini insisted that "we are trying to find a way of playing", implying that things would come right as players adjusted to his attacking approach.

The visit of Tottenham Hotspur, on November 24, would prove very significant. City not only won 6-0, but their second-half display was scintillating and the match inaugurated a long unbeaten run.

Spurs had come well-placed in the table with only six goals conceded so far. Yet there was a dramatic start with Jesus Navas scoring his first goal for City within fifteen seconds- which he celebrated jubilantly by leaping over the corner flag.

After the Citizens jeered Howard Webb when he denied a blatant penalty, Pellegrini for the first time took a ref to task, loudly complaining not only to the fourth official but to Webb himself. Humane and cultured though the Chilean clearly was, he'd needed to show steel in the face of unfair treatment. With his grasp of street English now really improved, he never looked back , from then on, when standing up for his team from the technical zone.

The six goals included a great team goal for the fourth with Fernandinho's one-two with Yaya, Yaya's great surge, Negredo's brilliant trap and feed to allow Yaya to continue before he passed to the parallel runner, Aguero, to strike home.

There was nearly another with a sublime chip by Nasri which came off the underside of the bar, then there was Alvaro Negredo's superb strike when he turned Dawson inside out before pivoting and delivering a rocket shot.

In Silva's absence, Nasri performed splendidly, Negredo was magnificent and Navas was well and truly starting to fulfil his talent whilst the returning Fernandinho was absolutely key, working all out to link defence with attack. Here the attacking football which Pellegrini had promised at the start of the season was beautifully delivered. Spurs conceded as many in a single afternoon as they'd done all season and Andre Villas Boas had been exposed as a mere novice in comparison to Manuel Pellegrini, with twenty-five years of managerial experience.

City's defeat of Viktoria Plzen was relatively straightforward but it confirmed that, for the first time, City would figure in the knockout stages of the Champions League.

Sceptics had constantly raised the issue of City's away form yet the team prevailed at The Hawthorns where Vincent Kompany returned after a ten game absence. Their fluent attacking tore West Bromwich Albion to shreds with Citizens chanting "you should've gone Christmas shopping!" as they revelled in a fantastic team goal and then a beautiful individual strike from Yaya.

The final match in the group stage of the Champions League found City visiting Munich to play, once again, in the Allianz Arena. Both Bayern and City had qualified for the knockout stage with the only thing left at stake being who topped the group. Bayern were in pole position with three points more than City. Though they were not at full strength – with both Robben and Schweinsteiger injured – neither were City. Yaya was suspended and Pellegrini opted to keep Aguero and Kompany on the bench in view of the upcoming Premiership clash with Arsenal.

The match opened disastrously with City going two goals down in scarcely more than ten minutes. Lescott was all at sea and his clumsy errors had the home crowd jeering whilst, in the directors box, the influential Bayern triumvirate, Beckenbauer, Rummenigge and Hoeness, notorious for their hostility to City, were smirking with satisfaction.

After sixteen minutes Richards had to withdraw, having pulled up with a thigh strain. Zabaleta came on and this proved to be a turning point in the match. He refused to be intimidated by Ribery and his presence seemed to boost Lescott who bucked himself up no end.

After twenty-seven minutes, City pulled a goal back with a confident move finished by Silva. With Silva and Milner working well together and with Fernandinho and Garcia putting in a strong stint in the five-man midfield, City were more than competing with Bayern. What's more, Demichelis, playing in the very arena where he spent seven years of his career, was defending stoutly.

Almost on the hour, City equalised via the penalty spot. Kolarov, captain on the night, stepped up to the plate and converted. A few minutes later, City took the lead following a bad defensive error which Milner exploited with a calmly struck shot.

Though Bayern tried hard to regain parity, City were worthy winners on the night, putting the supercilious Bavarian hierarchy firmly in their place. Despite this, Manuel Pellegrini was promptly subjected to trial by media. Eagle- eyed Sky anchorman Jeff Stelling pounced on remarks which the City manager made in the post- match press conference and which seemed to show he was unaware that a fourth City goal would've seen them top the group. Rookie pundit Jamie Carragher blustered that it was "an incredible mistake at this level" and the Skysters were quick to underline the point when, in the first knockout round, City, as mere runners- up, were drawn against Barcelona.

Pellegrini's objective, however, had been to demonstrate to the squad that they were capable of beating the European champions in their own backyard and thus had no reason to fear anyone. Unlike the pundits, who revelled in cheap jokes about " his maths", his vision was long-term.

Next up, on December 14, were Arsenal who topped the Premiership table and held a six-point lead over City. Arsenal were stronger than for several seasons with the Franco- German centre back partnership of Koscieny and Mertesacker giving defensive strength whilst, in midfield, Aaron Ramsey was a sturdy competitor and a regular goalscorer.

It was clearly vital for City to win and, in the event, they produced a devastating display, showing that anything Arsenal could do, they could do better. Though the final score, 6-3, was a shade harsh on the Gunners, the Sky Blues' football had been absolutely breathtaking.

Storming into attack, City kept Arsenal prisoners in their own half for a long period, opening the scoring with a startling, devastating Aguero volley.

City nearly doubled their advantage following a stupendous Kompany burst when he combined great ball control with rugged physical strength. It was a fine example of old-time attacking centre half play and it required a last-ditch Koscieny tackle to prevent a goal.

Unfortunately, on the half-hour, collective defensive errors gifted Arsenal an equaliser. But with Silva far outshining Arsenal's vaunted acquisition, the German Meszut Ozil, City regained the lead with a Negredo goal.

Early in the second half, City suffered the loss of Aguero who pulled up with a calf injury. Pellegrini didn't make the obvious like-for-like substitution. Rather than bringing on Dzeko, he opted for Jesus Navas who went on to trouble Arsenal with his pace.

Arsenal hit back with a brilliant Walcott lob following an eleven pass move – and City promptly topped it with a thirteen pass sequence which culminated in Navas' gully ball and Silva's lightning strike.

For a number of matches Fernandinho's tireless work in knitting together defence and attack had been a vital cog in the City machine. Now he turned up as goalscorer, delightedly bagging a brace with power shooting at the climax of tremendous runs.

With both Silva and Samir Nasri departing to standing ovations, City responded to Mertesacker's late headed goal by winning and converting a penalty.

This was a very significant match indeed in the development of the Pellegrini style. Arsenal, longtime proponents of cultured football, had been bested in a six-pointer and Arsene Wenger left the stadium ashen-faced and tight- lipped.

Those commentators who doubted City's credentials as Premiership title winners continued to point to defensive errors and to their inability to reproduce their stylish home performances when on the road. At Craven Cottage, Clichy slipped up and both Kolarov and Kompany were caught out of position for the first Fulham goal whilst a bizarre own goal from the skipper contributed the second. Yet City prevailed 4-2 with an unstoppable Yaya free kick, a goal from Kompany and two brilliant assists, Silva for Navas and Negredo for Milner. Yaya's free kick was his fifth of the season and he was converting more than half of his attempts! In refuting Jamie Redknapp's insinuation that Toure was a reluctant trainer, it was revealed that the Ivorian regularly stayed on at Carrington well after a session ended to practice free kicks, grateful for Pellegrini's encouragement.

The match was notable for two other things, Hart's long-delayed return and an immediate Zabaleta re-entry. This was Joe Hart's Premiership comeback after nearly two months on the bench. During his absence, he'd been counselled by Pellegrini and returned seeming both more relaxed and more focused.

Pablo Zabaleta recovered with astonishing speed from a hamstring strain suffered at Leicester during City's Capital One Cup victory. Long a heroic figure with the City faithful, he now had a song devoted to him, extolling his hardness and declaring "when we win the league, we'll sing this song again!" By now City lay second in the table so fans had good reason to be optimistic.

By this time Liverpool had supplanted Arsenal at the top, scoring more freely than any other team except City and benefiting by their absence from Europe. Manager Brendan Rodgers had converted Steve Gerrard into a deep-lying provider and had rehabilitated Luis Suarez. But, for the match on Boxing Day, Gerrard was unavailable as was the prolific Daniel Sturridge, once of City but transferred to Chelsea by Mark Hughes.

For only the second time in the Premiership – and the first at home – Pellegrini fielded a lone striker – Negredo. With Demichelis injured in training, Lescott returned.

City began well with Liverpool trapped in their own half for ten minutes and a header by Navas clipping a post. But, once they broke out, the Reds caused City real problems by the speed with which they transitioned from defence to attack. In Gerrard's absence, Suarez positioned himself deeper than usual and instigated a series of lightning counters which relied on the speed of Sterling. The third such move resulted in a Liverpool goal, scored by Coutinho.

Yet strong as Liverpool were in attack, they had a real weakness at centre back with Skrtel strong on the ground but inept in the air and trying to mask it by wild shirt- pulling at corners. What's more, the Frenchman Sakho was plainly not at ease with Premiership pace. It was no surprise that City took only seven minutes to equalise from a corner, Kompany being the scorer.

Just before half-time Liverpool's defence again let them down, goalkeeper Mignolet fumbling Negredo's chip and letting it go in over his head.

In the second half, Pellegrini firmly adjusted his tactics, giving the lie to pundits who'd claimed "he hasn't got a Plan B". City were directed to fall back in defence, to slow the pace of the game in order to deny Liverpool their foremost asset – pace -and to shorten their passes.

Though Suarez had been relatively quiet for a long period, he burst into life in the last fifteen minutes, beating Zabaleta and Kompany and delivering a cross to Sterling who had only Hart to beat but contrived to thump the ball high over the bar. Then, in stoppage time, referee Lee Mason denied Liverpool a stonewall penalty when Lescott pushed Suarez down.

This was a vital, hard-won victory for City, one achieved not by elan but by a tactical adjustment.

Pellegrini protested the scheduling which obliged City to play relegation strugglers Crystal Palace only forty-four hours after the titanic clash with Liverpool. He felt obliged to rest Zabaleta, Yaya, Navas and Negredo and to bring in Boyatta, Garcia, Milner and Dzeko.

Palace, under their new manager Tony Pulis, formerly of Stoke, parked the bus and a leg-weary and sub -strength City could only produce their weakest home performance of the season.The only benefit from this dreary encounter was the three points gained.

On January 1, 2014, City found themselves in Swansea, playing in torrential rain. And they would make heavy weather of defeating their hosts. With Dzeko having one of those days when his ball control let him down and Negredo slightly off the boil, both strikers suffered in comparison to Swansea's Ivorian spearhead, Wilfried Bony, who scored both their goals.

But, after a double substitution, one which would become characteristic of Pellegrini in being both attacking and defensive, the sub Kolarov's runs down the left wing were a significant weapon for City even before he scored. By now, the Serbian was turning the old fan hostility towards him right around.City went away deserved winners, 3-2.

Drawn against Blackburn Rovers away in the third round of the FA Cup, Pellegrini rang the changes and, with both Silva and Fernandinho having off days and a Pantilimon blunder gifting Rovers their equaliser, not to mention a sending off for the rarely used Boyatta, City could only draw.

It was an entirely different story in the Capital One Cup semi-final where City thrashed West Ham United 6-0. Citizens were treated to a glut of great goals, the first a superb volley from Negredo.' The Beast' then scored a powerful second and went on to complete his hat-trick. Yaya executed a majestic surge and strike and, to demonstrate the quality of the EDS youngsters, Marcos Lopes, the Brazilian -born teenager, pulled off a brilliant backheel volley to start a move from which Dzeko scored.

City travelled to St James Park on January 12 in what proved to be a very significant game. With Kolarov once again a fine attacking weapon, his assist provided Dzeko with a goal. But, just after the half hour, the game turned on a moment of controversy. Tiote blasted an absolute rocket into the net then Kompany urged Mark Jones to consult his linesman and the goal was disallowed on the grounds of offside interference with the goalkeeper's line of sight. Newcastle's choleric manager, Alan Pardew, reacted fiercely, contesting every decision and thus triggering hostile crowd reaction. When Pellegrini complained to the fourth official, Martin Atkinson, he was subjected to an astounding outburst of swearing by Pardew, caught in close-up by the television cameras so that every word he said could easily be lip- read. He snarled that Pellegrini was "a fuckin' old cunt" and even the minority of fans who hadn't taken to their manager were incensed to hear him vilified in this way.

Such was the context for Newcastle to turn ruthlessly physical with brutal fouls on Silva and on Kolarov. The worst was an appalling foul on Nasri who was carried off after being chopped down at the knee.

The outcome of the match remained in doubt until stoppage time when Milner's assist sent Negredo off on a great 40 yard run and strike. This was the moment when Ruben Cousillas' exuberant celebration, captured on TV, made him a cult hero with the Citizens.

The importance of the clash at St James's Park was that City had sustained their endeavours in the face of ruthless opponents roared on by a furious manager, facing a hostile crowd and, despite Yaya being off form, clinching a priceless victory. The pundit claim that " they can't hack it on the road" would be rarely heard after this.

The FA Cup third round replay saw several players rested in addition to Nasri. Expected to be sidelined for many weeks, he recovered well but never recaptured his sparkling early form. In the absence of both Kompany and Yaya, Pellegrini appointed James Milner as skipper, commenting that "he is a player of great character". It wasn't clear, however, whether the manager fully appreciated Milner's highly intelligent play not merely his phenomenal stamina and commitment.

After a dreadful first half where Dzeko perpetrated no less than four bad misses, enraging those supporters who condemned his erratic ball control, a flood of second-half goals enabled City to see Blackburn off.

By the time Cardiff City visited the Etihad, Malky Mackay was no longer their manager, having been dismissed by owner Vincent Tan in favour of Ole Gunnar Solskjaer, ex - Man U. Solskjaer thus witnessed at first hand the changing balance of power in Manchester. With United continuing to struggle under David Moyes, City were progressing on all fronts. Though talk of a Quadruple was premature – and something which Pellegrini himself never remotely suggested – they notched their hundredth goal of the season, scored by Dzeko – and flashed up on the big screen as '100 and counting'. Cardiff were duly seen off, 4-2.

The second leg of the semi-final of the Capital One Cup was a foregone conclusion with City taking a six goal lead to Upton Park. In the event, City added three more, one scored by Aguero after a brilliant slalom run from Lopes. Yet the match would be memorable for the wrong reasons. Negredo had scored a brace, including another fine long run and strike but, with only five minutes left, he fell awkwardly onto his shoulder in challenging for the ball at speed. Though he recovered physically, his brilliant early season form would desert him in future games.

In the FA Cup fourth round, City drew Watford for the second year running and, with star players rested, were two goals down before half-time. Pellegrini was obliged to take off the floundering Richards and Rodwell, to send on Kompany and Zabaleta and to move a reluctant Demichelis into midfield. City got back into the match with an excellent team goal but in the end prevailed solely as a result of a late goalkeeping blunder by the young shot -stopper Julian Bond.

It was a very different City – back at full strength except for Negredo – who visited White Hart Lane on 29 January. Aguero and Negredo had been a brilliant partnership but that didn't mean, as some mistakenly thought, that Dzeko couldn't combine with either of them. Indeed, for thirty minutes, City handed out a terrible drubbing with David Silva full of menace, majestically pulling the strings.

Sergio Aguero was also at the peak of his form in a display which melded power and finesse. He opened the scoring with a delicate side-spun shot and only the width of a post then a stupendous save from Hugo Lloris stopped him claiming a hattrick.

City's wonderful performance continued with a controversial but correctly awarded penalty converted by Yaya after Rose fouled Dzeko in the box. Strikes by Dzeko, Jovetic -in a rare appearance- and Kompany brought the score to 5-1, the same as it had been at White Hart Lane the year City last won the title.

By now the travelling Citizens had come up with the Sheikh Mansour Song with its surreal lyric about the Sheikh's mythical visit to Spain to recruit Manuel Pellegrini. He was said to have travelled in a Lamborghini-an inspired touch which implicitly hailed the iconic sports car as a symbol of elegant power and paid joint tribute to a generous owner and a top class manager.

The victory came at a considerable cost, however, with Aguero forced off with a hamstring injury. No-one could know at the time that this would be the last victory in City's wonderful run of twenty games unbeaten (eighteen of them victories) in all competitions -which had started in the reverse fixture two months earlier. It would also curb the scintillating attacking football – absolute Lamborghini style! – where Silva, Yaya and Nasri produced the midfield magic and Aguero and Negredo chalked up goal after goal.

On February 3, Chelsea, only three points behind City, arrived at the Etihad and the significance of the match was underlined by the presence of Chairman Khaldoun. In preparation City had sustained a late shock. Fernandinho had been injured in training and Demichelis was his midfield replacement with Nastasic in central defence.

It soon became clear that Demichelis was struggling badly against the young Belgian star Eden Hazard and the fast -running Brazilian, Willian. On this occasion, Pellegrini had clearly made an error of deployment. The problem was exacerbated by a nightmare display from Nastasic. He made a dreadful blunder early on, intervening when Kompany had matters covered. The captain retrieved the ball but fiercely bawled out Nastasic. The lack of a suitable central defensive partner was clearly putting the skipper under real stress. Demichelis had yet to adjust to Premiership pace and Txiki's attempt, in the transfer window, to sign the young Frenchman Eliaquim Mangala had failed.

Jose Mourinho sent out Chelsea to take a very physical approach, with Luiz and Ivanovic prominent as was the powerful young Serb, the newly acquired Nemanja Matic.

Completely taken aback by an atypically brilliant goal from Ivanovic, City were unable to get on the scoresheet –and Negredo, playing with painkilling injections, was a shadow of his former self. Jovetic came on as a substitute and forced Cech into a fine save from a powerful 25 yard shot. At the back, however, Nastasic's tribulations continued. Just before the end, he completely miskicked when well placed to score.

As the final whistle sounded, Sky commentator - and Citizen bete noire -Martin Tyler, blurted out in a husky-voice "and it's a Jose Mourinho masterclass!" But Chelsea's superiority on the night stemmed more from their physical approach than any tactical sleight of hand.

In the aftermath of this reverse, City laboured to a goalless draw at Norwich. Neither striker, Jovetic or Negredo, was at full fitness and their understanding was poor. Without a tremendous stint from James Milner, it's conceivable City might've lost.

Within a fortnight Chelsea had returned, this time in the fourth round of the FA Cup. With a heavy schedule and the visit of Barcelona in the Champions League looming, City got a lucky break when the midweek match with Sunderland was postponed due to gale force winds. Manuel Pellegrini made significant changes in his approach:

1. he opted for strength and security of tackle, dropping Demichelis and Navas and bringing in Lescott and Garcia. What's more, he instructed Vincent Kompany to drive into midfield and add his considerable muscle there.

2. he used James Milner in a double marking role, denying space to Hazard.

3. Jovetic's roaming movement meant that Chelsea could not concentrate their efforts on Silva.

4. City deliberately attacked at a slower tempo, depriving Chelsea of a springboard for the fast counters which they'd used so effectively in the Premiership clash.

This time City wouldn't let Chelsea get the better of them physically.Yaya, Lescott and Zabaleta were all prominent and Garcia did very well to get goalside of Etoo when the Cameroonian threatened while Kompany was ruthless against his fellow countryman, Hazard.

Jovetic had opened the scoring with a clinical finish and he was later substituted by Nasri- returning after a month out –who went on to score after a one-two with Silva.

This was a very significant game. City's progress in the FA Cup at Chelsea's expense had dramatically given the lie to those pundits who persisted in labelling Pellegrini as "cavalier", "inflexible" and "a man who has no plan B". This was a victory achieved not by liberating skilful players to deliver unstoppable attacking football but instead by astute tactical adjustments. It wasn't for nothing that he'd been dubbed ' The Engineer' in Spain!

The evening of February 18, when City faced Barcelona in the first leg of the Champions League round of the last sixteen, turned out very unhappily for the Sky Blues. The outcome of the match hinged on two incidents in quick succession early in the second half. After Busquets tripped Navas to thwart a City counter-attack, the referee, Jonas Eriksson, ignored the foul. Iniesta cleverly took advantage to feed Lionel Messi whom Kompany had allowed to drift away. Demichelis chased Messi who was one-on-one with the keeper and brought him down. Though Eriksson was of course correct in sending off Demichelis for denying his fellow -countryman a clear goalscoring opportunity, the offence took place outside the 18 yard line and should therefore have resulted in a free kick. Instead a penalty was awarded which Messi duly converted. As a result, City faced the pass masters of European football for fully forty minutes one down with only ten men.

Much criticism would be directed at Demichelis, the target of remorseless tabloid sniping, and, by implication, at Pellegrini for having selected him. But the Argentinian notably more comfortable at the slower European pace, had played superbly till then, notably when he jockeyed Sanchez out of the box before delivering a perfect tackle.

Eriksson's error was only one in a series of one-sided decisions which favoured Barcelona. He failed to call Busquets, Pique and Fabregas for ruthless fouls but halted Kompany for a straightforward shoulder challenge on Messi and Yaya likewise on Xavi. After he booked Kolarov for an alleged jump tackle on Busquets- in which he got the ball-Pellegrini protested to the fourth official.

Following the sending -off, Eriksson's one-sided refereeing continued. With Pellegrini shouting indignantly at him, he failed to book Busquets for a brutal bodycheck on Silva. Fortunately, his linesman was more efficient when ruling out a Catalan strike on the grounds of offside.

City came close to equalising with a superb move foiled only by an equally fine save. After Yaya's magnificent 50 yard high ball straight to Zabaleta, then Zaba's first-time chip -volley to Silva and Silva's instant strike when tightly marked, Victor Valdes plucked the ball out of the air at the last split second.

City had done well to hold out till the last minute of normal time when errors by Clichy and sub Lescott let Alves in to score.

There would be pundit criticism of Pellegrini for "giving Barcelona too much respect", a reference to his tactics of containing the Catalans and for having chosen two fullbacks, Clichy and Kolarov, in an attempt to limit Alves' effectiveness. In some cases, the comments stemmed from the very people who normally spoke of the Chilean coach as being "cavalier".

In the aftermath of the match, Pellegrini did not hesitate to criticise Jonas Eriksson. But he unwisely alluded to Eriksson's Swedish nationality, implying that referees from that nation lacked sufficient big-game experience. As a result, he received a UEFA ban.

The hangover from the Barcelona clash nearly derailed City in the league. A few days later, against a Stoke City parking the bus, with Aguero still absent, Negredo ineffective, Jovetic in and out again with a hamstring problem and a dreadful miss from Dzeko when unmarked four yards out left the Sky Blues needing a superb low cross from Kolarov which Yaya converted in order to secure the three points.

In the first half of March City had a three-game break from the Premiership whilst engaged in three knockout competitions. In the first of these, on a dull day at Wembley, City defeated Sunderland 3-1. The highlights of the match were two wonder goals in quick succession early in the second half, the first scored by Yaya, the second by Samir Nasri.

Till then City had laboured against the fully committed Wearsiders, going a goal down after only nine minutes when the Italian, Borini exposed Demichelis' lack of pace and brushed aside Kompany's surprisingly tentative tackle. By contrast, a magnificent tracking run by the skipper when Borini should've been called for offside but got clean away with a five yard start, was all that saved the Sky Blues from going two goals down.

Yaya's goal was a seemingly effortless 32 yard strike over a packed goalmouth, as devastating as a tennis ace's lob from baseline to baseline. Nasri's was an absolutely ferocious jump volley to climax a great team move which began with Pantilimon's targeted kick to the returning Aguero, his pass to Kolarov and Kolarov's dangerous low cross.

With City adding a late third by Navas, Manuel Pellegrini, looking drained though he was, smilingly received his first English trophy.

By contrast, the FA Cup sixth round home tie against Wigan Athletic went badly from the start and ended in a 1-2 defeat. With the second leg against Barcelona imminent, Pellegrini rested Fernandinho and benched Kompany, Silva, Zabaleta and Kolarov. Amongst those coming in were Lescott, Micah Richards and Garcia.

With Wigan ably marshalled by German manager Uwe Rosler – City's very own stalwart of yesteryear – and deploying three centre backs with the aim of foiling City's two strikers, the Sky Blues were all at sea in the first half. Garcia was tackling rashly, Yaya failing to assert leadership, Negredo sadly ineffective and Aguero not running freely.

Demichelis would be loaded with blame for both goals. The opener had stemmed from his lack of pace against Fortune and the clincher from his late reaction to danger. But he was by no means solely culpable. For the first, Richards had been out of position and Lescott slow to cover. For the second, Richards was almost static, Lescott not well positioned and Clichy indecisive before Perch scored.

After going two goals down, Pellegrini made a triple change, taking off Yaya, Navas and Negredo and sending on Silva, Milner and Dzeko. Milner's moral leadership was immediately apparent. He came on shouting "stop all this fannyin' about!" and immediately led by example, driving to the byline and executing a pullback with sadly no-one there to finish it off.

Dzeko, who enjoyed a freedom from injury not afforded the three other strikers, began to emerge as a key factor for the rest of the season. He reminded everyone of his power in the air with a difficult header against the bar (with Silva thwarted by the rebound) and he would later be narrowly wide with another header. But there remained a vocal minority of Citizens hostile to the tall Bosnian, some on the grounds of his suspect ball control, most because of what they perceived as casual attitude. So entrenched was this mindset that he was blamed for seeming to blaze the ball over the bar at point-blank range. It was only the big screen replay which confirmed that in fact Emmerson Boyce had brought off an incredible block.

Though Nasri scored, City couldn't pull the game round and, after the match, there was much criticism of Manuel Pellegrini from the more traditionally minded fans. They weren't having his prioritisation of the Champions League though in fact he was only taking on board the requirements of the owner.

It was soon obvious that elements in the widening City fanbase were being swayed by image. Garcia's pre-match appearance holding his baby daughter in his arms-admittedly a regrettable showbiz stunt for the benefit of BT cameras – and Pellegrini's pitchside gear were both cited as evidence of bad attitude. The coach's departure from his normal suit and tie to appear in a hooded club garment emblazoned with the letters 'MCFC' would be invoked in furious assertions that manager and players had treated the fixture with disrespect. And the Twittersphere was inflamed with smartarse tweets demanding to know "what's an old guy doing in a hoodie?"

City travelled to Barcelona on March 12 with Manuel Pellegrini banned from active participation. Having briefed the squad in their hotel, he left Ruben Cousillas in charge in the technical area. Lescott replaced the suspended Demichelis.

From the start, City took the fight to Barcelona and this time the refereeing issue was more one of inefficiency than perceived bias. Indeed Stephan Lannoy, the French official, made early errors which went in favour of City. He ignored Lescott's bodycheck on Lionel Messi and denied Barcelona a penalty after Lescott's clumsy tackle on Messi in the box.

With Barcelona on top in the opening stages, the truth dawned that Sergio Aguero was little more than a passenger. Scarcely mobile, he would be withdrawn at half-time.

Barcelona were understandably angered by Lannoy disallowing a goal where Jordi Alba's speed had defeated the City offside trap and Joe Hart needed to be in good form, making fine saves. Vincent Kompany, for his part, was doing remarkably well in his battle with Messi, considered by many critics to be the world's best footballer.

Shortly before half-time, City let slip a great chance. Yaya's marvellous 25 yard chip played in Silva and the little magician cleverly towed Mascherano across the box before delivering a wonderful backheel pass on the volley. But Nasri, to whom it fell, could only strike his shot straight at Valdes.

Joleon Lescott was technically out of his depth in the Camp Nou. One of his errors let Messi in to strike a post and, after he'd stumbled over his own feet and put the ball on a plate for the Argentinian super-star, Barcelona scored.

Citizens seated high in the gods valiantly chanted "we'll fight to the end" and City did just that with both style and substance. Only an incredible save from Valdes prevented a City goal. Dzeko had powered a tremendous header from a slowly dropping Kolarov cross but, as it flew towards the top corner, the keeper torqued backwards and just managed to put it over the bar.

With fifteen minutes to go, City's hopes appeared to be extin-guished when Lannoy refused a stonewall penalty for Pique's blatant trip on Dzeko. A group of City players protested vehemently and the Frenchman dismissed Zabaleta for dissent.

City, once again playing with ten men against the Catalans, scored with a couple of minutes left when Dzeko nodded on for Kompany to jab in an equaliser. But, in the very last minute, they were denied parity on the night when Alves got in from the right and scored. Yet Barcelona's aggregate margin,4-1, flattered them. It would scarcely have been achieved had City been able to call on a fully fit Sergio Aguero in both legs and had the Catalans not benefited from the one-eyed refereeing of Jonas Eriksson in the first.

After their three-week absence otherwise engaged, City returned to the Premiership at the KC Stadium against Hull City and needing to make up a nine-point deficit behind Chelsea.

Against a side enjoying a good run in the FA Cup, City suffered a huge blow after only nine minutes when Vincent Kompany was sent off by Lee Mason for pushing Jelavic down to the ground as last man. Mason had failed to call Jelavic's initial foul on the City skipper.

Pellegrini's response was not the obvious – instead of sending on Lescott and sacrificing an attacker, he switched Garcia to central defence. In the testing circumstances, the whole side responded well, three players in particular. One was Garcia who used his height to deal with Hull's long ball approach and another was his central defensive partner Demichelis. Indeed the long-haired Argentinian, bugbear of the tabloids, had an excellent game. By now he'd adjusted to Premiership pace and, significantly, in Kompany's absence, he took it upon himself to marshal the defence and to organise an offside trap into which Hull's naive attackers Jelavic and Shaun Long repeatedly fell.

The outstanding performance of the day, however, came from David Silva who took command and, within minutes of Kompany's dismissal, scored a fantastic goal with a 25 yard drive, the ball curling and swerving as if under remote control. Three times he laid on goal chances and, though Fernandinho and Dzeko each wasted one, Dzeko converted another at the close to clinch the victory.

Citizen fansites had taken issue on many an occasion with Sky's match coverage but Sky, at the least technically excellent, had never descended to BT levels. Vincent Kompany was hounded as he left the field and, still furious about being harshly dismissed, his kick against a wall was gleefully highlighted. What's more, BT focused on an incident between Hart and Boyd with repeated closeup replays lingering on whether or not Boyd had spat at the City keeper. This crude nonsense could not distract attention from a greatly improved City defence in which Demichelis had taken charge and bossed the field. The game at the KC was a significant turning point.

Against Fulham, Dzeko was taken ill on the morning of the match and replaced by Negredo. Sadly, the bearded Spanish striker, previously so prolific, couldn't buy a goal. In the event, a Yaya hat-trick, including two penalties and a wonder strike plus a tremendous stint from Milner demolished the relegation -threatened Cottagers five nil.

City next went to Old Trafford with City lying third, umpteen points ahead of a struggling United whose micro- revival was being bigged up by the media. With Van Persie's absence matched by that of Aguero, City scored in the very first minute with a brilliant team goal of which Silva was the main architect and Dzeko the finisher. Blatant refereeing errors by the Premiership's youngest official, Michael Oliver, might well've seen Welbeck sent off for dangerous play and should certainly have seen Fellaini redcarded for a violent foul on Zabaleta. Dzeko scored a fine second with a well timed run and, with Yaya scoring at the close to make it 3-0, Citizens cheerfully mocked a Stretford End banner saluting ' The Chosen One'. They made merry with chants about the hapless David Moyes, now slumped in gloom, and the dismayed Ferguson who'd nominated him for the succession.

Since they were beaten at the Etihad on December 14, things had not gone well for the Gunners. From a position of leading the Premiership table, they'd slumped to one where Champions League qualification was in doubt. Undoubtedly the long-term loss of Ramsey and Walcott had been a factor. But, though they'd been thrashed both at Anfield and Stamford Bridge, they remained strong at home and, on March 29, at the Emirates, both sides were boosted by news of Chelsea's shock defeat at Selhurst Park.

City scored early with a devastating counter-attack and nullified much of Arsenal's close passing. Though Demichelis once again played very well, marshalling the offside trap, heading powerfully out of defence and tackling decisively, Fernandinho was not quite at his best and was culpable for Arsenal's equaliser in the second half. After that, it needed a fine reaction save from Joe Hart to prevent Arsenal scoring again. But City came back into this brilliant cut and thrust encounter and, though plainly leg -weary from two big away games in quick succession, deserved their point.

At home against Southampton, City won a penalty in the second minute but shortly afterwards Nasri missed a good chance to increase the margin. After that City appeared to relax and the Saints equalised from the penalty spot and were looking good against a subdued atmosphere inside the stadium. Yet, in first half stoppage time, there was a complete U-turn with two fine goals, first Nasri's close range finish of a brilliant team move (albeit with an undetected yet blatant offside) then Dzeko's glancing header from a testing Kolarov cross. Pellegrini removed a below-par Fernandinho at half-time and sent on Garcia and later Jovetic who was on hand with a tap-in to finish an excellent team move and complete the scoring at 4-1.

With rivalry at fever pitch for a full week before City went to Anfield for a potential title decider – on the very weekend of the twenty-fifth anniversary of Hillsborough – Manuel Pellegrini aimed to calm things down, remarking "the team with the colder mind will win. It's about managing anxiety". But City's composure was undermined on the eve of the clash when Vincent Kompany was hurt in training after a collision with another player. Doubts would remain as to his participation until just before kick-off when he passed a late fitness test and emerged with one knee strapped.

Liverpool were riding the crest of a wave, topping the table after a tremendous run of nine straight victories. In an unprecedented display of hostility, the Kop were booing and whistling every City touch and they continued to do so for the whole game. After only six minutes, there were roars of delight when Suarez brilliantly created a goal for Sterling who calmly swerved past Kompany before planting the ball past Hart into the back of the Kop net.

In the early stages, Liverpool were rampant with Fernandinho and Nava desperately trying to cope with Sterling's pace. It would be thirteen minutes before the first City attack of any consequence took place and it ended badly with Yaya launching a shot wildly high and wide and hurting himself in the process. Within a few minutes, he went off with what looked like a groin strain. Meanwhile, the Reds had missed an excellent chance of going two goals up when, after Kompany slid to the ground vainly trying to tackle Sturridge, the striker sliced his shot wide.

Nevertheless, after twenty-six minutes, Liverpool did go two goals up after two corners in quick succession. At the first, Gerrard was unmarked as he rose for a header in the six yard box and City only survived thanks to a great point-blank save from Joe Hart. The reprieve was momentary with Skrtel pushing Kompany away at the second corner and scoring with a leaping back header.

After half an hour, the tide began to turn. First, Silva pounced on a misplaced Flanagan back pass and played Dzeko through only for Gerrard to save the day with a tremendous tackle. Next, City might well've had a penalty. Sakho, the slow-moving, Mohican –sporting Frenchman, completely missed his tackle on Dzeko in the box but Mark Clattenburg refused the spot kick. Just before half-time, City were inches from an equaliser when Mignolet failed to claim a corner and first Sterling and then Johnson had to head the ball away almost on the line.

Early in the second half, Pellegrini took off the ineffectual Navas and sent on James Milner. There was a major incident when Suarez confronted Demichelis wide of the penalty area and, having pushed the ball too far beyond him, went down, tumbling head over heels. With City players surrounding Mr. Clattenburg and demanding a second yellow for simulation, the referee decided against, explaining later that, as he saw it, Suarez fell due to glancing contact with Demichelis' trailing bootheel.

Three minutes later, however, City did score from a well worked move with Fernandinho finding Milner who promptly took advantage of Flanagan and Henderson having both switched off. He took the ball to the byline and adroitly pulled it back for Silva to finish

City survived a penalty appeal when Zabaleta challenged Sturridge following a high-speed breakaway. Mr Clattenburg, with the stadium in ferment, had noted that Zabaleta had got his studs on the ball.

Just turned the hour, City equalised after a sustained and confident attack, coolly working the ball into the box and producing an error from Johnson who diverted a shot into his own net.

With fifteen minutes left, City came close to seizing the lead when Garcia chested down a Mignolet kick and promptly played a ball down the touchline for Aguero, who came on as a sub for his first appearance in weeks. Looking momentarily like the old Kun, he turned Skrtel inside out, staggering from the impact of the Slovak's failed challenge. He steered a pass at high speed into the box for Silva but the little man, closing in fast, couldn't quite make firm contact.

A couple of minutes later, it was disaster for City thanks to a dreadful error from Kompany, a total miskick –under no pressure- which Coutinho promptly cracked into the net.

This was not the end of the drama. In the last minutes of stoppage time Henderson was redcarded for a studs -up challenge on Nasri. Then Garcia, sent forward to use his undoubted power in the air, boldly attacked a cement mixer cross amongst a knot of half a dozen players in the box. It appeared that Skrtel had decisively headed the ball away. After the final whistle, however, Sky pictures showed that Skrtel had used his hand to repel the attack. No one had appealed and Clattenburg, only ten yards away, hadn't noticed. Had he done so, however, the penalty would doubtless have been taken by Sergio Aguero who, very probably, would've scored.

Speculation aside, however, Citizens' title hopes seemed to have been badly dented and there was criticism of Manuel Pellegrini for not having taken a more cautious approach.Though Vincent Kompany was fit to play, he was clearly hindered by the knock he'd taken at Carrington. He'd been at fault, partly or wholly, for at least two goals. In normal circumstances, Kompany's sheer strength was more than a match for almost any opponent yet Skrtel had brushed him aside for the second. It would've been difficult, however, for Pellegrini to have overruled a captain who desperately wanted to play and who was regarded by his teammates as a talisman.

Three days after the Anfield defeat, the first of City's two rescheduled home games took place, with relegation -threatened Sunderland the opponents.Though City began well with Fernandinho scoring inside two minutes, they were unable to sustain their control with the same player volleying over when well placed. With Aguero tentative and Negredo ineffective, there was no real end product whilst the creativity of Silva and Yaya was badly missed.

As the match wore on, Sunderland gained in confidence and eventually equalised. With seven minutes left, they seized the lead following a speedy counter-attack. City were very lucky to get an equaliser when, with only two minutes remaining, goalkeeper Mannone perpetrated a dreadful fumble. Even so, they could've snatched a winner in stoppage time but Nasri blazed over from ten yards.

Supporters had left the Etihad in subdued mood after this unexpected loss of points and this was reflected in the next home game, against West Bromwich Albion, where there was a slightly reduced crowd but a very flat atmosphere. Meanwhile, Liverpool were storming on with their run of eleven consecutive wins.

Zabaleta scored after only two minutes and this time City continued to play more like their real selves. What was particularly encouraging was Aguero's brilliant opportunist strike from 25 yards. Then the Baggies equalised in a lightning break. But City soon restored their two-goal advantage with a tap- in from a badly defended corner. The scorer was Demichelis and it was remarkable that three Argentinians had all scored in one Premiership game.

Citizens were shocked to see the returning David Silva carried off halfway through the second half after what seemed like a minor knock but it was revealed afterwards that this had indeed been a precaution.

On April 27, those Citizens who'd made the long trip to Selhurst Park roared with delight as the big screen brought news of Liverpool's home defeat at the hands of Chelsea. It meant that, if City could beat Crystal Palace, the destiny of the title would be back in their own hands. This was no easy task, however, because manager Tony Pulis was being widely saluted for his work in bailing Palace out of relegation danger and lifting them to mid-table with five wins on the trot including away to Everton.

Injury swings and roundabouts meant that the Sky Blues were without Silva but that Yaya returned. Milner was now keeping his place at the expense of Navas whilst Garcia was brought in instead of the overworked and out of form Fernandinho.

For the third successive match, City scored in the first few minutes, a goal expertly created by Yaya for Dzeko to score with a ruthless header. The Bosnian had truly stepped into the breach in Negredo's prolonged goal drought.

With Palace unable to fathom their high line well marshalled by Demichelis, City laboured to increase the lead until, just before half-time, Yaya scored a magnificent goal, climaxing a 50 yard run from deep within his own half before curling a beautiful shot high into the far corner. He'd effectively defeated no less than seven Palace players. This was probably the Sky Blues' goal of the season so far and had Pellegrini's usually impassive face wreathed in smiles as he yelled "yes, YES!!!" Though City did not add to the scoring, they did what was needed to steal a march on Liverpool.

City visited Goodison Park on the penultimate weekend of the season in strange circumstances and found a muted atmosphere on an overcast day.

Everything was clear-cut but far from easy. Liverpool's defeat against Chelsea and the City victory at Selhurst Park meant they could clinch the title if they won their remaining games. But their record at Goodison was one of almost unbroken failure.

For most of the Everton supporters, however, the prospect of Liverpool winning the title was painful – many of them openly told the Citizens "we hope you do us today to stop THEM!". The atmosphere inside the stadium was subdued with many Toffees studying their mobiles even at kick-off.

Regardless of the fans' feelings, Everton boss Roberto Martinez immediately showed his intentions. On the touchline, scowling and bellowing orders, he would make sure that City had to sweat for victory.

After only ten minutes, there was a bolt from the blue, a stunning goal from Everton's Ross Barkley which would soon be compared with the teenage Wayne Rooney's famous effort against Arsenal. Standing 20 yards out and facing a packed goalmouth, Barkley struck an unstoppable shot low into the back of the far corner. It had Liverpudlians roaring with delight as they watched on Sky.

On twenty-two minutes, suddenly City were level. Sergio Aguero scuttled in on goal and hammered a bullet shot inside Howard's near post. At once, the curse which had plagued City all season – and Aguero in particular – struck again. Kun was forced off with an injury to his groin.

It took till two minutes before half time for City to take the lead and they did so with a tremendous Dzeko header. With Everton preparing to open a 'Wall of Fame' dedicated to Dixie Dean, this was surely the equal of anything from the Toffees' legendary master of the headed goal.

There was a breathtaking opening to the second half. First, the prodigious Barkley raced 40 yards right through the middle of the park with the Toffees' roaring him on. He bisected Kompany and Zabaleta to play Naismith through one on one with the keeper. But Joe Hart dived full-length and just got the tips of his left glove on it, averting a certain goal by turning it round for a corner.

Straight afterwards City took advantage of a positional error by Everton rookie John Stones and Dzeko scored with a tap-in.

On sixty-four minutes, Everton got a goal back with Lukaku's diving header but,

with a few minutes left, Joe Hart made another fine save. After a weaving run from Gerard Delofeu, Everton's Barcelona loanee, going past three men, the keeper hurled his body in the way of a close range angled shot and diverted it into the side netting.

This was a vitally important victory for City.

Two days later, in the Monday night game, the race for the title took a sensational twist at Selhurst Park when Liverpool threw away a three goal lead in the last ten minutes, emerging with only a draw against Crystal Palace. It seemed that the voluble Brendan Rodgers had been naïvely seeking to reduce City's goal difference instead of clinching three points. As a result, the situation was that City could afford to draw one of their two remaining home games and still take the title on a plus thirteen goal difference ahead of Liverpool.

The first match was a midweek rescheduled game with Aston Villa, contested in an intense, uber- Mancunian downpour. The entire first half was a stalemate with City enjoying almost continuous possession but unable to penetrate. On forty-five minutes, Nasri missed badly, shooting wide from four yards out. As the game wore on, some Citizens became more and more uptight, shouting with exasperation as Dzeko failed to control Yaya's glorious ball over the top. Throughout it all, Manuel Pellegrini remained calm but focused, giving instructions from the sidelines and insisting that City keep on playing football and the goals would come.

The breakthrough, when it came, on sixty-four minutes, produced an eruption of joy and relief. There was a perfect triangular move, David Silva's beautifully precise 15 yard through ball, then Zabaleta's perfect low cross ending with Dzeko sweeping the ball into the net.

With the floodgates opened, City scored three more times, a tap-in from Dzeko, a precisely placed shot by sub Jovetic and, in the last minute, a magnificent individual goal from Yaya. It was his twentieth of the season in the Premiership and City's hundredth. He ran maybe 60 yards from deep in his own half, beating two men en route, twisting this way and that, then fended off another and, from close by the penalty spot, blasted a shot inside Guzan, striking plumb centre in the back of the net. A goal reminiscent of Milan's (and all-too-briefly City's) great Liberian centre forward George Weah, it had everything : speed, control, strength, stamina – considering Yaya had played the full ninety minutes – and power of shot. Pellegrini acclaimed it with a wide smile, doubtless one of the best goals he'd ever have witnessed.

On 11 May Citizens went to the Etihad knowing that the only scenario which could deprive City of a second Premiership title would be one where City lost to West Ham and Liverpool beat Newcastle. Nerves were soon soothed by news from Anfield that Liverpool had gone one down due to an own goal by Skrtel. With West Ham scarcely able to get out of their own half but holding firm in defence, it took 39 minutes before Nasri broke the deadlock with a snapshot which the Hammers' keeper, Adrian, mishandled.

Early in the second-half, Kompany scored from a corner and, though news came that Liverpool had scored twice in quick succession, City looked secure. There would be no repeat of the incredible dramas the last time around. Though Aguero missed an open goal, Citizens were amused shortly afterwards by the spectacle of Liverpool's record signing, Carroll – later dumped on West Ham for half the price – being totally unable to control the ball from an easy cross.

The match finished with City victorious 2-0 and thus two points ahead of Liverpool. They'd narrowly failed to match the Premiership record goal tally but had achieved one more than the Reds – a total of 102 for the season.

Manuel Pellegrini had more than fulfilled what was asked of him when he was appointed. Despite an unlucky exit from the Champions League, he'd won two trophies, one of which, the Barclays Premier League, was a major prize. What's more, he'd done so with a style of football which was universally recognised as attractive – and one which had yielded no less than 156 goals in all competitions.

Pellegrini had been obliged from February onwards by injuries to Sergio Aguero, Alvaro Negredo (whose form also fell badly away) and Samir Nasri to row back from the high speed interpassing and positional interchanging which had characterised the first half of the season. With his leading strikers hors de combat, he relied on two main factors to sustain the goal rate – Yaya's formidable individual skill and Edin Dzeko's consistent poaching.

Thus it was not Lamborghini football alone which won the title. Once Martin Demichelis had adjusted to the hurly-burly of the Premiership and was acting as defensive marshal, in partnership with the outstanding Vincent Kompany, the City defence was notably more secure than Liverpool's and second only to that of Chelsea. Fernandinho, for his part, performed a vital role in linking defence with attack.

Beyond the elegant attacking and resolute defending, there was City's invincible team spirit. Trusted by the chain of command from Sheikh Mansour via Khaldoun Al Mubarak to Ferran Soriano, Manuel Pellegrini was perceived as the embodiment of the holistic approach. Yet Samir Nasri put it in much simpler language when asked what the difference was between this season and last. "The atmosphere, the manager and the confidence" he replied. "He "(Manuel Pellegrini) talks to the players. There is a trust in the philosophy, in the quality we have in this team. He is a perfect coach".

6

FROM AGUERO TO ZABALETA :
THE A-Z OF CITY HEROES

SERGIO 'KUN' AGUERO - KID ASSASSIN

How close City came to humiliation on 13 May 2012! One minute and forty seconds to go before Mr. Dean's final whistle would've signalled a monumental anti-climax, would've launched 'I told you so' snorts from pundits up and down the land and precipitated a torrent of sneers and an avalanche of abuse. That the Citizens were spared this ordeal and translated from dread to ecstasy was due to a collective act of will but above all to the ice- cool determination of the man who wore # 16 on the back of his sky blue shirt.

The title -clincher against QPR was Sergio Aguero's thirtieth goal of the season but it was the one which justified, at a stroke, the £38 million fee City paid for him to Atletico Madrid. Aguero had known what was expected of him and had summed it up perfectly when he said "this is an important club that made a decisive bet on me for their new project".

Argentinian by birth, of mixed Spanish and Lebanese ancestry, Sergio Aguero grew up in a shanty town on the outskirts of Buenos Aires. Quilmes is its name and he lived in its grimmest section, Villa Itati. The next youngest of seven children, his home was a clapboard shack with a tin roof on it and an old blanket for a front door. Neighbours' kids played out with cloth footballs and, by the time they were in their early teens, many were jail fodder, hooked on cocaine-base paco. But Sergio was both lucky and gifted-lucky to have caring parents and gifted with a ball at his feet. And, where most nippers only had rolled-up rags, that ball was a real football, bought as a Christmas present for him when he was three years old by his father Leonel – himself a more than useful footballer. Sergio slept with the ball under his bed in a room he shared with all his brothers and he cradled it during most of his waking hours. He had little in the way of formal schooling but he was quickwitted and confident and the standout player in the youngsters' teams who battled each other for pesos in the streets of Villa Itati.

It was his grandparents who gave him the nickname Kun. "It's a Japanese cartoon character's name" was all they said but they no doubt saw something in his expression- a playful confidence, a determination, a look that spoke of the fantastic skill in his feet and a belief that the world was his oyster.

Spotted by Independiente at the age of nine, his photo was taken as he sat on top of a filing cabinet in the club office, smiling boldly and lazily swinging his feet before signing junior forms. The club bought his dad a car to work as a taxi driver in the big city. Twenty quid a week was all he made but at least the family had enough for bread every day instead of making do with dried yerba leaves steeped in boiling water.

At Independiente, Aguero's career graph soared sharply upwards. Debuting in the first team barely a month after his fifteenth birthday, he would star in the defeat of bitter rivals Racing at the age of seventeen. That was when he carried out a Maradonaesque dribble and score, starting inside his own half. Short, sturdy-legged and skilful, brave and fast, delighting in twisting away from defenders and leaving them clutching the turf, he was a brilliant spearhead who seemed bound for a transfer to one of Europe's big-name clubs.

Liverpool seemed the likeliest destination but, in a decision which was shrewd in the short term and beneficial to Manchester City in the long run, Rafael Benitez dismissed the scouts' reports and the agents' videos. Benitez was far too astute to give credence to the old saw "you can take a man out of the barrio but you can't take the barrio out of the man". But he was concerned that, at only eighteen, the lad could scarcely be expected to cope with the culture shock of a move to Spain- let alone England, where he didn't speak a word of the language.

Where Benitez feared to tread, Atletico Madrid rushed in. They filled the Independiente coffers with a debt- clearing cheque of €23 million. But, in his first season, Aguero's underperformance seemed to bear out Benitez' reservations. Half a dozen goals was a poor return for the club record signing. And, while Aguero's conduct never sank to the level of a Premiership dolt, he blew his wages on limos, gorged on hamburgers and was seen clubbing it till the early hours.

Suddenly he changed - totally and for the better. This was due to Maradona. Not Diego, idol of all Argentina's young footballers but Giannina, Diego's Italian- born daughter, a year younger than Sergio. They met in 2007. Giannina knew football from the inside. Her youth had been split between Italy, Spain and Argentina as her father moved from club to club and from Naples to Seville then Corrientes before returning to his native Buenos Aires. This was before her parents amicably divorced when she was fifteen. Aguero succinctly summed up how vital she was to him. "Giannina is the woman of my life, my support system, an enormous help" he said. Then he hit the nail right on the head when he added "she grew up in the football bubble and she knows all about it".

By 2009 Sergio and Giannina were married and their son Benjamin was born. Benefiting from a stable home life, Aguero's La Liga form came on by leaps and bounds.Atletico asked him to step up to the plate in the wake of Fernando Torres' departure. He did just that and, after five years at the club, he'd netted 74 times in 175 appearances.These included a brace and a virtual hattrick (baulked only by a penalty-yielding trip) in wins over Barcelona.

When Aguero sought to leave Atletico, both Chelsea and Manchester City made enquiries. Not surprisingly he didn't contact his father-in-law about the choice. It was unlikely that a man who'd spent half his life being routinely slagged off by Fleet Street hacks could've been objective over any English club. But Giannina gave her opinion. She would have no problem with Manchester, she said, and, with Pablo Zabaleta's encouragement, Aguero opted to sign for the most ambitious club in the world.

Newly signed and nursing blistered feet, Sergio Aguero, now aged twenty-three, remained on the subs bench as City jousted with United for the Charity Shield. But, as he idly dangled his legs in front of him, his face had the same 'Kun' expression as it did when he was a boy of nine and had first signed with Independiente. If turning out for his hometown heroes was then the height of his ambition, now he saw success with Manchester City as the beckoning pinnacle of his achievement.

He began against Swansea, coming on at just over the hour and scoring within a couple of minutes, hurtling in, with that low centre of gravity of his, to jab Richards' cross into the net. Then came the balletic touch on the byline to turn a seemingly lost ball back for Silva to score. And he finished with a 35 yard rocket!

At White Hart Lane, his fierce high speed swerve confounded the doughty Dawson before his explosive finish left Friedel helpless. After the Wigan game he was delighted by the Premiership custom of keeping the match ball if you've scored a hat-trick. And his last-minute winner against Villareal in the Champions League set City up a treat for the trip to Old Trafford.

In the Demolition Derby he scored the third - the epic third - when he converted the superb combination play of Yaya, Balotelli, Milner and Richards and darted past Smalling to prod the ball home.

His goal glut continued virtually unabated and when Norwich visited the Etihad, his strike revived memories of his father-in-law's against Belgium in the Mexico World Cup - full stretch trap, huge swerve to leave the burly Barrett tumbling at his boots like a butchered steer and an uber- cool double nutmeg on Crofts and Naughton to squeeze the ball in at the far post.

The new year saw him at the heart of the heroic fightback in the Third Round Cup Derby, reacting to Lindegaard's bungled parry before Smalling had even registered it and ramming the ball over the line; he saluted the Citizens behind the goal, his shock of jet black hair plastered over his mug in the relentless Mancunian rain, shouting not 'Vamos! " any more but' Come on!".

Interspersed between the key goals in vital matches were fantastic near- misses. If he got the chance, only if the team situation would allow it, he'd essay the Maradona dribble and strike. When Newcastle came to Eastlands and City had already gone two up, he swivelled round Stephen Taylor, jinked past Coloccini and, as Simpson got to him, fired on goal from point blank range. It rebounded off the diving keeper Krul's chest and Kun had almost got on it when the Dutchman snatched it off his boots. Then Aguero sank down gasping, head in hand, like a man who has seen an exquisite china vase drop from a shelf, dived to retrieve it only to see it slip through his fingertips and smash.

On an ice cold winter's night in Wigan, gloved up against subzero temperatures far removed from the balmy Barcelona where Lionel Messi operates, only a banal blunder by a teammate, Edin Dzeko, robbed Aguero of a truly Messi-anic goal. Silva had split the Wigan defence with a beautiful pass straight into his path. Kun was on his own just inside the Wigan half heading for goal and, as the chasing defenders caught up with him at the edge of the box, he began a fantastic, high-speed dribble. He checked, he shielded, he jinked, leaving Figueroa on his backside.Then he swivelled abruptly, grounding Cauldwell, before he veered sidelong, flummoxing the goalie Al Hamsi who went slipping and sliding beyond his defenders as he tried to second-guess Aguero's next move. As Al Hamsi fell onto Kun's boots, the Argentinian stumbled for a moment but he kept his balance and was pivoting ready to crack the ball home. But, at that very moment, Dzeko, who'd been the close quarters decoy throughout it all, unaccountably intervened and shot, a woeful effort which Al Hamsi was relieved to gobble up.

Dzeko knew at once the enormity of his blunder, raising his arms in disbelief. Aguero looked dumbfounded, open- armed yet remarkably restrained in his mild rebuke to Dzeko. This was the measure of the man, determined and clinical but without that edge of raw aggression which has characterised many of the great Argentinian players. The travelling Citizens acclaimed the goal that never was, chanting Aguero's name. But, in truth, it was as if a rogue radio DJ had interrupted an intricate Johnny Marr guitar solo to sample a brass bandsman belching into his tuba.

The climax of Sergio Aguero's season, his winning goal against Queens Park Rangers, hinged on his running off the ball. Having dropped deep to pick up de Jong's pass, he disconcerted Derry with a feint before prompting Balotelli and setting off on an uncanny jig through the Hoops' defence. Going for a one-two with Balotelli, he reacted instantly to Ferdinand's tackle in the D- which grounded the Italian- and to the pass which Mario calmly made while slumped on the turf. Two defenders were blocking Aguero's path but he was round them in a trice, turning to hurdle Onuoha's lunging tackle. As Hill and Derry desperately rushed in to block the cross shot, he changed his mind and drove it home between Kenny and the near post. It wasn't that the QPR defenders weren't vigilant. They were. But Aguero's speed of thought and movement, his decisive execution, was simply too much for them.

Long ago and far away, on the shabby streets of Villa Itati, a boy his nan nicknamed 'Kun' dreamed of fame and fortune on the football fields of Europe. Round about that time, the loyal supporters of Manchester City could only pray for deliverance from the double- dip relegation nightmare wrought by a series of dodgy managers and a myopic chairman. But, on May 13, 2012, the man who still wore his boyhood nickname on the back of his Sky Blue shirt spied a chance, seized on it and delivered a dream of a trophy to everyone who hailed him in the City of Manchester Stadium.

In the season between the titles, Sergio Aguero was stretchered off in the first home match and would be plagued by injuries to his knees and hamstrings. He was also saddened by the breakup of his marriage. He and Giannina announced their separation in January 2013 and she returned to live in Madrid with Benjamin. Despite muckraking efforts by tabloids, the Agueros kept the reasons for their separation to themselves and Giannina conducted herself with dignity by refusing to hurl blame at Sergio and ensuring that his contact with his son was fully maintained.

Though season 2013-14 was one of anti-climax in terms of goal return, there was a wonder strike at home to Liverpool-when, from almost on the byline and twenty yards wide, he tricked Reina and chipped the ball over Skrtel into the empty net.

Aguero began the second title- winning season in sparkling form and, for fully five months, he rode rampant over almost all Premiership and C.L. defences. In the opening match, against Newcastle, sent away by Dzeko's backheel flick, he fended off Taylor and cracked the ball home. Then his brace in Pilsen helped shut up Sky's carping pundits. And, in the home derby, he applied a dynamic finish to Kolarov's cross, twisting like an acrobat to lash the ball home. Once again he ended the match with a brace.

But he was strangely hesitant against Bayern. He didn't seem to like it when he was told to drop back into midfield, he resorted to petulant fouling and was taken off. Then, against Everton, he was annoyed with himself for narrowly failing to convert a brilliantly planned triangular free kick routine. For once the executioner lacked ice in his veins.

But Aguero was soon back to his best in a white-hot goal glut. Thriving in partnership with Alvaro Negredo, he notched a brilliant strike at Upton Park, perfectly reading Negredo's dummy. And, after another Champions League brace, this time in Moscow, he scored a tremendous goal at Stamford Bridge striking at pace and with surprise from a sharp angle.

Having netted twice in the six- nil hammering of Spurs, he scored against Arsenal with a fantastic shot, a ferocious blow as sudden and total as a knockout by the great Argentinian middleweight Carlos Monzon. Early in the second half he had to go off when he pulled up with a calf injury but, after a few weeks out, returned as menacing as ever.

Aguero was at his absolute peak in the destruction of Tottenham at White Hart Lane. He nearly scored a superb solo when he drove Dawson across the D, waltzing past Chiriches to explode a fierce shot which shivered the far post but just went out.He opened the scoring with a delicate side spun shot as cool as a Selby snooker pot and he was foiled only by Hugo Lloris' stupendous save from his fierce point-blank header. Unhappily, this was the very match in which he was forced off with the hamstring injury which hobbled the rest of his season.

Aguero came back prematurely and was ineffective in the lost Cup tie against Wigan. Saddest of all was his appearance in the Camp Nou when he could make no impact at all due to his tightened hamstring and was taken off at half-time.

Out for many weeks, he came on once again at Anfield and looked like the Kun of old as he turned Skrtel inside out on the touchline and, staggering from the impact of the rugged Slovakian's challenge, adroitly recovered his balance to set Silva up with a lovely pass into the box.

There were more signs of his former brilliance in his low back lift strike against West Bromwich Albion from 25 yards. And, at Goodison, his scuttling dash, low centre of gravity carriage and sudden hammered strike was reminiscent of his title -winning goal against Queen's Park Rangers in 2012. Though he injured his groin in the process and had to go off, this was once again a crucial contribution in a decisive match.

Sergio Aguero is one of the greatest talents in world football. Standing a rung below the spot occupied by his all-time great compatriot Lionel Messi, his gifts are such that his near misses are more memorable than most players' goals. Unlike many South American stars over the decades – and in the case of Luis Suarez now – his temperament is agreeable. He has a rare calmness to go with his startling speed of thought and devastating execution. In that way he's still the same 'Kun' who delighted his grandparents as a boy with an attitude which suggested the world would be his oyster.Lethal as an assassin in front of goal, he's still a kid at heart.

Aguero has been at the heart of City's success since he arrived at the Etihad. Untimely injuries have prevented him, as yet, from repeating his Premiership form on the world stage. But he has all the qualities to lead City to ultimate success in the Champions League

GAEL CLICHY - THE MAN WHO CHANGED HIS MIND

When Gael Clichy signed for Manchester City in the summer of 2011, the media cast up the words he'd used two years before. Those words were : "if you're a player who thinks only about money then you could end up at Manchester City. You have to think if you want to play for a big club and have your image or if you want to play for a good club and still earn good money".

But Clichy was no hypocrite and no fool. He knew there'd been a big change at Eastlands since that day in 2009 when his Arsenal teammate Emmanuel Adebayor put pen to paper on his £25 million City contract. The time of the megabuck megastar signing, both real and attempted, was long gone. It had lasted barely a year. In September 2008, with the Abu Dhabi takeover imminent, Robinho was reeled in from Real Madrid for £32.5 million. Suddenly Al Fahim, Abu Dhabi point man for the buy-out, was barking his head off about which 'world class ' footballer would be coming to City next. Wanna buy Berbatov from United? No big deal! Wanna grab Villa from Valencia? No problem! Except that SAF personally drove the big Bulgarian from the airport to Old Trafford to stop him listening to temptation. And Valencia said no dice about Villa. Even though Abu Dhabi smoothly phased out Al Fahim, there was still Garry Cook. In the 2009 January transfer window, a bid was made of over £100 million to bring Kaka from AC Milan and when Kaka said no, Cook had the nerve to claim " Milan bottled it". In the summer of that year, Carlos Tevez swapped Old Trafford for Eastlands for a fee quoted at anything up to £47 million and Cook plastered Tevez' mug over Deansgate.

But change was in the air-partly because of the need to abide by UEFA Financial Fair Play Regulations but greatly because of Chairman Khaldoun Al Mubarrak, whose pronouncements were dignified even as he vigorously transformed the decrepit facilities at Eastlands But, though Al Fahim was out and Cook restrained, the image of Manchester City as a club which preferred a headline-grabbing quick fix to organic teambuilding didn't die overnight.

What's more, in Summer 2009 when Clichy made his original remark, the City manager was still Mark Hughes and the French international, who'd been with Arsenal since 2003 and was a member of the 'Invincibles' squad, was leery of joining an outfit run by the ex-boss of 'Black Eye Rovers'. But Hughes, hired by Shinawatra, was fired by the year's end and, when Roberto Mancini approached Clichy eighteen months later, he made clear his admiration for Arsenal 's style but stressed the need for greater defensive discipline.

It's unlikely that Clichy was unduly worried by misbegotten media mischief over the unjust imputation of hypocrisy. Any more than he was by Internet trolls smirking about his relationship with the glamorous French Umbro model, Charlene Suric. If any man had learned to shrug off brickbats, it was Gael Clichy. At the age of fifteen, Gael had narrowly survived death as a junior at FC Cannes. A freak accident at the training ground left him with a mutilated finger and, during an emergency operation to repair the damage, a serious problem arose with his lungs. Indeed his heart stopped beating and was restarted in what the operating theatre team would describe as "a miracle recovery".

Coached as a boy by his Martinique-born teacher father Claude, Gael gravitated to the famous football academy at Castelmaurau in southern France. Spotted by Arsene Wenger while at Cannes, he transferred to Arsenal as an eighteen -year-old. It didn't take him long to learn fluent, fast -talking English and his participation in the title- winning Arsenal squad of 2003-4, the Invincibles, meant that he had the kind of trophy -winning experience which Roberto Mancini wanted within his City squad. So far from being a two-faced acceptance of the Etihad petro-dollar, Clichy's signing was the realisation by an astute professional of a total change in the Premiership balance of power.

Wing-back was, for Mancini as for all Italian managers, a vital role but one so physically demanding that rotation was essential.So Clichy took his turn with Aleksandar Kolarov.The sturdy Serb could do things which Clichy could not-in particular his fierce and flighted free-kicks. But Clichy was the better defender and, as the season progressed, he slowly but surely regained his Emirates' attacking flair. In the title race run-in, he showed up well and truly-sometimes unspectacularly, as when he harassed West Brom's big Swede Olsson, flummoxing him so Aguero could rob him and play Silva through for the final goal.Then in scintillating style, at Molyneux, when he nutmegged Kightly on the flank and curled a wonderful ball round Bassong first bounce right into Aguero's path for the opener. This came at a time when Wolves were putting up doughty resistance and was a signicant step on City's path to the title.

But Gael Clichy struggled to adapt to Manuel Pellegrini's high defensive line and made a number of serious mistakes, notably when he switched off against Bayern Munich and kept Thomas Muller onside for the second goal. There was also the penalty he gratuitously gave away against CSKA Moscow.

Though he was being overshadowed by Aleksandar Kolarov's spectacular attacking performances, Pellegrini had sufficient faith in Clichy to keep him in the rotation and thus lesson the workload on the Serbian.

During the second half of the second title winning season, Gael Clichy recovered his form and was an invaluable member of the squad, well liked by teammates and supporters as he's always been. Easy-going and friendly though he is, he was astute enough to recognize immediately the difference between the likes of Al Fahim and Cook, on the one hand and Chairman Khaldoun Al Mubarak on the other.

Graham Gordon

MARTIN DEMICHELIS - FROM ZERO TO HERO

Signed in the last hours of the transfer window, Martin Demichelis was crocked on his first day in training. It was early October before he made his City debut, at Stamford Bridge. Greeted by BBC commentator Jonathan Pearce with the less than charitable words "it's hard to know how Demichelis can get a game yet Joleon Lescott's only on the bench", his potential detractors were alerted to what seemed undue preference for a foreigner – no megastar but, at £4 million, a basement buy. Demichelis had played for Pellegrini at Malaga and, for those so inclined, his purchase and selection would, if it didn't work out, be a potential stick with which to beat the Chilean.

It wasn't long before trolls were infesting the City fansites making rude remarks about Demichelis. "He looks like something straight out of a seventies porn movie" jibed one while another sneered that he was "a long-haired Argentinian prick !" Demichelis certainly sported a ponytail but, as GIFs by those who wanted to give the guy a chance indicated, his voluptuous, bikini -clad model wife, Evangelina Anderson, was proud to smile contentedly as she reclined in his arms.

Demichelis' debut was solid, with powerful tackles on the likes of Torres and Oscar. The doubters were soon back in full voice, however, as he struggled week in and week out to adjust to Premiership pace.

It was in the Allianz Arena, the very stadium where he'd spent seven years in the colours of Bayern Munich, that he showed his true class. In the slower pace of European football, his intelligent reading of the game was a real asset. Yet in the nine goal thriller with Arsenal, he'd been at fault – jointly with Pantilimon – for the Gunners' equaliser when the big Rumanian failed to call and Demichelis intervened unnecessarily, blocking the goalkeeper's line of sight

Demichelis' worst moments began against Chelsea when he was drafted in at the eleventh hour to replace Fernandinho in midfield and, out of position, struggled badly against Hazard and Willian. Then, against Barcelona, he was sent off by the inept Swedish referee Jonas Eriksson for tripping Lionel Messi. To add insult to injury, a penalty was awarded when, in fact, the offence had taken place outside the eighteen yard box. In fact, till then, Demichelis had played superbly, notably when he calmly jockeyed Alexis Sanchez out-of-the-box before delivering a perfect tackle.

BT pundits would have a field day during City's elimination from the FA Cup by Wigan Athletic. True, Demichelis had been slow to confront Fortune and had then dived in to bring him down in the box. But, in the lead -up to the resulting goal, Richards had been slow to cover and Lescott hesitant to back up. Yet they escaped with slight criticism. Once again, it appeared to BT that Demichelis was the sole culprit when he reacted slowly to the move which led to Wigan's second goal – regardless of Richards being almost static, Lescott not well positioned and Clichy indecisive. Host Jake Humphrey's mere mention of Demichelis' name was enough to make pundit Steve McManaman throw his head back and roar with laughter!

But the much maligned Argentinian would later make his critics eat their words. The turning point came, in adversity, at the KC Stadium when Kompany was sent off after barely ten minutes. Demichelis rose splendidly to the occasion and was in his element, marshalling the defence and trapping Hull's strikers offside time and again.

After this, he never looked back. He was excellent at Old Trafford and again at the Emirates, notable for his powerful headers out of defence and his resolute and well timed tackles. What's more, his dependability relieved Vincent Kompany of the burden of compensating for the central defensive mistakes of others.

In the crunch match at Anfield, he coped far better than most expected in dealing with Luis Suarez and, himself a player who contradicted stereotypes about Latin American footballers, comported himself with notable composure in the face of the Uruguayan's provocation.

Demichelis, in the second half of the season, went from zero to hero in the eyes of many previously sceptical supporters. His performances in the title run-in were exemplary, notably against West Brom, where his superb tackle stopped what look like a certain goal from Anichebe. He then scored himself, thus completing a remarkable series of strikes from all three members of City's Argentinian contingent in the same match. Martin Demichelis had well and truly justified his signing and, as Paolo Zabaleta threw a comradely arm around his shoulder, he'd joined Zaba and Kun, comprising three ches who could be relied upon to give everything in the cause of Manchester City

EDIN DZEKO - A DIAMOND IN THE ROUGH

In the film 'Ulysses' Gaze' there are scenes depicting the Siege of Sarajevo. In some of the shots, the screen glows orange as Bosnian trucks explode on being hit by the shells of the Yugoslav army investing Sarajevo from the surrounding hills. In others the city's enveloped in a wispy grey as the fog descends to provide temporary relief from the bombardment. In the mist, people gather in parks to hear bands play or actors rehearse a performance. One thing you don't see is boys playing football in the street. Because, if the fog should suddenly lift, they'd be prime targets for the Bosnian Serb snipers.

When the Siege of Sarajevo began, Edin Dzeko was six years old and, when it finished, he was ten. Bombed out of his parents' home, he was one of an extended family of fifteen sheltering in his nan's basement flat. During those four years the future star of Manchester City played out only once in the open air. That was when his mother called him in a few seconds before a bomb exploded on the waste ground where he and his mates were having a kickabout. At the very age when boyhood soccer trickery is perfected in the street, the years when David Silva, Sergio Aguero and Samir Nasri first developed their superb skills, Edin Dzeko never kicked a ball. And that's probably why- for all his intelligent positioning and often accurate passing- he can look clumsy and lose control.

When the war ended, Edin, who was a bright lad, made progress fast in high school and it was there that he learned English. But he opted for football, playing for his hometown club, Zelejnicar, as a midfielder. Tall, gangling and slow to trap a ball, he was nicknamed ' Lamp Post ' and they laughed when Czech club Teplice paid €25,000 for him. But, in the Czech Republic, he was converted to a target man and he had a strike rate of a goal for every three games. German club Wolfsburg came in for him and he made his name in the Bundesliga, winning the title with his club and upping his strike rate to better than one in two! Same thing in internationals, one in two for Bosnia-Herzegovina and a goal against United at Old Trafford in the Champions League. With 66 goals to his name in 111 matches for Wolfsburg, he was brought to Eastlands by Roberto Mancini for £27 million.

In Dzeko's first half season in a Sky Blue shirt, he didn't set the house on fire. Indeed he notched up only two Premiership goals. As Uwe Rosler explained, he needed a period of adjustment to the more physical demands of the English Premier League as compared to the Bundesliga. Still, he made a vital contribution to City's Cup run. With only ten minutes remaining at Meadow Lane, he scored at full stretch and forced Notts Forest to come to Eastlands. Vincent Kompany hailed that strike with these words - "this was the goal that kept us going in the Cup campaign".

It was on August 28, 2011, at White Hart Lane, that Edin Dzeko really came good. In City's red and black striped away kit, reminiscent of AC Milan, his boyhood football heroes, he scored four times in the 5-1 crushing of Spurs. First, he pounced on Nasri's clever chip and held off Kaboul before extending a telescopic left leg to prod the ball home. Next, he called on Nasri for a cross and, when it came, he took off like a VTOL jet plane and, though facing away from goal, steered a stupendous header beyond the hapless Brad Friedel. The third was a tap -in, yes, but Dzeko had anticipated Aguero's clever delay and Yaya's rolling pass across the goal mouth. Left foot, right foot, header ; this was a rare perfect hat-trick. The fourth was an effortless drive beyond Friedel from 22 yards, a relaxed and utterly confident strike.

Dzeko's second moment of glory came in the Demolition Derby, the 6-1. When he replaced Balotelli, the score was 0-3 and United were down but not yet out. Edin surged right into the action, picking up a good pass from Aguero. He shot promptly and a snick off Smalling diverted it with de Gea helpless. The big man with the # 10 shirt on his back was thoroughly attuned to the Premiership by now and showed it as he shook up Big Jones and got himself booked. Then, after United had pulled a goal back and led their crowd to believe that 'normal service will shortly be resumed', it was Edin Dzeko who stifled their cheers as he scored the fourth goal. It was certainly not a moment of classy skill - it went in off his knee -but it was a nail in United's coffin without doubt. There should've been another one straight afterwards when Silva sent Dzeko clean through on goal but, with only de Gea to beat, he spooned his shot over the bar. Still, with United staring humiliation in the face, not many of their fans were laughing at the miss. Then came a moment of real ball skill as he provided a key assist, nonchalantly nutmegging a floundering Ferdinand and playing in Silva for the fifth. A few minutes later, the lanky Bosnian read Silva's wondrous through ball and sprinted away from two United defenders. His finish was certainly not devastating - de Gea got a hand on it - but it found the net alright and it rang up the 1-6 scoreline which would reverberate around the world.

Dzeko's introduction would have a major impact on the title race. Mancini had seen that United's defenders were tiring fast and bewildered by the inter-passing of City's ballplayers. But he wasn't content merely to beat his rivals – he sought to destroy them. And Edin Dzeko's fresh legs – and deceptive speed – would be his means of doing just that. The goals scored after the Bosnian came on as a substitute at Old Trafford in October would be a significant factor in City's eventual triumph on the last day of the season, just as Sir Alex Ferguson had feared all along that they would.

Though Dzeko was overtaken in the pecking order by Mario Balotelli in the second half of the season, he had one final major contribution to make to City's title bid. Remember how it was on 66 minutes after City were caught stranded and QPR got their second.

That was when Mancini and Platt conferred grim- faced on the touch-line and came up with the only possible answer - get Dzeko on! So much beautiful football in match after match must not be robbed of its just reward in the final harrowing minutes. By all means necessary! – including forcing corners and relying on Dzeko to power goalbound headers. Edin did his best - he tried to get on the end of one Silva corner but couldn't. Marked closely by Ferdinand, his shot narrowly missed, so close it seemed to many Citizens for a moment as if it was a goal but it had only brushed the side netting. Another corner, Nasri's this time, not well enough floated to find Dzeko's napper.

Then came the denoument. In stoppage time, Silva pulled out a truly testing corner, high, and dropping slowly into the dead centre of the QPR goalmouth. And that's when the man from Sarajevo set off on a stealthy corkscrew run and, soaring above the Hoops' defenders with both legs tucked under him like a Balkan mountain stork honing in on its prey, sent the ball thumping in off his brow, an unanswerable rocket into the back of the Londoners' net. There was no time for celebration, of course, beyond a brief "Da!" from the striker to himself - but here was the platform for Kun Aguero, a minute later, to seize the title for Manchester City.

In the close season, speculation grew that Dzeko might be sold and it was then, when the Manchester Evening News polled them, that 80% of City supporters responded with a plea that he should remain on the books. Yes, there were moments when his failure to trap the ball, the legacy of his lack of boyhood street football, brought groans. But there were many others when his attributes - his acceleration, his heading, his reading of the game and above all his vital goal-poaching - made the chant of ' EDIN DZEKO ' reverberate round the Etihad.

In the season between the titles, Dzeko's goals to games ratio declined slightly but not significantly. What's more, he scored a fine breakaway goal against Real Madrid in the Bernabeu. Despite Mario Balotelli's departure in mid-season, Roberto Mancini seemed to have doubts about Dzeko long-term value to the club. It may well be that, if Mancini had remained at the Etihad, Dzeko would've been transferred. But, when Manuel Pellegrini took over, he assured Dzeko of his faith in him.

Dzeko began the season well. Against Newcastle, his deft backheel flick sent Aguero away to score. What's more, he led the line with assurance. At Cardiff he scored with a rare long-range shot. But, when he was substituted at half-time in the game against Hull and reappeared wearing T-shirt and jeans, it was interpreted by some as casual or sulky attitude. Dzeko had little of the spontaneity of City's Latin players and he would be slagged off by a vociferous minority on ' Blue Moon' for whom he could do nothing right.

A war of words developed on the forum involving his compatriots for whom he is a national hero- a UNICEF ambassador, an intelligent man who speaks four languages, is studying Sports Science at the University of Sarajevo and who does much excellent work in his native Bosnia, not only coaching youngsters but insisting on the kinship between former Yugoslavs, regardless of religion and ethnicity. This is something he's exemplified at the Etihad through his friendship with Aleksandar Kolarov.

Though Dzeko was clearly benefiting from Pellegrini's vote of confidence, he was soon eclipsed by the superb displays of Alvaro Negredo and it was the newly -signed Spaniard who became Sergio Aguero's principal strike partner. But, with Aguero's season disrupted by injury, Dzeko was regularly called back into first-team action.

Some said he didn't work well with Negredo but, at St James's Park, in the Capital One Cup, a fine move between them gave the lie to that.

And, also at St James, he finished a lovely move involving James Milner and Silva with a brilliant strike when he turned sharply at high speed and boldly slotted a reverse shot.

He reappeared against Liverpool on Boxing Day and nearly scored from Yaya's pass only to be thwarted by a lucky deflection off Sakho's boot. But he scored the vital winner when City were struggling against Crystal Palace.

There were days when his ball control would let him down. One such was at Swansea and he was even worse in the first half of the FA Cup replay against Blackburn Rovers, missing badly no less than four times in the first half – though he scored in the second.Perhaps his worst gaffe came when he contrived to miss an open goal from four yards against Stoke – furious with himself, he kicked a post in frustration. Still, he'd scored at St James Park in the Premiership after being set up by Aleks Kolarov and he notched City's hundredth goal of the season against Cardiff City. He began to emerge as a key factor from March onwards, benefiting from a freedom from injury not enjoyed by Aguero and Negredo.

Versus Wigan, only the smallest margins denied him three goals. There was his powerful header against the bar and a second header which narrowly missed. Another time it looked like he'd blazed the ball over at point-blank range. With voices raised in undeserved rebuke, it took the big-screen replay to confirm that, in fact, Emmerson Boyce had denied him with an incredible block.

Dzeko had a really good performance coming on at half-time in the Camp Nou. From Kolarov's slow dropping cross, he levered a tremendous header straight towards the top corner only to be denied by an outstanding Valdes save- torquing backwards and flicking the ball over almost from under the crossbar.Then, with fifteen minutes to go, he was refused a stonewall penalty by the French referee Lannoy when

Pique blatantly tripped him as he was preparing to shoot. What's more, it was his knock down which enabled Kompany to equalise.

He became the sole spearhead effectively from the Hull game onward with Aguero hamstrung, Negredo out of form and Jovetic rarely available. And he was the one who clinched victory at the KC Stadium with a late goal from Silva's perfect pass. At Old Trafford, in the first minute, he finished a brilliant team goal – and in the selfsame game he scored again with a well timed run from Nasri's corner.

Against Southampton, in first half stoppage time, he scored with a glancing header from Kolarov's cross but, in the same game, he missed badly. The Saints' keeper had parried his shot straight back to him but he miskicked ludicrously, skewing his shot over the far touchline.

At Goodison Park, in possibly City's most vital game of the season, he scored with a stupendous header worthy of the Toffees' historic hero Dixie Dean. Feigning disinterest then calling to Milner for the ball, he was all of eleven yards out as he soared into the air and thumped it first bounce over the goal-line with Tim Howard helpless.

There were some who still moaned at him when he failed to control Yaya's fine through ball against Villa but then he finished a perfect triangular move, sweeping Zabaleta's low cross into the net.

Dzeko would be a vital factor in City's regaining the Premiership title. Unlike many players with a suspect first touch, he can usually pass the ball accurately and he's always aware, seeming languid when in fact lurking with menace. At 6'4" tall, he's very mobile and powerful in the air. Where he comes unstuck is in controlling a bouncing ball played towards him, in particular a high dropping ball. But he's a notable goal poacher with a knack of getting to the right place at the right time, he's not easily shaken off the ball and is hard to injure.

Edin Dzeko has long been known in his homeland as 'The Bosnian Diamond '. There were those among the Citizens who considered this an affectation and would never accept his right to rub shoulders with the likes of Sergio Aguero and David Silva. Manuel Pellegrini did not share their view. He believed that there are certain exceptional players, who crop up every now and again in the world game, and who, deficient though they may be in close control, have every other attribute of the top-class striker – anticipation, awareness of others, stealthy movement, heading power and close range finishing. In some ways Edin Dzeko would remain a diamond in the rough. But he would totally repay Pellegrini's faith in him during the critical weeks in which it looked as if Liverpool's seemingly irresistible run of form would deprive City of the title but, where, in the end, the Sky Blues triumphed.

FERNANDINHO - A BRAZILIAN OF THE OLD SCHOOL

The announcement, on June 6, 2013, that a certain Fernandinho had signed for £34 million wasn't met with the enthusiasm which might've greeted the acquisition of a Brazilian international at most other Premiership clubs. The fact was that City supporters didn't have the best memories of Fernandinho's fellow countrymen. Giovanni had been lacklustre, Jo's end product was in inverse proportion to his transfer fee and Robinho, eased out by Real Madrid, had seemed miffed that he wasn't going to play for Chelsea and live in London. His City career descended as rapidly as the exiting crowds on the spiral walkways after a home defeat.

Elano, by contrast, got off to a brilliant start, the wondrous 35 yard freekick with which he scored against Newcastle United remaining in the fans' collective memory for a long time. But, though he flourished under Sven Goran Eriksson, he didn't adjust to the very different methods of Mark Hughes – or, in the opinion of many Citizens, Hughes failed to cater to Elano's talents.

Fernandinho had been signed from top Ukrainian club, Shakhtar Donetsk, just as Elano had been before him. What's more, showing what seemed to some a distinct lack of ambition, he'd spent no less than eight seasons there, after leaving Brazil at the age of twenty – more or less the peak years of a footballer's career. Indeed Luis Fernando Roza from Londrina seemed to be merely one of half a dozen anonymous footballing Fernandinhos. There were more than a few who wondered whether he was coming solely for one last bumper payday. That suspicion, at least, was dispelled when it was confirmed that he'd forfeited a £4 million bonus by transferring to City.

There remained a widespread belief, shared by the supporters of all the leading Premiership clubs, that only second-rate Brazilian players are willing to come to England-the likes of Anderson and Kleberson, who both failed at United, or Lucas, a competent, hard-working player, distinctly lacking in panache, who Liverpool supporters found it hard to warm to.

To some extent these disappointments reflected the tendency of the visual media to hark back to the fabulous Brazilian World Cup stars of the seventies. But after the failure of Tele Santana's gifted but defensively suspect side in the 82 tournament -and a sparkling but unsuccessful showing in Mexico 86- Brazilian football had fundamentally changed, with an emphasis on function not flair. The deadly dreary style shown in the 94 World Cup Final in the USA was certainly effective but it was about as appealing as an hour at the dentists under local anaesthetic.

Brazilian football writers christened the nineties the ' Dunga Era' after the team's remorselessly physical captain who went on to manage the national team-this time with neither spectacle nor success- between 2006 and 2010.Before that, there were of course the traditionally Brazilian flair players who starred in their country's fifth World Cup triumph, in the Far East in 2002 -Ronaldo, Rivaldo, Ronaldinho and Roberto Carlos. But their individual skills could not disguise Luiz Felipe Scolari's ruthless functionalism.

There was one member of the triumphant 02 Brazil squad who came to England. Gilberto Silva may have been solid rather than spectacular but he would be a key member of Arsenal's Invincibles. Fernandinho resembled Gilberto Silva physically and, it was hoped, would perform a similar role for City.

Fernandinho didn't start well. It was obvious at Cardiff that he hadn't adjusted to Premiership pace and the same could be said about his home performance against Hull.

But in a matter of weeks not only had he improved markedly but the overall team performance was boosted in proportion. What Fernandinho did was to link defence with attack and, in so doing, to free Yaya Toure to drive forward. The first time it really showed was in the home derby and then it was his greatly improved form which was key to the first away victory, at Upton Park.

'Ferna' –as he became known- was rarely absent injured but, when he was, he was badly missed. His unavailability at Sunderland was reflected in a poor team performance and when City suffered their first home defeat for two years, against Chelsea, it was his late with-drawal through injury which badly undermined them. It was the same with his rare off days, such as the one in the Cup at Ewood Park.

Against Spurs at home, he was absolutely key, working well to meld defence with attack and combining with Yaya in a one-two which was integral to the wonderful fourth goal.

It was against Arsenal that he produced his best performance. Not only was his box to box running liberating Yaya but he delightedly bagged a brace with power shooting at the end of his 30 yard runs. Throughout the season he outshone his much vaunted compatriot, Paulinho, at Spurs and was restored to the national squad.

Fernandinho's form began to suffer in the last weeks of the season. He was culpable for Arsenal's equaliser at the Emirates and, after being taken off at half-time against Southampton, he lost his place to Garcia. He was stretched to the limit at Anfield trying to cope with Sterling's pace and he bungled a freekick against West Bromwich Albion which led to their breakout and score.

It wasn't surprising that his form had dropped. He'd maintained a truly formidable workload and, with Barry on loan to Everton and

Rodwell injury- prone, there was no ready-made replacement. Basically, his temporary decline was due to sheer fatigue after his herculean efforts in City's cause.

Fernandinho adjusted well to life in Manchester with his partner and their three-year-old child. He spoke Spanish with his Argentinian teammates and got on well with them. He also speaks Russian and Ukrainian and rapidly got a working knowledge of English. A quiet, relaxed guy, popular and with a sense of humour, he joked about holding a barbecue in his garage in the shivering Ukrainian winter.

In some ways Fernandinho is old school Brazilian. And in other ways he is not. Socrates, the selecao playmaker in 82, said " Beauty comes first. Victory is secondary. What matters is joy". But, since the elimination of the 82 Brazilians in the Spain Mundial (on a par with Hungary 54, they were the best team never to win the title) Brazil has rejected Socrates' ideal. Where he, Zico and Falcao embodied a Corinthian attitude and comported themselves with dignity, subsequent high-profile Brazilians - Ronaldo, Ronaldinho and Robinho – often seemed little more than pampered superstars fawned on by certain sections of the media. The very name 'Brazil ', once synonymous with glorious attacking teamwork, is now uttered with a routine intake of breath by commentators who can't or won't adjust to the mundane realities of a functional Brazil.

Fernandinho is modestly skilled in comparison to the heroes of a bygone age and, when representing his country, has adapted himself to Scolari's ruthless methods. He would doubtless find Socrates' aphorism more of an embarrassment than an inspiration. But he's modest, hardworking, humorous and without showbiz attitude. In that sense, at least, he's a Brazilian of the old school.

JAVI GARCIA - THE IMPORTANCE OF JUST BEING THERE

Probably the least skilful player in the City squad, Javi Garcia contradicts the usual concept of the Spanish footballer. He has a limited range of passing, is slow, not always perceptive and hardly ever scores – just twice in seventy-one appearances! Slagged off on Blue Moon Forum, he was described by one poster as follows: "he turns slower than a battleship and runs like he's cacked himself!"

Not only had Garcia been a disappointment to the man who signed him, Roberto Mancini, but he continued in the same vein for the first half of 2013-14. He played badly at Cardiff on August Bank Holiday Monday when, with Nastasic now injured as well as Kompany, he was sent into central defence and badly exposed for pace – twice needing Joe Hart to bail him out. What's more, his performance in midfield alongside Jack Rodwell in the Britannia Stadium was abysmal.

Yet Manuel Pellegrini, who'd known Garcia from his brief time with Real Madrid, persevered with him and the player's personal turning point came in Sunderland when he bravely recovered from Larsson's potential leg breaker. From then on he showed what he could do, executing simple midfield tasks well, notably in the difficult away game with Bayern.

There were still times when he slid back into his old ways. His misplaced pass at home against Palace could've been costly but, thanks to Ward's impetuosity, it went unpunished. And he had a notably poor game in the Cup against Wigan. His appearance pre-kick-off holding his baby daughter was a regrettable show business stunt though he'd doubtless been put up to it by BT. Afterwards, possibly eager to show he was no softie, he tackled recklessly. What's more, a foolish square pass nearly let Wigan in to score again.

Yet Pellegrini was convinced that Garcia was a useful squad member and, bit by bit, he began to justify his manager's faith. He did very well in the Cup game against Chelsea – especially when he got goalside of Samuel Etoo, who was looking to score. But his finest performance came at the KC Stadium after Kompany was sent off. Once again he went into central defence yet this time, with Martin Demichelis organising, he used his height to good advantage to thwart Hull's long ball approach.

Towards the end of the season, beginning against Southampton and continuing from Selhurst Park onwards, he replaced the overloaded Fernandinho and did a really solid job of work.

At Anfield, his performance was mixed. He was all at sea when confronted by Sterling yet later on he chested down a kick from Mignolet and promptly played the ball down the touchline for Aguero to start a move which nearly ended with a goal from Silva. Indeed, he might've won a late penalty equaliser had Mark Clattenburg noticed that Skrtel had handled his powerful header from a cement mixer cross.

Javi is the exact opposite of his cousin Luis Garcia, ex-Liverpool. Where Luis was slight, mobile, neat on the ball, sometimes infuriating but likely to break the deadlock with a startling piece of improvisation, Javi is burly, ponderous and unimaginative yet he diligently and reliably carries out his coach's instructions to the letter. In so doing, he unquestionably made a contribution to City's second Premiership title.

At his best, Javi Garcia works unobtrusively. Supporters say of him "he's just there, isn't he?" And there are times when that's what fits the bill.

JOE HART - THE FALL AND RISE OF A SHROPSHIRE LAD

Probably the most mocked and parodied poems in the entire English language can be found in 'A Shropshire Lad'. Penned in 1896, these morbid tales of athletes and soldiers cut down in their prime struggled to survive the grim realities of the First World War and, by the time Joe Hart entered Meole Brace School in Shrewsbury in 1998, they'd endured a hundred years of mockery.

Little if any time would've been wasted on 'A Shropshire Lad' at Meole Brace, a school which specialises in maths and science and of which Joe Hart became Head Boy. No swot, no creep and nobody's fool, he was popular with his peers, a natural leader, and well -liked by his teachers. A budding county cricketer, six foot tall at sixteen, he was a lad whose fiery fast bowling few willingly faced.

Two themes marked Joe's childhood – activity and public performance. His father Charles was a qualified P.E. teacher who moved into the burgeoning fitness training business and his mother Louise was a singer and dancer. In the first defining moment of Joe's life, his dad threw the two-year-old a ball down the full ten yards length of their garden. Joe not only caught it unblinkingly but threw it right back -an astonishing demonstration of motor skills for a boy of his age.

Turning his back on rugby, the sport in which Charles Hart had excelled, Joe made use of his height and weight advantages as well as sharp reflexes to become a goalkeeper. Signed by Shrewsbury Town when barely out of school, he was spotted by Tim Flowers, City's goalkeeping coach and he moved to Eastlands at nineteen. Lauded by Sven -Goran Eriksson as the brightest goalkeeping prospect in England, Hart didn't find favour with Mark Hughes who preferred to spend £8 million on Newcastle's Shay Given.

Given wasn't a dodgy keeper. Far from it. As a shot -stopper, there were few better and his stalwart penalty saves included a blinder from Frank Lampard against Chelsea. But he didn't command the area with total authority and he lacked the decisive goalkeeper personality of United's Van der Sar, Chelsea's Cech and Liverpool's Reina. It was hard to imagine Van der Sar or Reina allowing the likes of Emmanuel Adebayor to block his line of sight and concede a senseless own goal such as Given did against Chelsea. Hart was far more assertive and, at 6'5" tall-even larger than City's splendid seventies keeper Joe Corrigan-he had natural advantages which Given lacked.

Unconvinced about Hart, Hughes sent him out on season loan to Birmingham City, a side which would struggle in vain against relegation. Hart's finest performance in a dark blue shirt came when he foiled pacesetters Chelsea at St Andrews.He was symbolically linked with another great City custodian, Bert Trautmann, as he dived bravely at an opponent's feet only to take Kalou's boot studs, by accident, in his head.It needed the Brummie trainer to fire staples into his scalp to seal the wounds. Like Trautmann, his shot stopping was formidable and he defied Chelsea's renowned forwards time and time again.

The second defining moment in Joe Hart's life came in August 2010 when, aged twenty-three, he stood in the City goal at White Hart Lane and single-handedly won a point for the Sky Blues with a fantastic series of saves: from Crouch's downward header; two from Defoe at point blank range, one a fierce hook on the turn, the other a sharp low jab; from Huddleston's venomous volley; and, incredibly, from Assou-Ekotto's fierce and deflected long range strike. Hart's blocks, parries and tip-overs were all that stood between City and a psychologically damaging heavy defeat in the opening game of the season. On the bench, a snickering Adam Johnson marked Shay Given's card as he sat next to the Irish keeper. Tentatively preferred by a Roberto Mancini who knew little of him, Hart saw his chance and he took it.

Hart followed up with a double block from Ngog and Fernando Torres in the opening home game against Liverpool at a time when the Reds were fighting back. He continued with a wonderful full-length save from Coloccini's volley against Newcastle and his tremendous save from Robin van Persie's curling shot at the Emirates helped to win a point.

His Premiership form was equalled in City's triumphant Cup campaign. His fine block from Berbatov in the Cup Derby Semi prepared the ground for City to knock out United and, in the final, he reacted promptly to retrieve Lescott's potentially deadly error against Kenwynne Jones.

There were, of course, cockups as well: a dreadful misunderstanding with Kolo Toure which allowed Blackburn to equalise and, at Leicester, the misjudgement of Gallagher's cross which let in King to score. They were the occasional blips of a young keeper and they were few and far between.

In the title-winning season it was soon obvious that Joe Hart had matured into a potentially great keeper. His finest display came at Anfield when, on a rare collective off-day for the Sky Blues, he single-handedly ensured that they came away with a point.

Of the other great goalkeepers in City's history, the one Hart most resembles is Frank Swift, the innovator of the throw- out, and, like

Frank, Joe Hart knows how to initiate such an attack. Like Swift too, he's something of a dressing room joker or, at least, an able adjutant to the irrepressible mirth -making of Les Chapman. That said, his jocularity worked against him in an England shirt when, in the Euro 2012 quarter-final shoot-out, his simian antics a la Grobbelaar, designed to flummox Andrea Pirlo, saw Pirlo stare coldly before despatching an unsaveable Panenka.

On the Champions League stage after that, Joe Hart was a spectacular and mostly successful keeper. In the Bernabeu he made excellent saves from Cristiano Ronaldo and Higuain to keep Real Madrid at bay for long periods- before a misunderstanding with Kompany led to a simple late winner for Real. At home, against Borussia Dortmund, he single-handedly won City a point denying Reus and Gundogan and leaving Mario Goetze tearing his hair out after being foiled for the third time.

But there were negative consequences from these fine displays. Roberto Mancini took fierce exception to Hart's post -match comments in Madrid and, from then on, their relationship soured. There was also the praise Hart received, much of it over the top. Wayne Rooney crassly tweeted "Joe Hart is the best keeper in the world" – a remark that smacked of English insularity rather than a compare and contrast analysis with Neuer, Casillas, Valdes and Buffon!

By now Joe Hart was certainly established as 'England's Number One ', a position he'd made his own by power of performance but where he also benefited from a paucity of competition. At the Etihad his blond locks and guardsman physique emphasised his Englishness in contrast to City's diminutive Latin ballplayers and he attracted the attention of advertisers. Soon he was starring in a ' Head and Shoulders' anti-dandruff ad and he became enmeshed in the celebrity culture which surrounds the England squad. Fawned on by the media while he was on his game, he would later be pilloried after high-profile errors in the England jersey.

From then on, tabloid slagging slowly began to sap Hart's hitherto boundless confidence. Where previously he'd once shrugged off Vincent Kompany's praise for a fine save by barking "you can BANK on me!", he now became prone to misjudgement. Once almost immune from media criticism by virtue of his England status, his City performances in the Premiership were now rigorously scrutinised after he started to slip up in internationals.

The early months of Manuel Pellegrini's management coincided with a severe loss of form by Joe Hart. One of the goals conceded at Cardiff came from his blunder and, at Villa Park, he came out of his goal too quickly, thus facilitating Villa's winner. At home to Bayern, he made a bad error early in the game when his weak hands, on going down to a speculative Ribery shot, cost City a morale-shaking goal. And, in the second half, he made a similar error against Arjen Robben. It looked as if he'd turned a corner with his excellent point-blank save in Moscow, just before the final whistle, which clinched three Champions League points and saw him warmly congratulated by his teammates.

He then turned from hero to villain, at Stamford Bridge in a last-minute mixup with Nastasic, which went viral on YouTube. The centre back wasn't blameless but Hart was the more culpable of the two. And, as television cameras focused mercilessly on his blunder, he was captured looking distraught inside his goal yelling "I shouted, I fuckin' shouted!"

After the Chelsea fiasco, he was benched for two months. He was supplanted by his deputy, the gigantic Romanian Costel Pantilimon – a solid keeper virtually ignored by Mancini. During his banishment, he showed up in a good light, being very supportive of Pantilimon. While he was out of the firing line, he was doubtless counselled by Manuel

Pellegrini and there seems to have been a full examination of his technique by new goalkeeping coach Xabi Mancisidor.

He returned at Craven Cottage after two months out and seemed at once older and wiser - even while he was on the subs' bench he'd been following play intently, not laughing and joking with Joleon Lescott and Micah Richards any more. In short, he took his temporary demotion well and learned from it. He would no longer be content with happy-go-lucky gymnastics but would be a student of goalkeeping science.

After he returned it soon became clear that he was tending to punch rather than to catch and it was also evident that Mancisidor had been encouraging him to practice targeted kicking. At Old Trafford, he found Silva with one such long kick and the Spaniard put Dzeko clean through only for Big Jones to save the day with a lucky lunging tackle. For the most part, however, City supporters remained unconvinced about Hart's kicking. This was in contrast to Pantilimon who succeeded at Wembley in the Capital One Cup Final when he splendidly found Aguero in the move which led up to Nasri's goal.

At the end of the season Hart would praise Manuel Pellegrini as "a very measured man" and there's little doubt that he benefited from the Chilean's counselling in ways similar to those described in detail by players at Villareal and Malaga.

Possibly the first sign of Joe Hart's new, relaxed composure came in the Boxing Day clash with Liverpool when he reacted calmly and maturely after Luis Suarez' ostentatious apology for a late challenge – all right, mate, forget it, let's just get on with things.

His bravery had never been in doubt and it was once again confirmed against Crystal Palace when he sustained a black eye and had to have six stitches – what's more, he pulled off a great save in that game.

In the Champions League, he showed for a second successive season that he wasn't fazed by the big occasion and made several good saves in the Camp Nou.

At the KC Stadium he was hounded by BT cameras obsessed by whether or not George Boyd had spat at him after he swore at Boyd and accused him of having dived for a penalty. Though Hart had briefly lost his temper verbally in the face of gross provocation, he'd restrained himself from lashing out.

He went on to make a significant contribution to City's title challenge when he produced a fine reaction save to stop Arsenal taking the lead at the Emirates.

But his finest hour came in the crucial game at Goodison Park. He couldn't possibly have saved Barkley's wonder strike but in the second half he brought off a great full-length diving save (it was in these kind of saves that he'd previously been suspect whereas his gymnastic ability in leaping saves had never been in doubt) to deny Naismith and save a certain goal. There was another fine late save from Delofeu after the Catalan loanee had gone past three City players – Hart came out at the right moment and got his body in the way of the shot diverting it for a corner. This was a critical moment in his career- one in which mere impetuosity had been superseded by bold judgment.

Joe Hart's unlikely to have ever turned a single page of A. E. Housman's cycle of sixty-three pathetic poems. But he's doubtless sampled the 'Shropshire Lad' real ale made by Wood Breweries of Craven Arms. He enjoyed growing up in historic Shrewsbury and likes to return from time to time to enjoy the peace and quiet of rural Shropshire. He would never've been a true hero for Housman, a writer who scoffed at football, advised athletes to die young so as never to outlive their fame, and celebrated soldiers who perished in battle. But, in his bold and brave goalkeeping displays behind the Sky Blue shirts of Manchester City- and, above all, the way in which he re-emerged after a period of tribulation-the boy from Shrewsbury is a 'Shropshire Lad' for the twenty-first century.

ALEKSANDAR KOLAROV - A MAN FOR SERIOUS BUSINESS

When Aleksandar Kolarov's 30 yard piledriver of a freekick thundered into the Leicester City net to give the Sky Blues the lead at the King Power Stadium in the Capital One Cup, he showed little of the ostentatious jubilation which goalscorers are expected to register. " Hey! Hey! Smile, huh!" said Pablo Zabaleta, gesturing that Kolarov should give his face a holiday. But the master blaster from Belgrade had scarcely been known for his levity since he arrived at the Etihad from Lazio in 2010. There were times when the Serbian's characteristic frown relaxed somewhat but that was about it.

At Christmas 2012, his teammates hit on the idea of him making a Christmas video and he duly obliged with a rendition of 'Jingle Bells '. The novelty of his sombre features and deadpan delivery in a heavy Balkan accent proved so intriguing that the video promptly went viral, featuring 600,000 hits on YouTube. The following year, the whole thing was played for laughs from the start with the black- bearded Kolarov's stern rendition of 'Santa Claus is Coming to Town ' produced against a background of thunderclouds and ravenous wolves. Only at the end did Kolarov's wink signify to the kiddies that there was really no reason to be scared of the unsmiling man with the funny accent.

Aleks Kolarov can of course do menace for real as he showed in the course of a bruising clash with Everton at the Etihad. The Toffees were flying high at the time and, in the wake of City's defeat to Bayern Munich, there was no shortage of pundits predicting a sky blue comeuppance. When Naismith's sly challenge resulted in Kolarov and Nastasic clashing heads in midair, Kolarov got to his feet first with blood pouring from a cut over his eye. Though Nastasic consented to an apologetic handshake from the Scotsman, Kolarov gave him a blood- freezing stare which precluded any repetition. Reluctant to leave the field to get his brow stitched, he looked like a welterweight boxer indignant that the referee's stopped the fight when he's still got knockout shots in his fists. Kolarov's defiant commitment on a day when he wore his wound as a badge of pride was an emblem of City's determination to prevail, come what may.

When Edin Dzeko arrived at the Etihad a few months after Aleks Kolarov, there were outsiders who believed that this was a recipe for dressing room dissent. After all, they argued, these were children of the former Yugoslavia but Dzeko was a Bosniak and a Muslim while Kolarov was a Serbian and an Orthodox Christian. Nothing could've been further from the truth. In next to no time they were happily chatting together in Serbo-Croat and it wasn't long before they were referring to one another as brothers. The sceptics might just as well've claimed that Aleks Kolarov- who, at the age of twelve, hunkered down in the basements of Belgrade while NATO warplanes bombed his city- would've harboured resentment against his English teammates.

Truth to tell, Kolarov failed to set the Etihad alight during his seasons under Mancini's management. In preferring Gael Clichy for the left back role, Mancini was signifying his disappointment with a player who, at £16 million, had been an expensive purchase. The manager's misgivings were more than matched among the spectators, many of whom conceded that he was good going forward but prone to fail in basic defensive duties. Others simply took a dislike to him based on his odd gait when tracking back, an eccentricity of movement which was wrongly construed as laziness. Indeed his surname itself, mispronounced as 'Collar Off', sounded, when shouted out, like a bizarre new swearword invented solely to bemoan the Serbian's defensive lapses.

It wasn't surprising that Kolarov tended to perform better away from home, most notably in the Bernabeu when, out of the blue, he produced an absolute thunderbolt to give City the lead against Real Madrid. Nevertheless, 2012-13 ended on a sour note for him with an outburst of fan hostility during the final home game against Norwich City.

Aleks Kolarov greatly benefited from the arrival of Manuel Pellegrini and was soon transformed from a defensively dubious full-back to a dynamic wing back. In the derby against United, at home, he cut through United's ranks like a rapier, spreading alarm with his low whipped crosses. Soon United skipper Nemanja Vidic would be rollicking Valencia for not marking Kolarov touch -tight.

Kolarov's defensive wobbles were fewer than in previous seasons, although he was caught out, as was Lescott, early in the Everton game when a quick long ball put Lukaku through to score.

As the season wore on and Kolarov's speedy overlapping runs and menacingly precise crosses – from which Aguero and Dzeko notched goals – became one of City's major attacking weapons, hitherto sceptical elements in the crowd warmed to him more and more. The old cry of 'Collar Off !! ' was heard less and less.

In the Allianz Arena, with both Kompany and Yaya rested, Pellegrini chose Kolarov to captain the side. He stepped up to the plate in no uncertain fashion and when the Sky Blues were awarded a penalty, he calmly dispatched it.

Those who claimed he still couldn't defend were proved wrong in the Boxing Day match against Liverpool when he halted Sterling with a fine tackle after it had seemed that the Liverpool flyer was bound to score. In the second half, however, Kolarov was lucky to get away with a moment of overconfidence when he rashly chose to dribble Luis Suarez, of all people, in the City six yard box – and was only reprieved by a foolish intervention from Henderson.

In 2014, he went from strength to strength. Brought on as a sub when things weren't going well at the Liberty Stadium on New Year's Day, his runs down the left flank unhinged Swansea and he also scored. Then he had a fine game at St James's Park, where he shrugged off some brutal fouling and laid on a goal for his pal Dzeko. Another stalemate which was broken by Kolarov was at home against Stoke City when it was only his superb low cross to Yaya which finally prised Mark Hughes' miserly defence open.

It was just the same in the Champions League.He had a good game in the Camp Nou when he fed Dzeko with a sumptuous, slow dropping cross leading to the Bosnian's power header which forced an incredible save from Valdes. And, in the title run-in, Kolarov replicated this against Southampton, laying the ball on a plate for Dzeko with the keeper powerless to intervene this time.

Towards the end of the season, Alex Kolarov's contributions were less spectacular. The corollary of this was that he'd become a solid and dependable defender. More than any other member of the City squad, more even than Samir Nasri, he benefited from Manuel Pellegrini's transformation of his role. Always effective and often decisive, he'd become, in his value to the team as in his demeanour, a man for serious business.

VINCENT KOMPANY - HALF HERCULES, HALF AMBASSADOR

Vincent Kompany is the new Manchester City in flesh and blood. Club captain since August 2011, he's a dependable, skilful and quick-thinking centre back -not to mention an intense and analytical man. Fluent in four languages, he's taking a Masters in Business Administration at Manchester Business School. Had he not been a gifted footballer, he might well have become an executive in his native city Brussels, seat of government of the European Union.

Vincent's parents were not athletes. His Congolese father, Pierre, was a dissident who fought against the bloody dictatorship of Mobutu, emigrated to Belgium and married Vincent's mother, Jocelyne, a Franco-Belgian from the Ardennes who became an employment adviser to the Belgian government. But Vincent's early days were spent in one of Brussels' worst districts, a vice- ridden and drug- infested dump round the back of the railway station. The family escaped when Pierre, who financed his studies by all- night taxi driving, qualified as an engineer. Whilst his parents were pleased that Vincent was a promising youth footballer, they urged him to stay on at school to complete his A-level equivalent, the Baccalaureat. This had many advantages -not least, from a City viewpoint, that it saved him from the clutches of Manchester United who already had him on their radar. His studies completed at university level, he transferred to Hamburg but his career in the Bundesliga was stymied for a full two years due to back and Achilles injuries.

Scouted by the Mike Rigg team while playing for Belgium at the Beijing Olympics, Kompany arrived at Eastlands in August 2008 in the last days of the Shinawatra regime, a bargain at £6.7 million. A remarkably mature twenty-two-year-old, he soon sussed the magnitude of the Abu Dhabi takeover. Speaking of Sheikh Mansour, he remarked that "he clearly didn't come in just to buy a bunch of players - he came in with a vision, a project, something far more rewarding than just winning a trophy".

On the ball as he was about Abu Dhabi, he was just as smart in realising the special character of Manchester. Shopping for a bed at the Trafford Centre, and expecting a clinical slumberware spiel such as he got in Hamburg when he kitted out his pad, he found himself chatting to the saleslady about eggs. "D'yer boil 'em, fry 'em or poach 'em? D'yer like 'em scrambled?" she said. It was, Kompany later commented, "a conversation about meaningless things and it makes everyone so relaxed". And he bought the bed!

Halfway through Kompany's second season at Eastlands, City sacked Hughes and appointed Roberto Mancini. It wasn't long before Mancini spotted that the young Belgian was just the kind of player to be at the heart of the City revolution, someone who'd listen to and learn from tactical discourse. Indeed he was in many ways a younger version of Patrick Vieira whom Mancini knew from their time at Inter Milan and who was his first acquisition at Eastlands. But, for all Kompany's technical ability and long- limbed tackling skill, Mancini deployed him in central defence. It reflected Mancini's Italianate conviction that good football builds from the back rather than the faith of Arsene Wenger, Vieira's Arsenal boss, in direct attack.And, though Kompany preferred midfield, he adjusted splendidly.He acknowledged Mancini as "tactically a mastermind" and spoke of his own liking for "responsibilities and pressure".He was clearly a captain in fact long before he became one in name.

Though Mansour and Mubarak were at the helm, Manchester already in his heart and Mancini in his ear, Vincent Kompany was well aware of a major fly in the Eastlands ointment- tabloid preoccupation with the private lives of players in the sky blue shirt. Already avid for sensation and watching even the most boring low-profile clubs in the hope of digging dirt, the redtops fastened with undisguised glee on the new City, funded by Arab petrodollars and managed by a demonstrative Italian coach. Incident piled on incident, real and rumoured, some trivial, others anything but, regardless of the culpability or otherwise of the players involved.

It was at times like these that Vincent Kompany's cool head was much needed in the dressing room. Grave of countenance and in a steady relationship with his future bride Carla Higgs, from Irlam, he was of zero redtop interest and able to comment philosophically about tabloid antics. "What happens in the media is like a piece of theatre" he reflected "once you come out, real life begins again" and he added that "footballers are a normal section of society but seen under a magnifying glass"

It was not only the tabloids that needed to be watched and Kompany's calm assessment of matches proved invaluable at a time of sustained scepticism bordering on attack following the loss of three consecutive games in late October and early November 2010. Although Carlos Tevez was club captain, a move made by Roberto Mancini who clearly saw him as someone who led by example and was always in the thick of the action, Tevez spoke little English, didn't participate in social life and, worse, was constantly in dispute with the club after the departure of Mark Hughes. It came as no surprise when, at the beginning of the 2011-2012 season Vincent Kompany was appointed to succeed him.

One of the sternest tests of Kompany's captaincy was the onfield management of Mario Balotelli, who had been under the wise mentorship of Patrick Vieira. If Balotelli was provoked by an opposition player, jeered by an away crowd or even told off by a teammate, there was always the possibility of him reacting so strongly that a red card would be produced. For the most part, Kompany succeeded in calming potentially serious incidents and his diplomacy was there for all to see in the 3-3 home draw with Sunderland when, with a firm hand on the shoulder, a direct stare and a few well- chosen words, he effectively defused an incident between Balotelli and Aleksandar Kolarov.

Vincent Kompany's maturity as a person was matched by his development as a player. He made it his business to study the strikers he would be marking, comparing himself to "a Formula One driver who goes into a race - he knows about each corner and what speed he should be taking it". In similar fashion such high profile strikers as Didier Drogba and Fernando Torres were analysed by video. His contributions were rarely spectacular but his mistakes were few. As for his main defensive partner, Joleon Lescott, strong but technically limited, installed by Hughes, he benefited considerably from Kompany's presence. The captain could be ruthlessly physical himself if need be and his skeletal grimace as he launched himself into tackles on the likes of Andy Carroll, then of Liverpool, daunted the Premiership's hardest targetmen.

One of Kompany's finest performances in a sky blue shirt came in a heroic but ultimately unsuccessful rearguard action at the Emirates in April 2012. Arsenal were in a rich vein of form and Robin van Persie was the Premiership top scorer, approaching thirty goals and coveted by the top clubs in Europe. Time after time Kompany screened the ball from van Persie, leapt above him to head the ball away, threw his body in front of goalbound shots and launched last-ditch tackles. Had it not been for a careless pass from Gareth Barry with only three minutes left on the clock followed by Mario Balotelli's stoppage time red card, City would've hung on for a potentially vital point. Earlier in the season his value to the club was clear when, following his unfair dismissal by Chris Foy in the Cup Derby, his subsequent four match ban (at a time when

Yaya Toure was away at the African Nations) saw City eliminated from the Carling Cup as well as from the FA competition.

It was Vincent Kompany who scored the sole and decisive goal to beat United in the title run-in. His contribution had been massive anyway with his total subjugation of Rooney but no one who saw it will forget his truly titanic winner when he rose high in the goalmouth, body torquing, to crash home an unstoppable header. Nor the class with which he dedicated it to the Citizens before calming himself instantly and gesturing to his teammates to do likewise.

In the season between the titles, his performance in the Bernabeu, when he ducked out of a cross and let in Ronaldo for a soft winner, was one of his rare weak displays. As the season progressed, however, he evidently became disillusioned with Roberto Mancini- a crucial deterioration in the relationship between captain and coach.

In the new season, Kompany adjusted immediately to the incoming of Manuel Pellegrini and described his new manager as "a first-class human being". In the opening game, against Newcastle, he initiated the fantastic second goal by contemptuously robbing Papiss Cisse before surging into attack and elegantly finding Dzeko. He gave a superb demonstration of central defensive play – one which recalled Johan Cruyff's paradox- "what's essential for a team to play an all-out attacking game is a totally dominant centre back". Sadly, his performance was abruptly curtailed when, stretching for a tackle on the touchline, he injured a limb and had to go off. He was away for a number of weeks and his absence was keenly felt.

In the derby at home, his ruthless blotting out of Wayne Rooney left the stocky Scouser pointing to his dislodged headband and whining in vain to Howard Webb. From then on, the skipper's outstanding individual performances punctuated only by injuries, were a major factor in City regaining the title. For instance, in the battle against Everton, he dealt very firmly indeed with his menacing fellow- countryman, Lukaku – then had to go off with a strained hip.

His return after a ten game absence enabled City to regain full fluency in attack. And his wonderful tackle at the last split-second, in St Mary's Stadium, prevented Southampton taking a winning lead. Against Arsenal, he gave a fine example of attacking centre half play with one stupendous burst combining great ball control and rugged strength as he shook up Giroud, barged his way past Ramsey and exquisitely found Negredo – only for a last-ditch tackle from Koscielny to prevent a goal.

As captain, he showed both command and diplomacy notably at St James Park when he urged Mark Jones to consult the fourth assistant and, as a result, Tiote's rocket strike was chalked off. At White Hart Lane, his cool explanation (to a bewildered Andre Marriner) during the furore over the disputed award of a penalty, when Rose brought down Dzeko, contrasted with Michael Dawson's exasperated yelling. What's more, his authority was total. On New Year's Day, at the Liberty Stadium, he reacted furiously to being harshly booked by Phil Dowd yet sublimated his frustration by rebuking his teammates for an unduly casual attitude. They responded at once.

From even before the turn of the year, however, he was showing signs of stress, doubtless originating from the tribulations of his centre half partners, the inexperienced and sometimes indecisive Nastasic – they'd appeared to be on different wavelengths at Villa Park when the winning goal was conceded as a result of keeper Guzan's Route One style kick- and the veteran Demichelis who was taking his time to adjust to Premiership pace.

In the game against Chelsea, on February 3, after compensating for a ridiculous intervention by Nastasic, he bawled out the young Serbian so furiously that a shocked Joe Hart was moved to steady his arm. But, when Chelsea returned after a couple of weeks for the Cup tie, his ruthless tackling against his compatriot Eden Hazard was a big factor in victory.

Vincent Kompany was not at his best in the first leg of the Champions League tie against Barcelona, at home, and it was his uncharacteristic lapse of concentration in allowing Lionel Messi to drift away from him which led indirectly to Demichelis' dismissal. Three weeks later, in the Camp Nou, however, he fought a wonderful dual with Messi, led the team splendidly and scored a late goal. His verdict on the game was very apt – he said "we gave everything we have, there was nothing left in the tank".

In the Capital One Final at Wembley, his surprisingly tentative tackle on Borini contributed to Sunderland's opening goal. Yet later, when the referee failed to call Borini offside and the Italian ran away with a five yard start on him, he chased and caught him, delivering a perfect tackle in the nick of time.

At the KC Stadium, he was incredulous to see Lee Mason brandishing a red card after he pushed Jelavic to the ground when last man. He insisted, with some rectitude, that the Croatian striker had fouled him first and that Mason had missed that. Obliged to depart, he hid his feelings as he walked off the pitch – only to be hounded by BT cameras and commentators who chortled with classless glee as his stud marks on the tunnel wall masonry confirmed that he was human after all!

Ironically, Kompany's dismissal and subsequent suspension enabled Demichelis to come into his own. The hitherto deferential Argentinian, a tactically disciplined veteran of the Bundesliga and La Liga began to marshal the defence. Despite his lack of pace, Demichelis was a technically adept centre back whose style contrasted with Kompany's free roaming. When the skipper returned, they established an effective partnership with Demichelis bringing the ball out of defence in measured style while Kompany ranged deep to guard against long passes over the top.

On the eve of City's clash with Liverpool at Anfield, which most observers expected to decide the Premiership title, Kompany was injured in training after a collision with a teammate. His participation was in doubt until he passed a fitness test just before kick-off and he played with strapping on one knee. In the event, he was well below his best in the game, losing Skrtel at a corner for the second goal and handing Liverpool the winner on a plate by a total miskick which went straight to Coutinho.

But, at Goodison Park, in a match which turned out to be crucial to City's eventual triumph, his perfectly timed tackle on Everton's Ross Barkley prevented the prodigiously talented youngster adding a second goal to the spectacular effort which he'd already notched.

Vincent Kompany is a man of Herculean physical strength – so powerful that a short push on Yaya Toure's chest, when the huge Ivorian was testing Andre Marriner's patience to the limit at White Hart Lane– was enough to make him stagger. Yet he combines this with an ambassadorial presence which enables him to do interviews fluently in four languages and raise the profile of the club. He remains a titanic figure, saluted in song by Citizens when they borrowed the words and melody of Simon and Garfunkel's 'Mrs Robinson' to declare "here's to you, Vincent Kompany, City loves you more than you will know!!"

JAMES MILNER - AN EYE FOR GEOMETRY AND LUNGS LIKE STEEL BELLOWS

James Milner doesn't look like what he is. Granite jaw and bull neck – these scarcely fit the image of a middle class lad brought up in a pebble -dashed semi in the posh Leeds suburb of Horsforth, his father a quantity surveyor and his mum an estate agent. But he has an earnest gaze rather like the faces of the old-time footballers who stare out from the pages of Pickford and Gibson's 1905 classic 'Association Football and the Men Who Made It'.

It was a disappointment to his teachers and a shock to his parents when James opted not to stay on into the Sixth Form at Horsforth School, a Specialist Science College. He'd done brilliantly in his GCSEs and the elegance of his geometrical solutions led to forecasts of an A grade in A Level Maths. But he was also a junior cross country champion and represented Yorkshire schools at cricket. The clincher was that his football skills made Leeds United determined to sign him on pro forms.

Milner's path from Leeds to Manchester City came via Newcastle United and Aston Villa. During those six years a whole series of club managers, plus England boss Fabio Capello, paid tribute to his skill, intelligence, versatility, fitness, workrate and dedication. The sole exception was Graeme Souness, erstwhile Newcastle boss, who, in a comment that said more about the man who made it than about the one it related to, claimed that he would "not win anything with a team of James Milners". Despite this opinion, Milner is a player who's almost always available for selection. He's rarely injured and, in the course of a twelve year career, has only once been sent off. What's more, he's refused to have an agent.He was sold by Leeds because the club were in dire financial straits. His transfer to Villa came about because he thought he'd be bettering himself and his move to City because he knew he would be.

Souness' reservations were only partly echoed by Milner's team-mates in the North-East and the Midlands. After all, he was a dab hand at snooker and a mean darts player who could run world champion Phil Taylor close in Pro-Am events. But darts and ale frequently go together and in Milner's case they didn't. Since he spat out a sip of his dad's beer at the age of twelve, he's sworn off alcohol. And for many years he's been in a steady relationship with his low-profile live-in girlfriend, Amy Fletcher. What's more, while other Premiership players were busy tattooing the length and breadth of their forearms and biceps, James Milner's arms remained unsullied by ink. His was a private life diametrically opposed to that of many English foot-ballers and it came as no surprise when Jermaine Pennant, during Euro 2012, tweeted his objections to Milner's regular selection for England. According to Pennant, the City man's chief claim to a place in the national side was his habit of "running around like a nutter on the training pitch" Milner did not dignify the fatuous remark with a response.

Brought to Eastlands by Roberto Mancini, Milner renewed his friendship with fellow golf buff Gareth Barry- with whom he'd palled up when they were both at Villa Park -and became a straight man foil for Les Chapman's humour. Milner it was who organised the St. Andrews golf outing during which Barry, Hart, Adam Johnson and Shay Given where entrapped by a tabloid snooper while attending a students' party – one from which the teetotaller James had kept clear.

In his first season for City, Milner's contribution was rarely spec-tacular but often effective. Linking Johnson and Barry for an assist against Liverpool, intelligently instigating Tevez' counter against Chelsea, sending Richards through for a goal in the Britannia and cleverly working the ball back leading to Crouch's own goal in the vital game against Spurs - these were some of the subtle touches which marked his work though he could sometimes drive powerfully through on his own and score, as he did at Leicester.

The arrival of the richly gifted Samir Nasri in 2011 put pressure on Milner and, in the second half of the season, he became something of a peripheral figure. But, before that, his contribution to the 6-1 Demolition Derby was a vital one. Indeed he played a key part in the first three goals. For starters, at a throw in, United collectively switched off but Milner didn't. Spying David Silva momentarily unmarked, he promptly fed him, taking full advantage of Nani's ambling failure to track back. Milner went right into the free space to receive Silva's pass and pull it straight back towards the Spanish maestro. Silva dummied and Balotelli did the rest!

Next, it was Ashley Young who was caught napping and United were once again made to pay. When Young belatedly reacted to danger, Milner exploited the gap as Silva ran into it. Then Milner gestured for the ball, sussing Young would be too slack to go with him. Released by Silva, Milner spotted that Smalling had let Balotelli get away from him and he steered the ball carefully beyond de Gea right to the Italian's feet for him to jab it into goal. If ever there was a cameo of reading the game goal -wise, this was it!

Lastly, for the third goal, Milner picked up Balotelli's startling, instant, angled backheel and, seeing Young once again leave his post to confront him, he transposed it into a surgically incisive forward pass that sent Richards flying through and prompting Aguero's strike.

When City's number seven was finally substituted with only nine minutes left, United's humiliation was yet to be completed. But their defeat had been sealed and he'd played a vital part in that. The three goals apart, his work rate had been phenomenal. Seeing him leave the field, ashen- faced, knackered but indomitable, the Citizens saluted him with the only possible accolade - "there's only one James Milner!".

Now, of course, for thirty years and more, mediocre footballers up and down the country, from Plymouth Argyle to Carlisle United and all points in between have been lauded in this all -too -obvious manner. The difference is this: City fans were saluting a player who comes very close to being genuinely unique - the expert geometrician who's also a cross country champion! It was all there at Horsforth School when James Milner was a lad of sixteen and it came to fruition on the day City went to Old Trafford and demolished Manchester United.

Heroic as he is in reality, James Milner had a serious image problem even before he became the target of the Twitter parody 'Boring James Milner '- which depicts him as a dullard preoccupied with such things as missed phone calls and prone to making statements of the obvious.

In keeping with his image, there are many fans- both those who admire him and those who think he's just a squad player- only too ready to dismiss him as " a lad who'll run his bollocks off all day long". But any serious examination both of his contribution to City's 2013-14 title-winning campaign and his impressive Champions League and F. A. Cup performances will reveal the superficiality of such judgments.

Against Bayern, he came on with David Silva after seventy minutes at a time when City were facing total humiliation. He promptly made himself available for an incisive pass from Silva and only a world-class save from Neuer stopped him scoring. His example boosted team spirit at a vital juncture and, so far from a runaway German win, City narrowed the margin to 1-3.

A few days later Milner had a very good game against Everton. Told to close mark Leighton Baines, he effectively shut him out of the match. Tackling like a tank in midfield, one of his challenges sent two Everton players to the deck at once and took the wind right out of the Toffees' sails.

In the C. L. return at the Allianz Arena, Milner played a crucial role. He won a penalty from Dante after being played through by Silva. Then he scored, calmly exploiting Boateng's error.

He was made skipper for the FA Cup replay against Blackburn Rovers and fully justified Pellegrini's observation that "Milner is a player of great character". In the next round of the Cup, against Chelsea, he was deputed to a double marking job on Eden Hazard and helped take him out of the game. What's more, he showed real moral leadership when coming on as a sub against Wigan. He shouted his rallying call – "stop all this fannying around!" -and immediately led by example, driving to the byline and executing a pullback with, sadly, no one there to finish off. Had his teammates applied themselves with the same zeal, Wigan would never have got away with their easy victory.

In what looked for a while like the title-decider, at Anfield, he replaced the ineffectual Navas early in the second half and got into the action immediately, starting a move only foiled by a last-ditch tackle from Skrtel. Then he picked up on Flanagan and Henderson simultaneously losing concentration, took the ball to the byline and cut it back precisely for Silva to score. He was excellent at Anfield, not only for his work rate and imperturbable attitude but also for his experience in the hurly-burly.

James Milner is particularly effective in combination with David Silva. And this is not just a matter of putting in the slogging stints which complement Silva's silky skills. Typically Milner is able to read the Spaniard's ambitious passing and to facilitate the moves which Merlin has instigated. There seems to be a clear rapport between them and it's characteristic of Milner that he set himself the task of learning Spanish in order to communicate better not only with Silva but with all his Iberian and Argentinian teammates.

In complete contrast to his image as an unimaginative plodder, he helped set up Dzeko's goal at St James Park in the Capital One Cup and, in the vital clash at Goodison Park during the title run-in, it was his sumptuous, slow dropping cross which set up the Bosnian's decisive power header.

Sometimes described as a typically English player, James Milner in fact resembles a German footballer in the cold application of geometrical intelligence and in the ability to produce a warrior -like performance without losing his head as many English players do. One of English football's deepest taboos is any discussion of the class origins of players and the interrelation between class and confidence. Among the sundry factors evinced by football writers to account for England's early elimination from the 2014 World Cup, this rated scarcely a mention. Yet England continually fail to tap a pool of middle-class talent which, in any other country, would never be overlooked.

Once an England regular, James Milner fell out of favour with a hitherto conservative Roy Hodgson who increasingly came to prefer cavaliers. Just as Hodgson more and more consigned Milner to the bench, so the Twitter parody revelled in scoffing at the Yorkshireman's supposed bourgeois respectability.

At City, however, events took a different turn. Where Milner and Mancini had often clashed vocally on the touchline, Manuel Pellegrini, who'd long placed his trust in Jesus Navas, increasingly, in the second half of the season, began to rely on James Milner and was rewarded with sterling performances.

It's been all too easy for commentators to parrot the cliche "you know what you're going to get with Milner" without fear of contradiction since both his admirers and his detractors acknowledge his phenomenal work rate. What's more, the one genuine weakness in his game, paucity of goals, means it's highly unlikely that pundits will be confounded by a Milner spectacular. But glib judgements such as these completely undervalue a player who, as a morale -boosting teammate and a subtle passer, is worth his weight in gold to Manchester City.

SAMIR NASRI - LAUGHING FEET AND A LETHAL GRIN

Just outside Marseille, the roughest, toughest city in the whole of France, lies the notorious La Gavotte-Peyret, its deprivation aggravated by a 60% unemployment rate. When the French Interior Minister visited there in 2011, he promptly announced massive police reinforcements in the hope of restoring law and order. That night, Claude Gueant got his answer - as hand grenades exploded and Kalashnikov gunfire raked the streets.

It was in La Gavotte-Peyret that Samir Nasri was born and raised. But, unlike the composite English footballer from a background only half as dodgy as his, he didn't grow up to be an inked up to the eye-balls, hooker -shagging, Bentley -crashing, twaddle- tweeting perennial underachiever. Instead he parlayed his soccer skills into an upmarket pad in Hampstead which he shared with tennis ace Tatiana Golovin, the Peace and Sport campaigner who was then his girlfriend. His sublime skills lit up the Emirates and in time he stood on the podium at the Etihad, first in 2012 then in 2014, to receive his medals as an important member of Manchester City's Premiership title -winning squads.

Samir's dribbling skills showed up as a young boy along with the confidence which led him to be nicknamed "the Little Prince". This worried his mother, Oussila, who, from the windows of their cramped third floor apartment, watched him play out on waste ground. By the age of seven, he was already running with a gang. But his bus driver father, Hamid, believed football would be Samir's salvation and got him signed to a feeder club for Olympique Marseille. And Hamid Nasri would be proved right, though Ouassila still dreamt of him becoming a doctor, a perfectly reasonable ambition since Samir's teachers rated him not only an exceptionally quick- witted boy but one with genuine academic intelligence.

At the age of eleven, Samir was already regarded as a football prodigy. But his first interview angered him because he refused to accept the journalist's determination to pigeonhole him as the next Zinedine Zidane. Like Zidane - and other gifted footballers such as Real Madrid's Karim Benzema and Newcastle United's Hatem Ben Arfa, Nasri is of Kabyle descent, his grandparents having emigrated from Algeria to France. But pride of place on his old man's football video shelves was occupied by an Argentinian, Diego Maradona and, in particular, by his second goal in the 1986 World Cup Quarter-final when he dribbled round half the England team. It was one which Samir Nasri would later describe as "a wonderful piece of art".

Taken to Arsenal by Arsene Wenger for £12 million in 2008, Nasri played less often in midfield than he'd done at Marseille, mainly to accommodate Cesc Fabregas. But, as a winger, he stood out for his close control, aided by his high- stepping gait and uncanny balance – not to mention his nifty football brain. He was never to be a prolific scorer but he scored truly memorable goals. One came against Fulham in the Premiership when a fantastic, swerving, boot- hurdling, high-speed run with changes of feet send him past two defenders and the keeper and, when it seemed as if he'd lost control of the ball, he turned through 180 degrees and clipped it into the net. That strike took Arsenal, albeit temporarily, top of the league. Another great Nasri goal for the Gunners came against Porto in Round 16 of the Champions League. He played cat and mouse with one Portuguese defender, dawdling then accelerating before a wizard dribble where he ran rings round three others before firing the ball in off the far post. Roberto Mancini found himself on the receiving end of Nasri's skills when he set up one goal and scored another in City's three nil defeat to the Gunners. Nasri was indeed a formidable foe but also one who could become a prize acquisition.

Wenger's Arsenal were of course a team of peak highs and trough lows - beating Barcelona at the Emirates but bowing the knee to

Birmingham City in the Carling Cup Final. Nasri's skill, brains - and bravery (he said the worst Premiership cloggers bothered him far less than the boys he faced in La Gavotte- Peyret, some of whom played with knives in their jeans)- made him highly coveted. But the question which Mancini pondered, before deciding that £22 million could be invested in the Frenchman, was: how hard would he work and how tactically aware could he become? Season 2011-12 would provide positive answers although, when Nasri failed to track Mackie's goalscoring run in the crucial final game against QPR – and, even as time ran out, hesitated over a throw-in- the Italian maestro may well have doubted the wisdom of his investment.

The positive highlights of Nasri's season included his three -assist debut at White Hart Lane, notably the underspun backwards chip which enabled Dzeko to open the scoring. Then there was the way he turned the game against Wigan when he replaced a lacklustre Tevez. After a couple of minutes, two goals had been scored with Nasri mesmerising Wigan defenders as he read Silva's cute backheel, nonchalantly jumped out of a tackle and perfectly played in Aguero to finish. What's more, he could score vital goals in big matches as when he and Silva cut Spurs to pieces at the Etihad before he cracked the ball past Friedel. But his piece de resistance was the late decider against Chelsea when he and Carlos Tevez were two fine football brains who thought as one. It was Nasri who received Tevez' delicate pass, outwitted and outran Frank Lampard, flummoxed Luiz and sent Ramires into the middle of next week before his final swerving jump to put the ball past Cech.

At other times Nasri had much to endure in the cause of Manchester City - the ferocious outburst of abuse at the Emirates and the car ambush, as ridiculous as it was disgraceful, perpetrated by YouTube-filming yobs after the Carling Cup Semi first leg loss against Liverpool. But, at his best, in 2011-12, he illuminated the Etihad, a slight, pale but formidable figure infuriating his opponents with jaunty footwork that seemed to laugh at their clumsiness but delighting the Citizens with that irrepressible grin which signals his contribution to decisive strikes.

In the season between the titles, Samir Nasri didn't shine as he had done before. He came in for particular criticism when his perceived slackness in the City wall contributed to Robin van Persie's late free kick winner in the home derby. Some Citizens convinced themselves that Nasri had become distracted by his glamorous new girlfriend, Victoria's Secret model Anara Atanes. He himself attributed his decline to a reaction from turmoil within the French camp. His international career has been characterised by conflict with teammates, reporters and coach Didier Deschamps. Roberto Mancini seemed to echo Deschamps' strictures when he said there were times when he felt like punching Nasri.

The arrival of Manuel Pellegrini proved to be a boon as far as Samir Nasri was concerned. Pellegrini's paternal manner, which Nasri compared to Arsene Wenger, soothed rather than antagonised. Where Nasri had fired verbal volleys against Deschamps and run rings round Mancini with his fluent English, he respected Pellegrini's faith in him.

When David Silva was injured playing for Spain, Nasri stepped up to the plate in exemplary fashion. He was at the heart of City's triumph in the home derby, tormenting the likes of Smalling with his foot on the ball artistry. And, though his skill had never been in doubt, he matched it now with a tremendous stint and, into the bargain, he scored.

When Silva returned, Nasri continued to play well and was in splendid form against Spurs, Swansea and – despite the jeers of the Gooner boo-boys who'd never forgiven him for his departure from the Emirates – Arsenal.

Nasri's season might well've ended at St James Park where he was the victim of an appalling foul by Yanga- Mbiwa who chopped him down at the knee. Happily he recovered after a few weeks absence and he scored against Chelsea in the Cup after a neat one-two with Silva.

There were times when Nasri briefly relapsed into the player Deschamps spurned and of whom Roberto Mancini had despaired. Against Bayern at home, he lost focus, became stroppy and started to mouth off. Much the same happened when Wigan took City out of the Cup. And there were moments when he was mortified by his own failure. In the rescheduled Sunderland game, having been gifted a lucky equaliser by keeper Mannone's fumble, he squandered a chance to win when he blazed over from ten yards then, in the title run-in, he cursed himself as he missed badly against Villa from only four yards out. Saddest of all was his slip -up in the Camp Nou when, though his general play was good, he shot straight at Valdes when Silva had superbly set him up. Regrettable though these misses were, Samir Nasri could no longer be charged with inadequate workrate. Far from it, he'd beavered away with a zeal which, if Deschamps had followed his progress more closely might 've convinced the former 'water carrier' of Nasri's dedication.

Though it would be simplistic to claim that Nasri fails to deliver in games when City are up against it, he's certainly at his best when the team are on the crest of a wave. His finest moment came at Wembley in the Capital One Cup Final. Having seen his pal Yaya score a magnificent goal, he seemed inspired as he finished off a great team move in devastating style.

Pantilimon started it with a huge targeted kick which found Aguero within a yard. Kun trapped it and looked to dart inside. Silva pointed out Kolarov overlapping fast into empty space. And Aguero pinpointed a reverse pass. Kolarov then delivered a low cross, not whipping it as usual but cuffing it sideways. This is where Nasri took over.

Seeing Sunderland's Bardsley stumble after the ball brushed him, Nasri steamed in to meet it as it decelerated on the third bounce. Dzeko had read him and pulled up sharp leaving space. Nasri leaped into a jump volley, striking the ball with the outside of his foot precisely over Alonso's outstretched leg. Slight of frame but with perfect timing, Nasri hit the ball with immense force and, in a flash, it was nestling in the netting just inside the post, rippling it all the way to the back, then bouncing buoyantly between the stanchions as if the goal itself was delighted to receive such a ferocious yet exquisite strike.

Here was the Samir Nasri France never knew, racing about open-mouthed, wildly elated, arms pumping, veins bulging in his neck as a colossal roar of 'YES! 'erupted from the delighted Citizens. This was the goal which sealed Manuel Pellegrini's first trophy, the confidence-boosting victory which laid the foundation for Premiership triumph.

Graham Gordon

JESUS NAVAS - MORE THAN JUST A SPEED MERCHANT

If you'd asked Spanish football followers a few years ago which of their fellow countrymen might be transferred to an English club, the last name on everyone's lips would surely have been Jesus Navas.

Yes, Navas was a player of real skill and tremendous speed but his early career in his homeland had been blighted by psychological problems – homesickness and anxiety. In regards to that, he contradicted stereotypes because, though he comes from a family of Romanies, he felt uncomfortable away from his home in the small Andalusian town of Los Palacios. Indeed, in 2007, he declined to travel on Seville's pre-season tour of the United States for psychological reasons. And he rejected a potential transfer to Arsenal.

In time, however, Navas determined to overcome this self-imposed handicap and, though he did seek professional help, his own determination and will power were crucial factors. After he travelled with the Spanish squad to the World Cup in South Africa, he never looked back.

Navas' family also contradicted ethnic stereotypes in that his father, Paco, had a deskbound job, as a school administrator. Jesus had made good progress in school himself, shining at maths and science, before his high football skill confined his ambition to making a career in the game

Navas has remarkable sprinting speed, especially considering that, unlike most track and field star sprinters, he has a slim frame. But he's run a hundred metres in 10.8 seconds and once, in the Seville training centre, sped so fast on a treadmill that he broke it.

When Txiki learned of Navas' availability, he was surprised but moved to sign him unhesitatingly. Rather than just giving him a glowing picture, he confronted him with possible negatives about life in England

and in Manchester specifically – the distance from his family, the language and the rainy Mancunian climate. Navas was not put off.

It helped that his new coach, Pellegrini, was a Spanish speaker and that there was a real contingent of others, Silva and Garcia plus the Argentinians Zabaleta and Aguero. What's more, his friend and Seville teammate, Alvaro Negredo, would also be transferring to City. To top it all off, his older brother, Marco, had signed for Bury and would be living not faraway from the city centre hotel where Navas, his wife Alejandra and their baby son Jesus were staying.

Jesus Navas' early-season form was mostly good. In the opening match, against Newcastle, City supporters gasped at his speed and the way he was gelling with Pablo Zabaleta. Though he was not as comfortable away from home against Cardiff City (where he was double marked) he impressed in the 4-1 City home derby victory -not only as a speed merchant but as a man who was more than willing to track back. But he looked a forlorn figure at home against Bayern Munich where, instead of his Spanish-speaking buddy Zabaleta, he had Micah Richards alongside him on the right flank.

On Metrolink, on the way to the Etihad before the game against Spurs, one supporter loudly slagged off Navas, insisting "he'll be crap today – he's all right against the small teams but he never turns up against the big 'uns". Within fifteen seconds of kick-off, however, Navas scored his first City goal, reacting with typical speed of movement to an error by Lloris and also shrugging off the burly Kaboul before scoring with great despatch. His celebration was sheer jubilation – he nimbly leaped over the corner flag. He scored again later in the game and was truly starting to fulfil his talents.

He continued in the same vein and, though he didn't start against Arsenal, he came on when Aguero had to come off and he troubled the Gunners with his pace. Against Liverpool on Boxing Day, he popped up with an unexpected header, early on and clipped a post. Afterwards, Pellegrini successfully used Navas' pace to back track and neutralise the Merseysiders' startling speed on the break.

In the second half of the season, Jesus Navas' form somewhat varied and he had to compete for his place with James Milner. He scored the final goal in City's 3-1 defeat of Sunderland in the Capital One Cup. At Anfield, Pellegrini deputed him to try to contain Sterling's pace but he was ineffectual and was taken off early in the second half.

Though Jose Mourinho dismissed him as a mere pace merchant, using the derisive phrase ' Speedy Gonzales'- a possibly intended allusion to his maternal family name-Jesus Navas contributed many brilliant moments to City's second Premiership title campaign.

ALVARO NEGREDO - ' THE BEAST ' AND HIS BURDEN

You had to wonder how it might've felt when the nickname he'd borne successfully for fully five months suddenly ceased to become appropriate. How Alvaro Negredo might've reacted when he found the glittering half season, in which he'd scored 23 goals in 33 games for Manchester City, suddenly ended by injury. At Upton Park, when vigorously tussling for the ball on the touchline, a tackle sent him crashing to the turf in full flight. And his shoulder took the full impact of the fall. No, it wasn't broken and, yes, he could soon resume his place in the starting lineup. But, it was clear from his body language - and soon officially confirmed- that he was playing with painkilling injections. Seeming more and more bereft of confidence, he would endure a fifteen game drought.

Had the injury been worse, had he actually been hors de combat, the situation might've been easier to cope with. But, when you carry a nickname intended to symbolise raw power and indestructability but your capacity to deliver those qualities is abruptly cut short, you may well wince when the stadium announcer proclaims you 'The Beast '. And when fans welcome you, now a mere substitute, by chanting the B word over and over again. By contrast, Negredo, getting ready to come on as a sub against Southampton, smiled and waved as he warmed up by jogging along the touchline and heard shouts of "hey, Alvaro!", "Good lad, Alvaro!" and "all right, Alf!" In his response to such unostentatious encouragement, it seemed as if he yearned to shed the burden of the beastly nickname.

When he first arrived, in the final minutes of the opening game against Newcastle, he was simply Alvaro Negredo Sanchez. But he nearly got on the scoresheet against the Magpies, having a perfectly good goal disallowed. And, in the home derby, though he didn't find the net, he looked powerful even indomitable as he outmuscled Vidic and contemptuously brushed Ferdinand aside.

Coming on from the bench against Bayern Munich, he scored with a superb swivel and strike. A few days later, it was he who levelled the scores a few minutes after City had gone one goal down to Everton. He then gave the Sky Blues the lead, having kept his composure in an incident where Seamus Coleman lost his.

By now he'd supplanted Edin Dzeko as first choice strike partner for Sergio Aguero. And, in the course of Manuel Pellegrini's first away win, at Upton Park, his insouciant dummy opened up West Ham for Aguero to strike. If ever a move wrote a question mark against Negredo's beastly image, it was that. On Blue Moon Forum, Didsbury Dave was rightfully enamoured of it and started a thread in which posters vied to describe precisely how Negredo had bamboozled the Hammers' defence without actually touching the ball. It had been given short shrift on Sky but City supporters had demonstrated an appreciation of the subtler football arts which eluded the Skyster pundits.

It was not of course that Negredo wasn't rugged and competitive. Those were the very qualities he'd shown during his career in Spain, firmly getting the better of defenders and establishing, whilst with Seville, a highly impressive goals to games ratio of one in two. But those Spanish commentators who chortled when he was, as they saw it, shipped off to England to leap at long balls and thumped crosses, had long underestimated his skill. It had been all too easy to pigeonhole him as 'The Beast from Vallecas '– the working class Madrid suburb where he'd been brought up, one of three brothers who were the sons of an unpretentious but hard-working couple, Jose-Maria and Juana Negredo. Alvaro's dad was a taxi driver who worked hour after hour to provide a decent living for his lads while his mum was the heart of the home, cheerfully washing umpteen items of football kit which her rumbustious sons had dirtied playing out in the street.

Though his brothers Cesar and Ruben were uncompromisingly physical players, Alvaro was gifted with a delicacy of touch which belied his brawny physique. The first time he showed this in England was at the Britannia Stadium when he daintily toe- trapped a Joe Hart goal-kick before almost instantly delivering a beautifully flighted chip to Stevan Jovetic which the Montenegrin striker came close to converting.

Negredo's coronation came in the Champions League when he scored a hat-trick against CSKA Moscow. The word 'Beast!', repeated three times, resounded throughout the Etihad and some fans were so carried away they acclaimed his every touch. Other supporters preferred to anglicise his first name to 'Alf", a homely touch which seemed to suit the smiling Spaniard and was said to have begun on the streets of Alderley Edge where, bearded, burly and speaking just a little heavily accented English, he cut a distinctive figure.

The home game in which Spurs were demolished 6-0 was perhaps Alf Negredo's finest hour. His finesse was at the heart of a superb team goal in which Yaya's was the most spectacular element but it had been Negredo's brilliant one touch trap and feed which had enabled the Ivorian to flourish. But Alf would prove equally adept with ruth-lessness and raw power – that was there for all to see when he turned the hefty Michael Dawson inside out and, almost as if the blond bat-tler wasn't there, pivoted to deliver a rocket shot which left Hugo Lloris helpless.

In December and January everything seemed to go right for him. He scored against Arsenal, he brilliantly assisted Milner's goal at Craven Cottage and he scored against Liverpool on Boxing Day when Simon Mignolet fumbled his deft chip. In the semi-final of the Capital One Cup versus West Ham, he scored with a superb volley, notched another powerful goal and completed his hat-trick. At St James's Park, City had to draw on all their qualities of physical resolution to end the inflamed belligerence of the Barcodes and it was Negredo's great clinching goal in stoppage time – when he ran fully 40 yards before despatching the strike – which triggered an ecstatic celebration from Ruben Cousillas!

Alvaro Negredo's season rose and fell in one evening at Upton Park in the second leg of the Capital One Cup semi. He'd scored a brace, including another fine long run and strike yet, sadly, in the last five minutes came the traumatic fall which clouded the rest of his season.

It was fortunate that City had three outstanding strikers to choose from this year. Where Negredo had ridden the crest of a wave in the first half of the season, it was Dzeko who became the principal spearhead in the second half. Though Negredo was at his best when partnering Sergio Aguero, he and Dzeko could definitely play alongside each other and showed this more than once, notably in the Capital One Cup tie at St James's Park.

February, March and April were months of personal anti-climax for Alvaro Negredo. Yet, as he stood with his teammates on the podium to receive his Barclays Premier League medal, he could look back with pride on the tremendous contribution, in terms of both successful and beautiful football, with which he'd lit up the Etihad.

DAVID SILVA -   SPACEFINDER - GENERAL

When Roberto Mancini submitted his pamphlet ' Il Trequartista' to the Italian National Football Centre at Coverciano in 2001, Manchester City was, as yet, far from his thoughts. In defining and analysing the role of the playmaker, he doubtless had in mind such Italian exponents as Roberto Baggio and Allesandro del Piero. But, if you'd asked City fans just then to exemplify such a player, one name would've been on their lips.

As the millennium dawned, Georgi Kinkladze was languishing in Derby County reserves - on loan from Ajax. But the memory of his three magical years at Maine Road was spark- bright in the minds of all City supporters. He was the man you could depend on to brighten up the darkest winter's day - of which there were all too many in City's late nineties football purgatory. Acquired by Franny Lee, admired by an all -too- rapid succession of managers, mired in a dismal collective mediocrity and junked by Joe Royle, Kinkladze's balletic footwork and defence-piercing passing were the quintessence of playmaking. What's more, the little Georgian prefigured the cosmopolitan squad of the Mancini era. Where Uwe Rosler's German grittiness had already seemed close to traditional English virtues and likewise Shaun Goater's Bermudan opportunism, it was Georgi Kinkladze, with his sublimely deceptive shimmy-shuffle, who was City's first Latin-style hero.

Italian soccer parlance typically contrasts the trequartista and the regista or deep-lying midfielder - such as Andrea Pirlo who bewildered England to defeat in Euro 2012. But, in Colin Bell, City had both positions embodied in one man. Brought to Maine Road by Malcolm Allison who would describe him as "the greatest player I ever worked with", Bell was the heartbeat of the great City side which won five trophies in five seasons.His precise passing and powerful shooting allied to the unquenchable energy which drove him from box to box led the legendary Tom Finney to rate this self-effacing son of a Geordie coal miner " as good as anything I've ever seen". Statistics alone can never do Bell justice. Record books note his phenomenal tally of 153 goals in 498 appearances but it was a fans' poll which named a stand in his honour at the City of Manchester Stadium. It remains a unique distinction.

Long before Kinkladze's time and even before Colin Bell was born, the majestic Peter Doherty bestrode Maine Road. Nostalgic fans can watch 'Kinky' on You Tube and can get archive footage of 'Nijinsky ' in his prime but they'll find nothing there on Peter Dermot Doherty.

But Peter Doherty ought to be remembered alongside the historic household names who graced the old First Division, with Stanley Matthews and Tom Finney. But he isn't, for one simple reason. He was Irish. The Sperrins- born brickie turned bus conductor was twenty-two when he signed for Manchester City from Blackpool. He led the Sky Blues to the First Division title in 1936-7, scoring 30 goals, and, by the time the Second World War truncated his career, he'd found the net at an astonishing rate of better than one in every other game. He was described by Len Shackleton as having "the most baffling body swerve in football, able to perform all the tricks with the ball, owning a shot like the kick of a mule and having such an enthusiasm ... that he will run like a horse for ninety minutes". He was hailed by Matthews as "a genius of a footballer" and by Joe Mercer as "like a greyhound, very fast and elusive but with stamina". " He had a Rolls-Royce engine in him" Mercer added and "was unplayable on his day".As for his tactical astuteness, it would be there for all to see when he coached Northern Ireland, clean against the odds, to the World Cup Quarter- Finals in 1958. Without doubt, the rebellious red-blond Irishman with the rock 'n' roll hairstyle before the hour was the attacking playmaker incarnate.

Peter Doherty, Colin Bell and Georgi Kinkladze – such was the superb lineage of twentieth century City playmakers. But, when David Silva arrived at Eastlands in 2010, acquired from Valencia for £25 million, the man younger City supporters compared him to was Ali Benarbia. Born in Algeria, brought up in France yet overlooked by his adopted country, Benarbia was the pivot of Kevin Keegan's promotion-winning side at the start of the new century. Skilful, clever and strong, the popular Ali had all the playmaking attributes and it was a shame that he was in his early thirties by the time he reached the Premiership – where he found the hectic pace harder to cope with. Silva, by contrast, was only twenty-four, yet already a veteran of Spain's successful Euro 08 and World Cup 2010 squads.

Silva hails from the outermost margins of Spanish territories, a sleepy fishing village in Gran Canaria. He became obsessed with football as a young boy, possibly as a way of establishing his ethnic identity to locals who'd nicknamed him 'El Chino'. Dark -eyed and tiny, he was not, as they half- humorously reckoned, Chinese but in fact part Japanese on his mother's side. At four years of age, David was playing out in front of the house with potatoes and oranges he'd nabbed from the kitchen as his improvised footballs. Later on he pitted his dribbling skills down the alley against his older cousin and his mates with a rag ball his nan made for him. At school, David was bright and his mum entertained ambitions of him becoming a surgeon. But like Georgi Kinkladze's mother - who wanted her boy to become a ballet dancer - she was to be disappointed when he opted for a football career.

Silva would never have come to Manchester City had not three of Europe's most famous clubs deprived three of its greatest coaches of his services. First, Real Madrid failed to follow up the recommendation of Vicente Del Bosque when David trialled in the Bernabeu at the age of fourteen. "Too small !" they said. But Real's sizeism would cost them dear in future years when Barcelona built supremacy round immensely skilful but short- bodied players. Silva himself rose to prominence at Valencia alongside other small players such as David Villa and Juan Mata.

Next it was Roberto Mancini's turn to be dismayed. Watching the nineteen -year-old Silva playing what he called a "fantastic, incredible game" in the Champions League against Inter-Milan, he asked the Inter bosses to sign him but they wouldn't meet Valencia's asking price.

Much the same happened at Anfield in 2009. Rafael Benitez, who knew Silva from Valencia -and remembered how he calmly dealt with the muscular attentions of Chelsea's Terry - figured he'd have no problem adjusting to the Premiership. But Benitez was thwarted by the toxic regime of Hicks and Gillette who refused point blank to sign Silva.

At City, however, Mancini was working with perceptive directors neither motivated by greed nor prejudiced over size and, second time around, he got his man. But Silva's arrival in the Premiership was greeted with some scepticism by pundits who portrayed him as a Liliputian cast loose in a scary hurly burly of rugged hard men. Some Citizens fretted that he'd be clattered by Cattermole and his ilk, just as Kinkladze had once been victimised by Vinnie Jones. They needn't have worried. If he didn't succeed in hurdling tackles, he swerved out of them, and, if he was caught, he learned not to let it worry him. As Roberto Mancini commented, at the end of Silva's first season, "he needed to work hard and grow stronger on the pitch. and that's what he's done. He's still a magician on the ball but now you can't knock him off it so easily". Bit by bit, Silva's incisive passing brought key assists, first in the match at Bloomfield Road when he was brought on as a sub and turned the game; and later in the season when he set up goals for Mario Balotelli, Carlos Tevez, Adam Johnson and Yaya Toure.

In the Cup Derby Semi, he seized on Carrick's error to prompt Yaya's goal. In the Final itself, he evaded most of Stoke's tackles and was closely involved in the winning strike. True, he notched only six for the season, a mere four in the Premiership and it was a shame when he narrowly failed to finish a beautiful team move at Old Trafford. But his beautifully weighted left foot passing was a joy to watch and he finished the season with fourteen assists to his name.

Off the field, he was soon dubbed 'Merlin' by his new teammates and there were those in the media who suggested it referred as much to his invisibility on the social scene as to his magical footwork. Though the Mancunian climate was not easy for someone raised in the subtropics to endure, he appreciated the far greater privacy which, compared to Valencia, he now enjoyed. Closeted in the Cheshire stockbroker belt, he kept clear of Manchester's nightclubs and even hesitated to venture into the city's restaurants. When he was finally spotted scoffing paella at El Rincon de Rafa, he was amazed at the respect with which he was treated by fellow -dining Citizens.

Manchester City's rise to Premiership power effectively began in the 2011 Demolition Derby. In that 6-1 overthrow of Manchester United, David Silva played a key part. By the time he nonchalantly nutmegged de Gea to score the fifth, he'd been at the heart of all but one of the goals. Balotelli 's opener was prepared by his dummy and before that by his astute pass to Milner. And the second goal was a beautiful strike born in Silva's brain and instigated by his exquisite footwork. When Milner dashed beyond Young on the flank, Silva shunned the obvious move and passed back short to Richards, telling Micah to find James. Young naïvely steamed in to cover Milner and Silva promptly took his place. With Milner reading and finding him, he swiftly sussed his options. He saw everything at a glance -Fletcher on Aguero, Smalling leaving Balotelli clear, Milner surging free in the six yard box. Now he turned Anderson inside out and, at exactly the right moment, released Milner to feed Balotelli three yards from goal. Milner had been totally on his wavelength throughout but Silva's chess master reading of the game was the fulcrum of the move. The fourth was straightforward but it was the one which knocked the stuffing out of United. It was Silva's hoisted corner which flummoxed de Gea leading to Dzeko's point-blank finish.

The piece de resistance was the last: Silva deep in his own half, reacting at once to Ferdinand's misdirected header, arm raised aloft as if he was summoning the ball to do his bidding, instantaneous left foot trap, flick up and stupendous, levered half volley pass beyond Smalling, fully thirty yards but rolling to a stop at Dzeko's feet, inviting him to score, which he promptly did.

On that astonishing day, October 23, 2011, David Silva was the master of United's brawn, brushing aside Ferdinand and Fletcher, Evans and Evra, sowing confusion in their ranks with a fantastic dribble when the scores were level - just as he did at six years of age when he made fools of his cousin's hefty mates down the alleys of Argineguin.

If the Demolition Derby was the jewel in David Silva's crown, there were other glittering gems: his wildly swerving run at the Reebok when he left four Bolton defenders reeling in his wake like ninepins in a bowling alley to put the ball on a plate for Aguero; his fantastic strike at Loftus Road when he killed Dzeko's pass with the merest touch and effectively passed to himself as he sped beyond three hulking Hoops defenders before wheeling round and scorching it home; and his goal against Bayern when their defenders were expecting either a dribble or a pass but he danced into space and unleashed an unstoppable left foot shot. His tally for the season increased from six to ten but more important were the goals he provided for others - a total of twenty-one key assists in all.

In the season between the titles, he appeared less often, made fewer assists and scored even fewer goals but he was back to his best following the arrival of Manuel Pellegrini. After he opened the season scoring with a header against Newcastle, he did his hamstring playing for Spain in August and was badly missed during his layoff.

His re-emegence, from the subs' bench, against Bayern was a measure of his class. City had seemed in awe of the European champions and looked as if they were lurching to a humiliating defeat. But, after he arrived on seventy minutes, accompanied by Milner, he nearly turned the tide. Bayern sought to subdue him with rugged tackling but his beautiful nutmeg pass set up Negredo's swivel and strike then he sent Yaya clean through only to be brought down in full flight. He took the resulting freekick and beat Neuer to the wide but his shot cannoned off the bar.

A few days later, in a must -win game against Everton, he robustly stood up to the Toffees' abrasive challenges, dishing out as much as he received and, despite the gap in stature, ruthlessly tackling Lukaku. Then he cleverly spotted that Everton had lost focus after an incident between Coleman and Negredo- though Negredo had kept cool- and he promptly set up his fellow countryman's goal..

In the Capital One Cup at St James' Park he once again turned the tide, coming on after City had laboured with Rodwell struggling badly in midfield. In the Champions League, he was far too good for CSKA and departed to a standing ovation. But he was then out for four weeks with a calf injury and his absence showed in a poor team performance at Sunderland. Returning after six weeks out, he shone at the Allianz Arena and scored. Working very well with Milner as usual, he produced a fine pass to play the Yorkshireman through for a goal.

Against Arsenal he easily outshone Arsenal's vaunted Meszut Ozil and his rugged tackle on Ramsey prevented a dangerous Gunners' counter-attack.What's more, his lightning strike climaxed a thirteen pass sequence and he left the field once again to a standing ovation.

Though he had a rare off day at Ewood Park in the FA Cup Third Round, he orchestrated City's masterly victory at White Hart Lane on January 29. His splendid approach play paved the way for a goal by Dzeko and his determination to maintain the highest standards was shown when he rebuked Jovetic for failing to execute a one-two.

Against Barcelona in the Etihad, he was foiled of a goal only by Valdes plucking the ball out of the air at the last split-second. He played beautifully in the Camp Nou, notably when he towed Mascherano across the box before delivering a wonderful backheel volley from which Nasri should have scored and he was applauded by the Catalans as he came off.

He was absolutely outstanding at the KC Stadium after Kompany's dismissal. He took command and scored a fantastic goal from 25 yards out, the ball curling and swerving as if under remote control. Undaunted by Elmohammady's attempt to kick him out of the game, he laid on chances for Fernandinho and Dzeko which they both wasted. But, from his perfect pass, Dzeko scored late to clinch victory.

At Old Trafford he was the architect of the brilliant first minute goal and, against Aston Villa his beautifully flighted ball sent Zabaleta through to score. Citizens feared the worst when he was carried off in the rescheduled Sunderland game but it was only a precaution against his besetting ankle injury. He continued at the heart of events till City clinched the trophy.

David Silva is a man of relatively few words even in his native Spanish yet his off- field shyness contrasts with ruthlessness on the pitch, an intensity revealed in a visage as taut as a samurai warrior as he shrugs off abrasive challenges. Yet he remains susceptible to injury, notably to his ankle. In 2011-12 he had to go off at half-time in the Third Round Cup Derby and was absent for the first leg of the Carling Cup. City's bid for a treble of trophies was affected as a result and, had he remained fully fit throughout, the Sky Blues would, in all probability, have won the title with something to spare rather than at the last gasp.

There is one major weakness in Silva's game – he doesn't score as many goals as he should. His Premiership returns have been slight. In four successive seasons, his tally has been as follows: four-six-four-seven. And over that four-year period, his grand total in Europe is a mere four! This contrasts with his wonderful record of 61 assists in 183 appearances. His overall ratio of goals to games is 1: 6.7. If he could increase it to the 1: 4.15 he's achieved with Spain, it would be a very significant benefit which might well have a big effect on City's hopes of Champions League success.

Despite his modest goalscoring record, David Silva is one of the finest players ever to have worn the sky blue shirt. He is Spacefinder-General, a man who demoralises the opposition by literally running rings round them with the ball magnetised to his boots. He saps their morale by his surgically precise passing, his merciless left foot the soccer equivalent of a great boxer's left jab. The banners displayed at the Etihad emblazoned with the words in Spanish 'Silva es magico' bear witness to his status in the eyes of the Citizens.

Graham Gordon

YAYA TOURE - IVORIAN ARTIST

There was, they said, only one reason why Yaya Toure wanted to leave Barcelona for Manchester City. Only one motivation for his move from the balmy air of the Med to the Manchester murk. Of course, had he made the move a year earlier, instead of boldly snubbing United, few questions would've been asked. But his embrace of City depended, it was claimed, solely on his wages. Quoted initially at £185,000 per week but liable to rise by at least ten grand a time in subsequent media reports, it was swiftly pronounced 'obscene' as if Toure was on a par with some greedy bonus -grabbing banker cocking a snook at the recession.

Yaya Toure's personality and lifestyle made it difficult to sustain these cynical insinuations. A devout Muslim who worshipped at one of the Stretford mosques, he lived quietly at Wilmslow with his wife and family. What's more, he had a close bond with his elder brother Kolo, already captain of Manchester City for one year, and he wanted to play alongside Kolo at club level just as they'd done at international level for Cote d'Ivoire.

Seven years earlier it looked like the two brothers would play for the same Premiership team. Yaya had a successful trial with Arsenal but, due to work permit problems, they couldn't sign him. While Kolo enjoyed the glory of being a member of Arsenal's Invincibles, Yaya shivered in the Ukrainian winter, playing in Donetsk for two years before moving to Greece. Monaco spotted him at the 2006 World Cup and signed him. He moved to Barcelona a later and stayed three seasons. It was when he scored for the Blaugranas against Roberto Mancini's Inter in 2007 that Mancini first compared his mix of physical force, technical skill and positional adaptability to his old Sampdoria teammate,

Dutch ace Ruud Gullit. And Mancini determined to sign him one day if he could.

If kinship with Kolo was one of the main reasons why Yaya joined City, another was his wish to enter the ultra- competitive arena of the Premiership - but to do so with a rising rather than an established team. Impressed by Didier Drogba's Premiership- winning success at Chelsea, he'd heard Drogba's tales of toughness and endurance, of playing on Boxing Day and New Year's Day without a break, of battling it out at the Britannia and roughing it at Ewood Park and he wanted to pit himself against highly-rated midfielders such as Steven Gerrard and Frank Lampard - not to mention the out and out hard men such as Sunderland's Cattermole, a red card record contender.

The Toure brothers' early years had been spent in a home where discipline mixed with love but where poverty was ever- present. Kolo and Yaya played football barefoot in the sand in the old French Foreign Legion garrison town of Bouake. Though their surname is common in that part of the world, it's worth noting that they share it with Samori Toure, Mandinka Emperor and great general who kept the French at bay for nearly twenty years. Their soldier father Mory (the absolute spit of Yaya) didn't have the money to buy boots for all his boys - indeed he just about had enough to provide the family with one square meal a day. But, when they moved to Abidjan, the seat of government, things looked up and both boys went to the youth academy of ASEC Mimosas where they learned in the Ivorian official language, French, and were taught maths, sciences, English - and football! By the time the once- thriving West African country descended into civil war after years of drought and agricultural recession, the Toure brothers were in Europe, Kolo at Arsenal and Yaya at Beveren in Belgium. Beveren depended heavily on African talent but, unlike his partying teammates, Yaya divided his time between bulking up in the gym and studying football videos in his apartment. Serious and ambitious, that's how he came across.

Chastised by Kolo for listening to 70s pop soul instead of the strident R&B sounds favoured by Joe Hart, Joleon Lescott and Micah Richards, Yaya was not to be dissuaded from his musical preference and insisted it was vital in helping him relax before big games. In fact relaxation is the key to Yaya Toure 's game. Powerful as he is, he's also unflurried. As he surges out of defence into attack with that characteristic long, raking stride, his carriage is relaxed as he slows down and considers his options. This is what made him Roberto Mancini's second key signing, six months after Patrick Vieira arrived, and Mancini converted him from the defensive midfielder which he was at Barcelona into a vital attacking midfielder.

The first time Yaya Toure's qualities could be seen was at the Stadium of Light when he made a rugged tackle -riding run and then calmly put a prime goalscoring chance on a plate for Carlos Tevez. Tevez surprisingly missed but that took nothing away from Yaya. The travelling supporters at once recognised a major acquisition and, at the DW Stadium, where he scored in front of a throng of Citizens, he was mobbed on the touchline.

Key assist followed key assist -for Johnson against Juventus, for Tevez against Bolton, and for Barry at Villa Park. Toure dominated proceedings at Upton Park, scoring twice, he startled Blackpool with his skilful dribbling and, against Villa, he played in Balotelli for a goal then scored himself. At Goodison, he found the net almost effortlessly, one of the few to stay cool in a tension-filled game. But it was in City's successful Cup run that Yaya Toure did more than anything to endear himself to the fans.

In the Cup Derby Semi, he seized ruthlessly on Van der Sar's poor clearance, calmly set up Silva for a one-two and coolly netted. In the Cup Final itself, he was an absolute powerhouse, shrugging off Stoke's alehouse challenges and scoring the vital goal, his eleventh of the season.

In 2011-12, his understanding with David Silva illuminated the first half of the season and he enabled Silva, a man of slight physique whose game depended solely on skill and brains, to make incisive passes without being confronted by instant challenges. In the October Demolition Derby, it was Yaya Toure who instigated the third goal, suddenly spying an opportunity and delivering a perfectly faded 25 yard ball to Balotelli. He bullied Villareal at the Madrigal. And he won the game at Loftus Road, soaring high into the air over the hapless Gabbidon and imperiously heading home. When Liverpool came to the Etihad, Toure left Glen Johnson standing in the six yard box and when Johnson tried too late to make amends, he beat him to it and scored with a powerful header.

Precisely how vital Yaya Toure was to Manchester City was shown in January and early February 2012 when his African Nations commitment obliged him to miss eight games. During this time, City went out of the FA Cup, were eliminated from the Carling Cup and lost at Goodison. The effect of his absence was, of course, not total and City laboured to wins against Wigan, Spurs and Villa. But it was only on his return that they rediscovered their fluency and the goal tally began to mount once again. Likewise, City stuttered at the Emirates when he went off injured after only ten minutes but, at Carrow Road, whilst Tevez and Aguero made the headlines with their wonderful goals and sparkling interplay, the match remained in the balance until he was brought on.

It was sad for the Toure brothers that his supremacy coincided with the stalwart Kolo's gradual decline, exacerbated by a six-month absence after failing a test for substances. As boys, Yaya'd been the serious one and Kolo the joker - now he used both humour and compassion to help his brother through a difficult time. Another teammate who benefited from his encouragement was Edin Dzeko, a Muslim like himself, and when Dzeko completed his hat-trick at White Hart Lane, Yaya was the first to congratulate him - "Edin, see what you can do when you believe in yourself!"

Described by one of the Eastlands coaches as "a humble man, a perfect low maintenance superstar", Yaya is still an intense competitor, ever ready to argue the toss with referees. And a darker side to Toure the Younger could surface occasionally as it did at Stamford Bridge when Mark Clattenburg's refereeing blunder deprived City of a nailed -on penalty and then Meireles began to kick Silva. Charged with marking the brilliant Juan Mata - with whom he seemed to have had previous in La Liga - he looked like a man with the smell of rotten eggs in his nostrils. He jabbed the little Spaniard in the thigh with the toe of his boot and, after Mata got up and mimed a full-blooded kick, daring Clattenburg to dismiss Yaya, he boxed Mata's ears on the blindside. Later on, as the abrasive Ramires was darting away from him, he raked his boot down the Brazilian thin man's calf and got away with it.

Yaya was vitally involved in the title-clinching run-in, above all with his two wonderful goals at St. James Park and, though he was off the pitch injured in the moment of supreme triumph against QPR, he'd laid the foundation for that with his key assist to Zabaleta's opener.

In the season between the titles, Toure produced some outstanding performances, notably against Real Madrid in the Bernabeu. Yet, though his goals to games ratio remained the same, there was a section of the City support which became disillusioned with him.

Quite often, at the Etihad, when the cry of "YA-YA !" was heard, it came from fans groaning at Toure for what they perceived as moments of indolence. This was the obverse of the "go on, Yaya, go on !", the feverish shouts of encouragement which resounded when the Ivorian midfielder surged into one of his dynamic long runs, taxing himself to his absolute physical limits so that he was obliged to have moments of comparative tranquillity in order to sustain his overall match performance.

In 2013-14, Yaya added another dimension to his already formidable game – scoring with precisely executed free kicks which revealed both innate skill and the hours of practice at Carrington which, after the arrival of Manuel Pellegrini, he was happy to undertake. The first of these came in the opener against Newcastle and he never looked back after that.

Without doubt Toure benefited from the arrival of Fernandinho. More than Gareth Barry and Nigel De Jong, the Brazilian could be relied on to aid the defence, to interrupt the opposition, to win the ball and to transfer it promptly to Yaya.

But those who gratuitously grumbled at Yaya simply because he wasn't Superman were on stronger ground when they criticised his unsuitability, as formal vice- captain, to step into the skipper's shoes when Kompany was absent. At Cardiff, he really did appear to be sauntering for much of the time and he was lacklustre against Hull even though he made the points safe with a free kick. Yaya lacked Vincent Kompany's capacity to inspire his teammates and, in dealing with referees, tended to confrontation rather than calm enquiry. Once the skipper was back in the fold, Toure resumed what would prove to be a tremendous contribution to City's success.

His fantastic strike in Pilsen was as precise as a free kick yet delivered on the run.And he scored in the home derby, where United were completely unable to deal with him.

In the Champions League, things did not go so happily for him. He had a distinct off day against Bayern at home, seemingly nonplussed by ultra-tight marking. But what occurred when City were drawn against CSKA Moscow was on a different plane entirely. He was the victim of vile racist abuse, targeted by malevolent neofascist thugs in the Arena Khimki.

Back in the Premiership, he went from strength to strength.He was the fulcrum of the great team goal City scored against Spurs. That was when he surged forward, combined succinctly with Negredo and then passed for Aguero, on a parallel run, to score. By now he was scoring regularly from free kicks and he also had a beautiful individual strike at The Hawthorns.

He was dominant against Arsenal both with staggering challenges and a superb reverse flick – but he was furious with himself after allowing Ramsey to rob him, leading to the Gunners' equaliser.

In the Boxing Day game against Liverpool, he essayed a tremendous 40 yard surge, from touchline to goal-line, shrugging off Glen Johnson and then laying the ball on for Edin Dzeko who was unlucky not to score

In Swansea on New Year's Day Yaya looked casual – and on Match of the Day he was criticised by Didi Hamann who was echoing the views of a significant minority of supporters when he labelled Yaya "a liability". Robbie Fowler's rejoinder, humorous but pointed – "but what a liability to have!" -reflected the assessment of most City fans.

Against West Ham in the Capital One Cup, he delivered a majestic strike. True, he was off form in the critical game at St James's

Park – which City still won- and, against Chelsea in the league, he found an opponent willing and able to take him on physically. This was the brawny young Serb Matic and it was rare to see Yaya levered off the ball. But, against Barcelona at home, he executed a magnificent 50 yard crossfield ball which dropped out of the sky straight to Zabaleta and led via Silva almost to a goal.

Possibly his finest achievement of the season, given that a final was being contested, was his magnificent goal at Wembley in the Capital One Cup final against Sunderland. At a time when City were struggling, he calmly cased the packed goalmouth and perpetrated a seemingly effortless 32 yard shot, landing it with pinpoint accuracy in the far corner of the net – as devastating as a Rafa Nadal baseline to baseline lob.

Those supporters who felt that Yaya was a man for the big occasion who didn't always want to exert himself in more homely encounters got some ammunition from his poor performance, once again as acting captain, against Wigan in the FA Cup fifth round. Certainly he failed to assert leadership that day.

But, in the celebrated surroundings of the Camp Nou, warmly greeted by his former Barcelona teammates, his 25 yard chip played right to Silva's feet, was sheer perfection.

Against Fulham he scored a hat-trick comprising a brace of penalties and a wonderful shot and he wrapped up the scoring at Old Trafford. In what most thought would be the Premiership decider against Liverpool at Anfield, City suffered a bad blow when he was forced to leave the field after fifteen minutes, having twisted his groin attempting a powerful shot.

But, when theopportunity opened again for City at Selhurst Park, following Liverpool's fall from grace against Chelsea, it was Yaya who boldly seized the open door. First, his perfectly executed chip created an early headed goal for Dzeko. Then he scored a magnificent goal himself, climaxing a 50 yard run when he effectively took out seven Palace players. It evoked a touchline exclamation of delight from Pellegrini but, as he sank to his knees after another one -which didn't come off- Palace supporters snickered fatuously.

When City were looking to clinch the title in the run-in, against Villa, Toure launched a glorious ball over the top looking for Edin Dzeko who failed to control it. Later on he unleashed another wonder strike when he ran 60 yards, brushed past two defenders and blasted the ball through keeper Guzan – reminiscent of George Weah in his pomp at Milan! That strike completed twenty goals in a season, an astonishing tally for a midfield player.

It was deplorable that celebrations of City's Premiership triumph were marred when Toure made unsubstantiated remarks critical of the club. Yet nothing can detract from his achievement in a season when his formidable goalscoring sustained City's challenge at a time when three accredited strikers had been injured or had suffered a collapse of form.

Outside of the club context, his friend Samir Nasri has said that Yaya feels underappreciated and that, as an African player, he doesn't receive the acclaim which European and Latin American players, regardless of race, can expect to enjoy. Certainly descriptions of him such as Harry Redknapp's "the human train" are bound to grate with a man who sees himself as a football artist. Formidable as Yaya is in full stride, he's the epitome of relaxation and precision as he prepares to execute his devastating free kicks.

European football fans have had no trouble in appreciating the athletic gifts of African players, embodied by Eusebio's ferocious shooting and Didier Drogba's rugged menace, but have been less inclined to recognise the languid artistry of such as Kanu. As for the great Mario Coluna, architect of Portugal's outstanding 1966 World Cup team, yet born in Mozambique, he had almost faded from collective memory by the time of his death in February 2014. Like George Weah before him (the Weah that alas City never knew), Gnegneri Yaya Toure combines the power of Eusebio and Drogba with the sheer skill of Kanu and the vision of Coluna. If he began his time at the Etihad as a formidable athlete, he had, by 2013-14, added a whole new dimension of artistry.

PABLO ZABALETA - FROM BUENOS AIRES VIA BARLOW MOOR ROAD

Spanish supermodel Christel Castano had sometimes felt sad as she looked out from the windows of her Didsbury flat at yet another rain -drenched Mancunian day. She'd been well aware, of course, that the Manchester climate was not like Barcelona but she didn't know that Oasis nearly christened themselves The Rain. Nor that, in the weirdly English game of cricket, at Old Trafford, two whole five-day test matches, one in 1890 and the other in 1938, had been washed out without a ball bowled. She could've been forgiven for asking herself " how did I get here?" – or, more precisely, how did her Argentinian boyfriend Pablo Zabaleta arrive?

The answer could be found in the dossiers of Mike Rigg, former chief scout to Blackburn Rovers who became Technical Director after Mark Hughes was appointed. In the Eriksson-Shinawatra era, City had relied on video- touting agents hawking their piffling players around and the signing of Rolando Bianchi at £8.8 million – merely on the basis of a brief one-off scoring streak – was only the most notorious of the deals which went through. Instead Rigg used his contacts to set up a network of overseas scouts, one of whom hotfooted it to the Beijing Olympics where he spied Zabaleta, captain of the victorious Argentinian side, stuck in La Liga with modest Espanol and available at £6.5 million.

Castano's appearance at The Avenue/Spinning Fields hunting an Armani jacket at five quid less than a grand provoked Internet trolls to sneer at what they reckoned was a foreigner just like the average England thicko wag. Of course, they scoffed, she'd come over here to scoop the maximum loot from her bf's Abu Dhabi- funded wages. But Christel was a journalist as well as a model and Pablo Zabaleta was an open-minded man. They were more than willing to explore a new culture and he was a player ready to give every last drop of sweat in the service of Manchester City.

Balding and burly, 'Zaba' looked like the oldest twenty-three-year-old to don a Sky Blue shirt but his rugged and wholehearted play would soon make him a cult hero. Accepting Mancini's wingback rotation, alternating with Richards at right back and filling in on the left from time to time, he could score a thunderbolt as he did at Craven Cottage and he could be absurdly sent off as he was at the Emirates after showing restraint when Bacary Sagna squared up. He could also cross coolly as he did for Tevcz' scoring header against Wolves. In the Wembley Derby Semi, he was left with Paul Scholes' stud marks on his bloodstained thigh and Scholes was rightly sent off. At one stage in the Cup campaign he was given indefinite leave to visit his dad Pablo, who was in intensive care in Buenos Aires following a motorbike crash. Like son like father!- Jorge Zabaleta made a speedy recovery and Pablo hastened back to Carrington.

Zabaleta had thoroughly adjusted to life in Manchester. He learned formal English with his private tutor and Manc slang with Les Chapman. He watched the reserves regularly at Hyde, and, before moving out to Cheshire, he and Christel had spent a couple of years in the Didsbury flat. Though she couldn't be persuaded to sample the chippy on Barlow Moor Road, Zaba went there and he also played pool in ' The Barleycorn'. Around the time they got married, she didn't hesitate to say how much they both "loved Manchester and its people". And certainly the Zabaletas were the polar opposites of the superstar footballer and his diva wag.

Zabaleta's love of Mancunian life made it all too easy for his compatriot Carlos Tevez-who, with his wife Vanesa, closeted himself behind his own front door- to rely on him for translation. And, when Sergio Aguero initially hesitated over signing for City, it was Zabaleta who convinced him he'd be happy in Manchester. How appropriate it was that 'Zab' was the one to open the scoring against Q.P.R. on the day Kun finished it and City took the title!

Manuel Pellegrini remembered Zabaleta as a seventeen-year-old junior who was already on the books of San Lorenzo when he took over as coach. The Argentinian's transformation in the eleven years since they'd last been at the same club was something which the new City coach needed time to assess. Eager to give Micah Richards a chance and impressed with his speed, he seems to have soon realised that Roberto Mancini was not far from the mark when he described Richards as "cristalli" and queried his powers of concentration.

In 2013-14 Richards' proneness to injury meant that Zabaleta had to undertake a tremendous workload. Yet, on those rare occasions when Richards deputised, Zabaleta's absence was all too obvious. Stouthearted and popular though the former City junior was, his positional naivety was badly exposed at home against Bayern and in Sunderland. As for the fixture in the Allianz Arena, the turning point came when, after twenty minutes, Richards was withdrawn with a thigh injury and Zabaleta came on. Though Ribery tricked him at first, he refused to be intimidated, stuck to his task and, by the second half, the world-class French winger was reduced to shamming. Joleon Lescott was clearly boosted by Zabaleta's arrival and bucked himself up no end.

Zabaleta once again showed he was the heart and soul of the team in the opening weeks of the season when, with Vincent Kompany injured and the squad taking time to adjust to Pellegrini's preference for a high defensive line, City looked anything but convincing.

There was also the issue of the captaincy. For all the splendour of his attacking play, Yaya Toure, formally vice -captain, showed few powers of leadership. Many Citizens believed Zabaleta would do a far better job. He seemed mortified by the defensive errors at Cardiff, including his own, and had desperately sought to spark the team into life in the early minutes against Hull when the Tigers came close to snatching a two-goal lead. Pellegrini seemed not to share this view, possibly concerned about Zabaleta's tendency to confront referees.

Zaba's indomitable character and streetwise guile were in evidence many times during the second title -winning campaign. Treated for a profuse nosebleed against Everton, he went off, had the blood flow staunched and returned to work a crafty penalty which Aguero converted.

Then there was his astounding resilience. Forced off at Leicester with a hamstring strain, he returned at Craven Cottage only a week later and gave a good account of himself. Violently fouled by Fellaini at Old Trafford, he simply got up, dusted himself down and imperturbably got on with the job.

Above and beyond his qualities of character, Zabaleta was an excellent all-round full-back. Though he could sometimes be caught out of position, his tackles were well timed, notably the one in the box at Anfield when he halted a rampant Sturridge by just getting his studs on the ball. His creative play against high-class opposition was notable. Against Barcelona at home, he set up Silva with a first time chip-volley which forced Valdes into a world-class save from the Spaniard. In the Camp Nou, oblivious to the continuous whistling which, as a former Espanol player, he had to endure, he coped well with Andres Iniesta until he was harshly sent off for dissent by the inept French referee, Lannoy. And it was his perfect cross which provided Dzeko with the goal, in the run-in, against Aston Villa. He could also strike for goal with surprise and despatch. He nearly scored from 35 yards at the KC Stadium and he opened the scoring after only two minutes against West Bromwich Albion.

Pablo Zabaleta had long been a cult hero with City fans and, in Pellegrini's title- winning season, he established himself as an absolute talisman. The Zabaleta song rang out time and time again, both in the Etihad and on away grounds:

Paolo Zabaleta, he is the fuckin' man
He is an Argentinian, he' s harder than Jaap Stam,
He plays in blue and white for Pellegrini's men
And, when we win the League, we'll sing this song again.

Speaking of war, Napoleon remarked " morale is to the technical as two to one"

and Pablo Zabaleta effectively translated this to football when he said " the game is seventy per cent mentality". Not blessed with the technical gifts of his compatriots Carlos Tevez, Sergio Aguero and, above all, his great friend Lionel Messi, he is a man of honour in the best sense of the term.

7

THE REAL CITY NITTY GRITTY

The Nine Key Clashes in the Fight to Get the Title Back

1. The Dynamic Curtain-Raiser

City 4 Newcastle United 0

August 19 2013

Sunshine over Manchester on a Monday evening –Manuel Pellegrini's first Premiership game- against Newcastle-Sky out in force, sceptical pundits and all –of the new signings, Fernandinho starts and so does Navas, Negredo is on the bench-Aguero plays, seems to have recovered fom pre-season injuries

The Magpies leave out French playmaker Yohan Cabaye-his boss, Pardew, makes out his head's been turned by interest from Arsenal-Pardew's on his feet, bawling as usual, Pellegrini's seated, looking focused, slightly tense as he awaits kickoff, tightening the knot of his tie.

Dzeko first into action – leaps to win a header, shrugs off a second defender, lays it off to Zabaleta – Dzeko really leading the line, his new boss has praised him, seems like he feels wanted now.

City springing into life and threatening the Newcastle goal, Zabaleta – Dzeko – Navas – Navas' low ball across the box – Zabaleta gets on it and goes down under Taylor's challenge – look like a penalty but Zab didn't appeal – ball runs loose to Aguero – he shoots but Krul parries it – and Newcastle thump it clear – Citizens love it, the all-out attack!

Kompany great sliding tackle on the touchline – gets up and starts a move, looks like his old self – finds Navas – Jesus, can he shift!

Silva – Navas – he slips a pass through to Zabaleta – the Zabman squares it back to Dzeko – Dzeko shoots – and Krul turns it round – Navas' corner but it's cleared – he's a real live wire, the lad from Seville.

Space is the name of the game and City are finding it!

Out of the blue, Hatem ben Arfa's shot on the run –too erratic for the French squad, they say –but he needs watching, we know what he can do when he's up for it.

Navas' incredible scampering gait!

Goal! Six minutes – Dzeko on the left wing – stupefies that dodgy Debuchy – he crosses – Krul parries and Coloccini can't clear – it bounces up high to the unmarked Silva and he nails it like swatting a fly, a rare header from the little man, thumping it into the back of the Magpie net.- " VAMOS-KAMON!""
Pellegrini pumping his arms, smiling, but he composes himself at once, adjusting his tie.

BLUE MOON, you saw me standing alone, without a dream in my heart, without a love of my own.

Vincent Kompany utterly confident as Newcastle dare to attack – he brushes Gouffran aside and starts a move.

Gutierrez has to hang back to protect the gormless Yanga-Mbiwa fom the joint attack of Navas and Zabaleta – they've started off like a house on fire, those two, really gelling.

Suddenly there's danger, it's Ben Arfa again, who else would it be? – he dances past Clichy, brushes past David Silva, hurdles Lescott and puts Gouffran through. Andre Marriner blows up for offside– the baldheaded barcode sticks it pointlessly in the net.

Pundit favourite Papiss Cisse? Sky would love one of his longshot spectaculars– no danger, Vinny has him in his pocket already.

Contrast in styles, Newcastle hard -running, lung -bursting, City fluid and relaxed, wonder who they get that from, look at the touch-line, there's the answer, Manuel Pellegrini, standing, hands in pockets till there's a need to point something out. Contrast with white -headed Pardew, he's stopped his yelling now, he's stooped, arms folded, almost resigned to Newcastle's fate.

Nice move, Fernandinho – Silva – Dzeko – Dzeko's sweet little pass into the box for Yaya – and Debuchy, crew- cut, tattoo-crazy bluffer of a full-back pulls Yaya down – penalty, SURELY it must be – but no, Mr Marriner, the Brummie blunderer doesn't give it – it was just Yaya's momentum, you see – yeah right!

Free kick for Newcastle and there's Stephen Taylor, all staring eyeballs and zoom -white teeth going up for it, youse'll see me threr me furcan weeyut aboot –but there's nowt doin' for the Geordie hard man.

But you can't forget Ben Arfa – same as the pundits can't forget about him breaking his leg here a couple of years back, supposed to be an extra motivation – he dispossesses Silva – but Lescott gets in a good tackle and stops the move

A lull then Ben Arfa's at it again playing like he's dying to get away from Tyneside before the window closes – he swings a cross – but Zabaleta heads it clear on the run

Papiss Cisse right out of it, head down, staring at the Wonga shirt he didn't want to wear.

Two nil twenty-seven minutes – a fantastic goal – sheer dynamite – Newcastle had actually mounted a half -decent move and paid the price for their insolence – Coloccini – to Ben Arfa – to Cisse, almost the only three barcodes that can play – but Kompany contemptuously robs Cisse with an angled tackle – then the skipper surges forward, keeping possession with neat touches – he steers it through the empty centre circle to Dzeko who's lurking well back – Aguero's ready to run – Coloccini takes his eyes off Dzeko and appeals for offside, Kun's the one he's worried about – but Dzeko, yes Dzeko – executes a dainty little backheel flick – and Kun's clean away – Taylor's racing across to cover – gerrout o me furcan road, Argie boy-he's one on one with Kun – but this is the Aguero of old, in his pomp and fending Taylor off at the edge of the box– he places it clinically beyond Krul's full-length dive – it explodes off the inside base of the far post into the back of the net.

The whole beautiful move takes place within seven seconds-everyone on their feet, jumping for joy – SERGIO- SERGIO AGUERO! Yes, sure but Vinnie the K started it and what about that touch from Dzeko?

Seems like a surreal mélange of past World Cup brilliance across the nations with Kompany as Santamaria, Dzeko as Hagi and Aguero as Romario, that's how good it was!

Pellegrini pumps his arms in delight for the strike and applauds the beauty of it.

Bit of a lull then, on the half-hour, Dzeko's booked after a tussle with Yanga-Mbiwa, he pushes the ball past him – then Mbiwa pushes him down on the goal-line and pushes him again when he's on his knees – Dzeko gets up and he's angry, pushes the man from Marseille, palms on the chest – and here's Mr Marriner dashing up, he's having no more of this here pushing – yellow card for Mbiwa then a yellow for Dzeko – the big Bosnian's incredulous and Kompany protests- some pundit'll soon be saying "of course you know what you can expect if you raise your hands" Taylor tries to rile Dzeko who wisely ignores him

ONE EDDINZHEKO, THERE'S ONLY ONE EDDINZHEKO!

Navas' glorious crossfield ball to Kun – nothing comes of it but what a talented player the little Spaniard is, this green - eyed whippet from Seville!

A City slip-up, F ernandinho caught in possession by Gutierrez – he touches it to Gouffran – Fernandinho's aghast, desperate to stop a breakaway and he trips Gouffran – loose ball and Sissoko's onto it, Mr Marriner waves play on -but Sissoko can't control it and Clichy blasts it into touch – Mr Marriner goes back and books Fernandinho.

Sissoko hauls down Aguero, boos erupt – Mr Marriner books Sissoko– the barcodes know they're beaten and they're getting dirty.

Navas takes the freekick – he swirls it tantalisingly close to Dzeko's outstretched boot and it eludes the entire Geordie defence passing just beyond the far post-

applause ringing all around the stadium for City's classy football and utter dominance.

Zabaleta tackles Tiote out – Fernandinho picks up the loose ball – prompts Dzeko neatly – he bursts into the box but slips at the crucial moment – groans all round but more of disappointment really, not derision, as they might have been last season.

Nearly 40 minutes, Newcastle's first shot on target – sort of, Ben Arfa's shot was going just wide but Joe Hart pounced on it anyway, Hart's been a spectator all half, just wanted a piece of the action

Navas buzzing again and Mbiwa recklessly barges him after the whistle, over the touchline – "get yer book out, Marriner!" – but that would mean sending him off and he ain't going to do it – heavy boos all over the Etihad and it doesn't stop the Brummie whistler punishing Dzeko, giving a foul for just a strong tackle.

Dzeko turns away from Coloccini and hits a glorious ball to Aguero out wide – he finds Silva – back to Dzeko but he shoots wide from 8 yards.

Suddenly the barcode cracks open into a fissure, Hart's long, high kick from hand right out towards Aguero on the touchline, heads up with Taylor, Aguero tumbles, Taylor's sideswiped him over the head – Mr Marriner instantly dismisses Taylor, what else could he do?

Pardew looks miserable – he swigs from his water bottle, really it's brandy he needs, the Magpies are taking a helluva beating and now he's down to ten men

Half time, forty-five minutes of the new era, highly impressive display of fluid, interchanging football and relaxed attacking, never desperate but always persistent. And here's another difference from Roberto Mancini, Bobby Manc did a hell of a lot for Manchester City, no doubt about it, instilled will to win with painstaking lateral passing coming out of tight defence but, Italian to the core, he played without risk. Not so Manuel Pellegrini!

Lull after the resumption for a few minutes then nearly another goal, Tiote misses his tackle on Aguero and the ball runs to Dzeko – Dzeko plays in Navas wide in the box – Navas' cross eludes Coloccini, rebounds off the young Geordie sub Dummett to Silva – Aguero calls for a ball in the box – Silva provides it – Aguero turns brilliantly past two defenders – stands up a chip for Dzeko – who slips his marker and powers a header – goal, it MUST be – no, Krul saves it at point-blank range, tremendous stop – and Newcastle thump it clear.

Debuchy at it again – can't deal with Aguero so he pushes him down on the edge of the box
And it's three-nil direct from the free kick, Yaya flights it smoothly just over the crumbling wall, Krul can't get to it, shakes his head.
Pellegrini applauds hugs all round for Yaya, even one from Nasri, racing along the touchline with his sub's bib on, "VAS-Y!

Newcastle totally defensive in the face of City's utter dominance- Ben Arfa sacrificed in the interests of damage limitation.

Silva feeds Navas – this time he goes for the pullback instead of the cross – he finds Clichy in plenty of space, unmarked – Clichy shoots but Krul blocks it and it rebounds over the bar

On the hour, Aguero's done enough on his comeback and he goes off to be replaced by Nasri.

After a lull, Kompany storms forward past three men and feeds Navas –who forces a corner, every time he touches the ball Navas spells trouble for Newcastle.

Suddenly a dismal blot on a glorious evening, Ameobi breaking on the left touchline – and Zabaleta's not there – Kompany has to move over to confront Ameobi – he forces the ball into touch with a powerful sliding tackle and – OH NO! – the skipper's lying prone, grimacing in pain, hand to groin.

He gets up but this doesn't look good at all. Manuel Pellegrini looking very concerned indeed – Kompany limps off – Pellegrini summons Garcia – this is the last thing we needed.

Lescott a nervy clearance, reacting straightaway to the loss of his skipper-several minutes of City inactivity, collective reaction to the loss of Vinnie

Then it' s 4-0, dreadful Newcastle defending, Zabaleta steers a pass intended for Dzeko – and Mbiwa tries to pull Dzeko down but can't – the ball runs clear into bags of unguarded space – Nasri easily outsprints the dozy Debuchy – he's only got Krul to beat – and, cool as you please, he picks his spot from 15 yards-Nasri loves a laugh and he's grinning from ear to ear, ON Y VA!

MANCHESTER CITY, WE'RE TOP OF THE LEAGUE !- and this is literally true because United only won 4-1 at the Liberty Stadium yesterday.

Yaya starts a counter – Silva – to Navas out wide – Navas hoists yet another fine cross – Dzeko well marked by Coloccini but he outjumps the Argentinian and powers a header only just over the bar – Dzeko, he's done so much work this evening but hasn't a goal to show for it

Ten minutes left, Negredo on for Silva – applauded all the way – Negredo on the eve of his twenty-eighth birthday, none of your Liverpool moneyball nonsense here.

Fernandinho long ball to Negredo– he gets on it but not quickly enough to stop Debuchy forcing a corner, Debuchy's done his job for once and from that corner City should be five up, but the linesman wrongly flags Negredo offside and Mr Marriner doesn't overrule him.

Nasri took the corner, Garcia headed for goal – Krul parries it beyond Dzeko – but Negredo cracks it in in at the far post the big, rugged Spanish striker stands in front of the fans behind the goal, arms raised in jubilation till it's chalked off Negredo chokes his disappointment and salutes Fernandinho's initial pass.

Final whistle and Newcastle got what they deserved, indeed they were lucky to to be let off relatively lightly. Manuel Pellegrini shakes hands with all his players as they troop off the pitch, special word for Dzeko -seems like a man reborn under his new coach – and Navas too, a fantastic debut. Let's not forget Sergio Aguero, that finish was as good as any produced in the title year. And David Silva was here, there and everywhere with many a delicate, prompting touch – just like the maestro of old.

It'll be no easy task getting the title back, challenging Chelsea who've reinstalled their ruthless pragmatist Jose Mourinho, and, though Ferguson's quit the swamp, he's left Moyes with a strong squad. The only real cloud on the horizon is Vincent Kompany's injury. He may well be out for several weeks and centre-back's where City are weakest, already suffered one unlucky blow pre-season when the promising Mati Nastasic was injured in Asia.That leaves only honest but technically limited Joleon Lescott (alright when he's with VK), the cringeworthy Garcia and the erratic Boyatta.

But this still feels like the start of a new era, Manuel Pellegrini's mission statement, attacking football, fluid interpassing, positional interchanges – and GOALS GALORE! Yes, Newcastle played a full half with ten men but they were a badly beaten side long before that. Pipe down you pundits, don't dismiss this as "pretty football and it gets you nowhere!". This was beautiful winning football, the Geordies appreciated that but this was built from defence, high line but resolute, founded not on volatile enthusiasm, not on Keeganesque "go out there and drop hand grenades!" but on Pellegrini's calm conviction, his quiet self-belief, his presidential confidence coolly transmitted to his players.

2. Demolition Derby a la Vivaldi

City 4 United 1

September 22 2013

Summer's just ended but Manchester's bathed in warm sunshine as new United boss David Moyes, ' The Chosen One', brings his squad to the Etihad for the first time – and the news is that Robin van Persie's out due to a thigh strain. Moyes has chosen Welbeck to replace him, not Hernandez. He prefers Ashley Young to Kagawa and also keeps Nani and Cleverly on the bench. He signed Fellaini from Everton on the last day of the window and plays him now. Smalling's in at right back because Rafael's injured. So's Big Jones. Giggs, now player-coach, doesn't play today. Moyes sits next to Phil Neville, his new assistant. Somehow, the rollcall of their names sounds ordinary indeed!

City are still without Silva and Clichy with Nasri and Kolarov continuing to deputise. And Edin Dzeko, though he scored in Pilsen, stands down in favour of Alvaro Negredo.

Khaldoun has flown in for the big one and sits next to Ferran Soriano.

Howard Webb's in charge, much to the consternation of most Citizens.

Half a minute gone, hold your breath! Welbeck charges into Kompany's intended clearance and makes off with the ball – but Vince recovers at once – Welbeck loses the ball and it goes out for a goal kick.

Then Rooney, looking like a rugby league scrum-half with a heavy black headband covering his Carrington wound, prompts Welbeck who's gone wide of Nastasic – but the Longsight Laddie slips at the crucial moment.

Five minutes, and there's controversy already, Nastasic booked for a simple clash of heads with Smalling, Nasty launched himself into a straightforward aerial challenge but Smalling came off worst and he's lying flat on the turf. Mr Webb produces yellow – Yaya complains bitterly – roars of rage all round the Etihad.

Ten minutes, and City swing into action, Yaya – Negredo – a clever dummy from him – and Aguero's in – he feeds the overlapping Kolarov – Kolarov whips a cross on the run – and Vidic is forced to head it behind for a corner – Vidic looks worried, holding his head.

Nowt from the corner, de Gea punches it away but the crowd are roaring, delighted with what they see

More City pressure and more aggravation, Yaya tries a shot – it skims off Vidic's shins and goes for a corner – United desperate to get it out anywhere but Aguero's clear right on the touchline – Rooney chases after him and they tussle for the ball – Rooney pushes Aguero down – Mr Webb blows for a foul – Rooney's furious and he kicks the ball right at the prone Kun – roars of rage, " fuck off, you fat Scouse twat!" Rooney's palms up, WHO, ME? Mr Webb doesn't book him and Citizens are inflamed and rightly so. This was dissent and dangerous play all wrapped in one but Mr Webb did nothing.

Martin Tyler'll be going on about how Mr Webb must be the greatest ref in the world because he handled the World Cup Final. Of course, Webb looks like a top ref, brawny copper, shaven -headed, looking hard, keeping up athletically with the play and all the rest of it.

Nothing comes of the free kick and Rooney's throwing himself into the hurly-burly – he sends Young away – but Navas is tracking back and he dispossesses Young – really good how Pellegrini's using Navas' speed defensively as well as in attack

Sixteen minutes 1-0, and City's classy football breaks through with a brilliant goal, Nasri's skill on the ball is the fulcrum, Aguero's explosive finish is the end product, Nasri turns Smalling inside out, feinting, foot on the ball – and he does it slowly, craftily allowing Kolarov time to sprint into an overlap – then Nasri back- heels it to him – Kolarov's low cross on the run, guided between the central defenders and it drops just right for Aguero to volley – ah no, he's slightly behind the ball – no problem, he twists like a contortionist and lashes it home first time then he takes off in a wild run of celebration, eyes glazed, looks maniacal, gesticulating frantically, Kun the killer, now he's bear-hugged by Negredo and Navas – SI, SI, we mean yes, ARRIBA! Nasri and Kolarov created it, say it in French, Spanish or Serbo-Croat, this is one hell of a goal!

Pellegrini on his feet, smiling, arms pumping at a beautiful move, finished like exploding dynamite the crowd are ignited, they know what this means – and so does Vidic, their big, gloomy Serb skipper, he grimly calls Valencia over, pointing to the space where Kolarov ran free, unhindered by the little dozer from Ecuador.

No more than a minute later a long, sustained City move, could've been a great team goal – Kompany's header out of defence – he finds Aguero – Navas – back to Aguero – he delivers a crossfield ball to Negredo, don't these Spanish names sound like music! – Negredo thinks about a shot, changes his mind – lays it off to Zabaleta – United not breached yet, patience, patience – to Nasri – Yaya – he widens the play, finds Navas – Navas' cross to the far post – Smalling goes up for it with Zabaleta, just gets something on it but can only divert it to Nasri – Nasri's in space, he'll score for sure – he shoots, but no, it dips over the bar – Nasri grits his teeth in self -annoyance " FAKEEN SHEET- BAH!"

United try to hit back but Carrick's getting no midfield support from Young and Valencia, Fellaini's crude, Rooney's well pissed off with his teammates, he's working his socks off trying to get something going – he leaps for a ball with Kompany but big Vinny's all over him. He's just too big and strong for Rooney's Scouse scrapping – now Rooney's whining to the ref – but Mr Webb won't give a freekick, no, Wayne, can't oblige

A minute later, same thing, and Rooney's headband's off, his forehead's covered with a bandage, he's standing there with his headband in his hand seeking redress from Mr Webb – "'e's pushed THIS off, look wharrydone!" But Mr Webb jogs off – Rooney runs after him, "ahr eh, ref ?, AHR EH!" But Mr Webb's having none of it –"FUGSACHE!"

United's first good move, hell it's their only move and they've had to wait twenty-four minutes for it, a counter – quick transition from Fellaini to Welbeck – Welbeck shunts the ball towards Rooney – but Rooney hasn't bent his run – he's offside, flag's up, he shoots anyway but mishits it and Hart collects with ease, jeers all round for the comeuppance of a Scouser.

Next move, Negredo's on the ball – he prompts Kolarov – Kolarov's full steam ahead – he races into the box but loses control and collides with Smalling- and he goes down – Citizens scream for a pen – the ball bounces away for a corner – Mr Webb smiles, he's not deceived – Kolarov gets up, vigorously tapping his chest," NAAH -I bounce off 'im 'ERE, thassit!", worried Mr Webb's gonna book him for diving, Mr Webb smiles, he wasn't going to anyway, Nasri's waiting to take the flag kick, grinning his head off, ben' lors, faut rire, uh, you've got to have a laugh sometimes when tension's so high, he thinks, nowt comes of it.

Incident -packed, you can't take your eyes off it for a moment, free-kick now just outside the box – Kolarov'll take it and he takes it short, a training ground move -but Evra's read it, he easily clears, some in the crowd groan- "COLLAR OFF!"

Rooney sends Valencia away – and Kolarov loses him – the moaners again, "WAKE UP, COLLAROFF, will yer!"– but Nasty bails him out, thing is there was a lot of pundit talk beforehand about Kolarov's susceptibility against Valencia – but Pellegrini, he knew Valencia from Villareal, knows his skill but knows his lack of concentration too, he doesn't like the defensive work and Pellegrini's instilled it into Kolarov's mind, attack him, drive him back, he'll switch off and he won't bother you.

Just before the half-hour and Rooney's booked, now there's a laugh, most Citizens reckon Mr Webb's too chummy by half with the Roonster but now he's booked him when it was actually Vince who fouled HIM – Rooney can't believe it, he's gurning his head off, cheers from the crowd, "shut yer cake 'ole, Shrek, stupid sod!"

But Moyes is indignant, no wonder really, and he's glad to be up and about having something to shout about, till then he's been slumped in his seat, gobsmacked from the shock of it all but now he's jumped up and he's got plenty to say to Mr Mullarkey, the linesman – nothing doing so he goes over and speaks to Mr Oliver, the fourth official, still to no avail.

What about Fernandinho? – unspectacular player, easy to overlook him, but he's made no mistakes today, seems to be getting the hang of the Premiership pace and allowing Yaya to get forward – and when Yaya gets forward the opposition quail!

United get the ball to Young – he's in space, out wide, where he likes to be – but all he does is to thump a futile cross straight into Joe Hart's gloves – what is it with Young? Is that all they ever taught him at Villa Park? or is it because Moyes has had words with him, told him off about his diving, you know, The Man Who Fell to Earth, he's on good behaviour and it's inhibiting his game.

Couple of minutes before half-time and Jesus Navas is breaking away just within the touchline – but Mr Mullarkey thinks he's over-stepped the mark – he's flagged for a throw in – and Navas is angry, how dare you impugn my ball control !– Mr Webb overrules Mr Mullarkey and there's a hiatus –

just the time for Pellegrini to come right to the touchline, he has a word with Zabaleta, it's in Spanish of course, one last push, let's get a second before half-time.

Zabaleta taking the throw-in which Mr Webb awarded, he sees United are perplexed and have switched off – quick throw in to Navas standing completely unmarked – quick thinking and you can say the same for Navas – he stoops and heads it back to Zaba who took off as soon as he threw – he forces a corner

In stoppage time, 2-0, Nasri's corner, well floated-Negredo's pulled away from his marker, twelve yards out, then he leaps and beats Smalling to it and heads it down, danger and disarray in the United defence, Ferdinand's dosing, he's deserted his post – Yaya steals in, connects on the far post, knees it into the back of the net

Pellegrini up smiling and pumping his arms, "BRAVO, BOYS!"

Yaya runs away, a huge grin of sheer delight, then he's spreadeagled on the turf, his teammates beside him gently pulling him up, Gulliver the Great, not one of his most artistic goals, no it certainly isn't but, in the time moment, in the context, it sure as hell is a great goal !

Second-half, Moyes has made no changes and Pellegrini didn't need to!

3-0 within a minute City score again – Kompany breaks United up – Aguero – Navas – wide to Nasri – he cuts sharply inside and slides a sweet pass to Negredo – Negredo leaves Ferdinand for dead – Vidic desperately challenges him in the box– and they tussle for the ball shoulder to shoulder all the way to the byline – Vidic, rugged as he is, simply cannot shift Negredo off the ball – and just before the line, Negredo turns him and, all in one movement, crosses it low into the centre of the goalmouth – Aguero's steaming in – he stabs a volley – de Gea tries to palm it out – but there's too much sting in it and it's in the back of the net –

Aguero with his second goal, doesn't react like the first time, he just smiles broadly, laughing his head off at the way United are being dismantled –

he races behind the net, saluting the Citizens, then comes back on the pitch to be hugged by Negredo and Nasri, the ones who created it, Citizens in absolute ecstasy – de Gea palms down, arms outstretched, SOMEONE TELL ME, HOW CAN I COPE WITH THIS ?? –

Ferdinand head down, humiliated, speechless. Moyes on the bench, slumped, head in his hands, then he stirs himself and motions to Cleverly to warm up, he's making a change but why on earth didn't he make it at half-time ?, that's their problem, who cares, blue moon, BLUE MOON!

Three minutes later and its 4-0, a United attack fizzles out and Kompany surges out – he sends Navas clean away down the flank – Navas' tremendous burst of speed, Navas the treadmill- buster – and there's Kompany himself, storming forward, running the whole length of the pitch, uberdecoy– Navas gets into the box – Fellaini can't get near him, Ferdinand can only stand and watch– Vidic is distracted by Kompany going right on into the six yard box –   Navas looks up, and looks up again, this lad's got a brain as well as lungs –Negredo's waiting to pounce – but he hears a call from Nasri, lurking a few yards behind, LEAVE IT! – and Negredo ducks out – thing was, Valencia was bewildered and hadn't marked Nasri – so the Frenchman calmly waits for the ball to drop to him – and he promptly volleys it into the net

Nasri takes off for the corner flag and punches it in sheer delight – open-mouthed now, he's in a world of his own, LOUFOQUE, HUH! while Vincent Kompany, whose lung -bursting run sowed terror in United's ranks, is on his knees on the goal-line, arms raised in triumph, face wreathed in smiles.

The stadium's in uproar, Pellegrini's beaming.

Moyes is slumped, averting his eyes, his head in his hands. Rooney stares, expressionless, dry-mouthed in shock.

behind the goal, they're doing the Poznan again, Blue Moon, you saw me standing alone without a dream in my heart, without love of love of my own

Then merciless humour takes over, " there's ONLY ONE DAVID MOYES, there's only one David Moyes!!

Couple of minutes later and there's nearly a fifth – Yaya skies a clearance – but Negredo traps it on his toes with a delicate touch – he immediately lays it off to Aguero – he dashes away, City steam forward – Aguero to Navas – Navas lays it off to Negredo – he's right in and he must score – but no, Vidic's tremendous last-ditch tackle saves United from total humiliation.

Evra makes a run down the left – he crosses – but Kompany heads it clear, steers it actually, starting a brilliant move – to Yaya – who lays it off to Aguero and surges forward – Kun's tackled – but he plays Negredo in – Ferdinand runs out to confront Negredo – he's desperate now, pushing, shoving and shirt -pulling but Negredo holds him off with contemptuous ease – he waits for the right moment and calmly passes back to Zabaleta – then Zaba feeds Yaya, full steam ahead – Yaya's round Fellaini as if he wasn't there – he shoots but, what a shame, his shot's not the best and de Gea just manages to turn it round for a corner, a magnificent team move which deserved a goal.

One thing though, just over the hour and City's pace has slackened, inevitably, they put so much into that hellfire opening, they've been so completely on top, playing dream football.

United start to come into it, they've got possession, but it's just vacant possession – they can't do anything with it, their passing's laboured and predictable where City were fluent and imaginative

United make a move, get a freekick just outside the box – Rooney steps up but he can only blast it lamely into the wall, roars of delighted derision all round.

The first City substitution – Milner's on for Jesus Navas – Navas is applauded off, quite rightly so – he shakes hands with Pellegrini

Nasri, still well up for it, probably his finest game in a sky blue shirt – he barges Ferdinand out of his way like he was shoving aside a snotty- nosed kid in the back streets of Marseilles – the ball runs to Negredo – he shoots – but slices it high and wide

Fifteen minutes left and signs of anti-climax, for all their improved ball possession United can't really put together an incisive move

Negredo off, replaced by Dzeko – warm applause for big Alf and a warm handshake from Pellegrini too – the so-called 'Beast' has well and truly imposed himself in the physical challenges – probably why he was picked – but he's shown many subtle touches as well, not to mention providing a key assist for two goals.

City break – a through ball to Dzeko – he drives a shot – it's straight at de Gea but powerful – and the keeper fumbles it – it's out of his grasp and it's going to trickle in at the right-hand post – but de Gea scrambles and clutches it just before it goes over the line – WHOAA!

Last ten and United are now doing some useful work against a tiring City, Valencia forces a corner – Evra leaps high and heads it -it thwacks off the post – Dzeko tries to blast it clear but only finds Rooney – Rooney drives the ball back into the ruck but Hart saves.

Nastasic fouls Rooney – looks worried, because he was booked in the first few minutes – but Mr Webb takes no action

4-1, Rooney takes the freekick, twenty yards out – it's an unstoppable drive, hit precisely over the wall, accelerating into the top corner, Hart has no chance with it, no keeper would've done

Behind the goal, the Rags muster a cheer, United are beaten, humbled, but it's stopped short of a tennis scoreline, a lot of that's due to Rooney's industry even before his goal, Rooney knows it, he sees no point in the slightest celebration, just shoots a glance at his teammates, I DONE MY JOB, wharrabout YOUSE?

Stoppage time and Fernandinho steams past Valencia – and sets up Dzeko-Dzeko shoots, just inches wide, soft groan from Citizens, last chance to add one more.

Final whistle, an ashen- faced Moyes steels himself to shake hands with Manuel Pellegrini -who has totally triumphed today!

Vincent Kompany " here's to you-City loves you more than you will know!"
Courtesy Photo Works: Shutterstock

Sergio Aguero "up steps an Argentine who scores a goal in Fergie time!"
Courtesy Jagget Rashidi: Shutterstock

David Silva "he is the maestro of Maine Road!"

Courtesy Photo Works: Shutterstock

Yaya Toure "oh, before you break away and you score!"
Courtesy Jagget Rashidi: Shutterstock

Pablo Zabaleta "he is an Argentinian, he's harder than Jaap Stam!"
Courtesy Maxisport: Shutterstock

Graham Gordon

Postscript

To mark the occasion, the official club site issued videos featuring slow motion footage of City's victory, one silent, the other featuring close-ups of the fans accompanied by extracts from Vivaldi's 'Four Seasons'.

These videos, for which no one was credited, are works of art, elevating football skills alongside cinematic technique and beautiful music. Where a lesser producer would have dumbed it down with electronica or rock, here someone chose the dazzling ebullience of Vivaldi violins.

What shines through is City's high individual skill (Nasri's foot on ball, extreme swerve mastery) devastating finishing (Aguero's acrobatic, explosive volley), intelligence (Negredo choosing exactly the right moment to cross for Aguero's second goal, Negredo responding to a call from the better placed Nasri for the fourth).

United, pundit -boosted, are revealed (following the departure of their inspirational Clydesider who made them more than the sum of their parts) as distinctly second-rate, desolate in their mediocrity.

Apart only from Yaya's ostentatious bellyflop after his knee-in, City's celebrations are without show business – there's just the sheer jubilation of Aguero and Nasri and the comradely hugs which follow.

Above all, however, it's the Citizens who are the stars, their faces captured in close up as they thrill to City's sparkling performance. This is old school crowd celebration, far removed from the hooligan-blighted Eighties, reaching back to the days of Joe Mercer and even to Wilf Wild. Though there are, of course, a few glimpses of ritual aggression - of 'bragging rights' in the pundits' cherished, banal phrase-there's a notable absence of machismo as the cameras concentrate on mild-mannered young blokes, notably the chubby lad moved to tears and comforted by his dad, and the initially sceptical then incredulous older geezers.

And, amongst the City supporters, it's above all the women who stand out. There are unforgettable shots of: a young blonde in a pink shirt with red and black diagonal stripes, nervously pushing her hair back from her face then blowing out her cheeks in relief at danger which has passed; a dark -skinned brunette, teeth clenched with tension, eyes lighting up with the expectation of a goal; a white-haired older lady in glasses and with earrings, covering her mouth with her knuckles, worried at first then beatific, delighted at the turn of events; another older lady with grey hair in a purple cardigan, a nan with her granddaughter, clenching her shoulders in fear of something going wrong then wiping tears of joy from her eyes.

Young and old, men and women alike, these were the ones who'd suffered in the Swales Era and in its aftermath, those who made jokes about it just to survive it, all those who endured jibes about 'Noisy Neighbours' and 'The Temple of Doom ', uplifted now by the renaissance a great club.

Here is something far nobler than World Cup fanaticism, TV showbiz and nerd play –there are no flags, no wigs, no face paint, no religiosity, no dumbass selfies, no silly totties, all bare midriff and blowing kisses to the cameras. This has been a Demolition Derby, right enough, but one achieved by scintillating football, purveyed by Manuel Pellegrini and his players for the Citizens of Manchester and captured on film against the classic strains of Antonio Vivaldi.

3. The Master and the Student

City 6   Tottenham Hotspur 0

November 24 2013

Tottenham arrive, well placed in the table, only six goals conceded so far. City make changes after the dismal defeat at Sunderland – the return of Fernandinho from injury (how badly he was missed in the Stadium of Light!) Zabaleta replaces Richards, another big plus. Clichy comes in for Kolarov, Nastasic returns and Jesus Navas starts.

Andre Villas –Boas, the young Spurs boss, surprisingly selects the half -German Holtby ahead of the clever Belgian Dembele and the Argentinian Lamela at the expense of England highflyer Andros Townsend. His Danish playmaker Christian Eriksen was injured on international duty but French international keeper, Hugo Lloris, returns.

On Metrolink before the match, a bloke was slagging off Navas, claiming he didn't turn up for the big games and couldn't take a knock. He will be proved dramatically wrong inside fifteen seconds.

Kick-off, the ball goes back to Lloris – his kick's crap and Aguero pounces – he shoots – Lloris parries it – but, with extreme speed and despatch, Navas races in, heedless of the bulky Kaboul, and flights a perfect chip over Lloris' head to nestle just inside the far post.
This is Navas' first Premiership goal for City – he takes off in a wild run, face lit up with delight and leaps over the corner flag in sheer jubilation- SI-SI-SI-SI-SI!
Lloris goes white as a sheet and, on the bench, AVB looks stunned.

Within two minutes Spurs come close to equalising – the balding, bearded Brazilian Sandro sends speed merchant Kyle Walker storming down the right flank – he gets past Clichy – he steers a low cross through the six yard box – almost disastrously Pantilimon and Demichelis both go for the same ball – Pantilimon manages to push it out – Lamela gets on it and shoots from an angle – keeper and centre back once again in a muddle – but Demichelis kicks it off the line-what a let-off!

Five minutes, and City trouble Spurs again, Aguero should really score – Negredo puts him through – but he tries to dink the keeper – and, as he falls, Lloris sticks up a hand and pushes the ball away

Despite the defensive rick, Manuel Pellegrini's smiling broadly, looks like he's pleased the way City are moving.

Next up, City are denied a penalty by the dreaded Howard Webb, Negredo puts Nasri through – and Sandro tackles him from behind bringing him down – but Mr Webb ignores the appeals – Nasri gets up and pulls one hell of a face, like a full binbag's been held to his nostrils – a storm of booing – "E'S BIASED, I'm tellin' yer, old baldie –headed Yorkshire get !"

It would be comic if it wasn't at City's expense – the two Tottenham Brazilians, Sandro and Paulinho, collide and, as Sandro falls, Mr Webb awards Spurs a freekick – Vertonghen takes it but shoots straight at Pantilimon.

Twenty-five minutes gone, and a bizarre incident as Sandro, already booked, sinks to his knees, he's been ill during the week and he throws up now

"Eh, you, dontchew puke on our pitch !"

couple of minutes' delay while Sandro gets treatment onfield, during which Pellegrini calls Nasri over and gives instructions – Nasri nods.

City pressing unconvincingly forward –   the crowd want more action – " SHIFT YERSELF YAYA, CHRISSAKE!"

Just past the half-hour,, City go two nil up via a Sandro own goal – another weak Lloris' clearance finds Nasri – to Aguero – he forces a save from Lloris – it rebounds to Negredo – he lashes it goalward – Kaboul clears off the line – but it only rebounds off Sandro into the net – Negredo does an uncharacteristic knee slide, almost as if pre-empting the Dubious Goals Committee – still it's announced as an own goal.

Sandro in the thick of events – Navas darts past Sandro who's fouling him – Mr Webb plays advantage – it peters out and Mr Webb fails to go back and book Sandro – which would mean his dismissal, of course- Citizens erupt in anger.

Spurs trying to get into the game – Mr . Webb books Vertonghen for fouling Zabaleta – but fails to act when Dawson bodychecks Aguero – Pellegrini comes to the touchline and complains to Mr Webb – Citizens jeer the allegedly Rag- loving Yorkshire cop.

Five minutes left before halftime and City take a three nil lead – Zabaleta points Navas to run into bags of space wide right – and presents him with a good pass- Navas steers a neat ball across the six yard box – where Aguero's lurking unmarked – he opens his body and slots the ball home. VAMOS!

What a strange half of football, that fantastic start then anti-climax, yet City are three goals up, despite not playing to their best. Howard Webb's been the fly in the ointment, of course, and Pellegrini took too long to protest his one-sided decisions. Even so, City have been too good for Spurs and the boss has finally spoken out.

Second-half and AVB has decided to replace Holtby with City reject Emmanuel Adebayor – Joleon Lescott comes on for Nastasic who's taken a knock, despite having little to do in marking the totally ineffective Soldado

Four minutes in and City score a wonderful team goal of which Yaya's gut -busting surge is the fulcrum – Fernandinho one-two with Yaya – Yaya dodges from behind Kaboul and Vertonghen and darts forward – Negredo reads him and calls for the ball – he gets it, toe-trapping it instantly and scooping it precisely into Yaya's path as he steams forward at full tilt – Walker rushes back and tries to stop him by fair means or foul – but Yaya's far too strong for him – Aguero' s made a parallel run – and moving at full tilt, Yaya clips a precise pass across the box behind Michael Dawson – Kun extends his leg and pings the ball home

Citizens roar with delight at this fantastic strike, Negredo goes over to lift Yaya whose momentum has sent him to the turf, in this instance the assist is more vital than the strike. What an enigma Yaya can be, turning it on like that after his lacklustre first half!

in the technical area Manuel Pellegrini's beaming broadly – BRAVO BRAVO !!

A couple of minutes later, it could've been five, Aguero finds Nasri-Nasri, half-crouching, flights a sublime chip over Lloris' head but it rebounds into play off the crossbar – Nasri flops to the turf in disap-pointment – someone says the Frenchman didn't mean it, it came off the outside of his foot and someone else reckons he intended a cross – not so, he faced the keeper directly and anyway there was no-one to pass to- what's more, Nasri's always quick to laugh about strange turns of events – but he was deadly serious over this one!

A few minutes after that, City do indeed go five goals up with a superb individual strike – it's Alvaro Negredo, he calls for the ball – Fernandinho steers it towards him – in one move, Negredo turns Dawson inside out and tees the ball up at the back of him, almost as if he's passed to himself ! – Dawson desperately tries to stop him, palm-ing him right in the face – Alf shrug it off- pivots- and explodes an absolute rocket beyond the helpless Lloris.

BEAST! BEAST!! BEAST!!! BEAST!!!!

Strange in a way that this nickname has followed Alvaro Negredo from Spain, yes, he's a big, rugged bloke but his touch is exquisite and his football brain is sharp as a blade.

On the hour AVB resignedly brings Dembele and Sigurdsson on for Paulinho and Soldado, far too late in reversing his early selection blunders.

Pellegrini gestures City forward, he promised, when he first came in, that he'd never let the team rest on their laurels-and he keeps his word!

Zabaleta attacking space, he wants in on the goal action – he cuts in and shoots hard – but Sandro desperately gets in a full stretch block and sends it looping for a corner.

Navas tormenting Vertonghen down the right flank-low cross into the six yard box – Nasri almost on to it- Spurs get a block in, just.

Aguero off to an ovation, he's replaced by Garcia-still there's no let-up in the action, Navas stands up a cross for Negredo – but, though he's unmarked, he heads the ball just over-he grits his teeth in annoyance.

A long crossfield ball sends mighty mouse Navas away- he delivers a fine low cross to Yaya driving in just outside the box, marked by Sandro and Dawson- they can' t stop Yaya fizzing in a sidefoot shot –it beats Lloris and curls an inch over the bar.

With fifteen minutes left, Samir Nasri comes off - to sustained and fully desrved applause – a tremendous stint in the continuing absence of Silva.

this is the end of a long white hot spell by City, fully thirty minutes of the second half it's lasted, with a five goal lead, the pace inevitably slackens sooner or later.

Ten minutes left, Fernandinho misses an absolute sitter – he totally fluffs his lines only five yards out and unmarked, a shame really as he's done a lot of hard grafting today, fetching and carrying for Yaya.

Spurs force a belated corner – ironic humour from their fans "we only sing when we're shit !"

But their humiliation is not yet complete, a couple of minutes into stoppage time – a huge 50 yard lofted ball from Milner, aimed for Navas – Vertonghen should really cut it out – but he fails – Navas is clean through, one-on-one with Lloris – he takes his time and slots it past the French keeper, Navas grins from ear to ear,   MUY CONTENTO ! -this has been his best game in a City shirt.

So Spurs have conceded more in one afternoon than in the whole of the season till now- and the thirty- six year old Andres Villas Boas, only four years into his vaunted coaching career, suffers by comparison with Manuel Pellegrini who has a quarter of a century's experience to draw on. It's a question of master and student really !What's more, Daniel Levy's spending spree with the money received from Real Madrid for the sale of Gareth Bale looks ill-advised in comparison to City's astute purchase of Fernandinho, Negredo and Navas. Seven players have been brought to White Hart Lane for a total of £105 million yet each one has failed to shine or gell with teammates.

Manuel Pellegrini's reluctance to challenge referees has been his one real weakness in the campaign so far and he signally failed to confront Mr. Webb at Stamford Bridge. Now he's done it and, intriguingly, the ex- Yorkshire cop, Sergeant Webb of Rotherham, made no errors in the second half. Turning to the squad, they've known Pellegrini's qualities as connoisseur, tactician and father figure right from the start. And, on this day, when they saw him standing up for them in the heat of battle, they responded with a scintillating second half display.

4. Anything You Can Do, We Can Do Better!

City 6   Arsenal 3

December 14 2013

A vitally important clash with Premiership leaders Arsenal arriving at the Etihad boasting a six-point lead over City. In the Champions League, they played one day later, losing in Naples whereas City won in Munich. Midfield revelation Aaron Ramsey, benched against Napoli, returns. Both Theo Walcott and Bacary Sagna return after injury but Mikel Arteta is suspended while Santi Cazorla is benched.

For City, James Milner, Aleksandar Kolarov and Jesus Navas return to the bench despite fine performances in Munich. Samir Nasri and Gael Clichy are preferred with the two rested strikers, Aguero and Negredo, returning.

Manuel Pellegrini and Arsene Wenger shake hands amicably. They last met in the Champions League semi-final in 2006 when Arsenal narrowly prevailed over Pellegrini's Villareal.

City surge into the attack straight from the kick-off – they win a freekick which Sagna clears. Next they win a corner which Nasri takes, heavily booed by the solid phalanx of Gooners in the South Stand, his perceived desertion not forgiven. Another City corner – Mertesacker, skipper in the absence of Arteta, clears it, just about.

Arsenal are trapped in their own half with Aaron Ramsey aggressively scrapping for the ball, Ramsey, he's been at the heart of the Gunners' renaissance this season, the year of his personal resurrection after three years of trauma, his leg stove in by Shawcross at Stoke, not just a midfield competitor now but a freescoring attacker as well.

Pinball in the Arsenal goalmouth, seven and a half minutes before Arsenal can break out, they win a freekick – but Negredo heads the ball clear.

City attack again, Silva – Zabaleta overlapping – he crosses low into the box but Flamini hacks the ball clear. Fernandinho prominent for City.

Ten minutes of all-out action, now Walcott – fed by Sagna – causes City problems, goes past a defender – he crosses – it's deflected into the goalmouth – Wilshere traps it – but he swipes it impetuously – Giroud's at the near post but he can't get on it, Olivier Giroud, Arsenal's new hero, praised by Wenger as a footballing reincarnation of the old English centre-forward- "that charming striker" they called him in his native France, sounds more like Morrissey than Tommy Lawton.

Arsenal reply with a long ball towards Giroud – but he can't control it –still the lino's flag stayed down and the Citizens vent their anger at this.

Aguero – good pass towards Negredo – but Koscielny, a man who looks permanently surprised, heads the ball behind.

corner taken by Nasri – Demichelis' late run-he leaps up and nods it to the far post – Koscielny's slow to react and Arsenal are punished with a fantastic volleyed goal from Aguero – the ball drops sharply and he leans right back under it and abruptly thrashes it right footed into the roof of the net – as instantaneous and fierce as Carlos Monzon, the great Argentinian middleweight, knocking out a fighter who'd dropped his guard and Kun proudly pats his chest as he runs off in front of the Gooners-" LIL BAARSTED-LIL FACKIN' BAARSTED !!"

1-0, fourteen minutes, Manuel Pellegrini on the touchline, delighted " BRAVO!!"

Per Mertesacker blameless, skipper for today, he remains calm, a dominant figure at two metres tall, resolutely rallying his comrades, the Gooners sing about him-"BIG FACKIN' GERMAN , WE'VE GOH BIG FACKIN' GERMAN".

From the restart, Arsenal attack – out wide left to Ramsey – he crosses to the far post – Pantilimon drops it – but he reclaims it before Walcott can pounce – unusually animated, the Romanian giant gestures two closed fingers at the lino, claiming he was fouled twice but Arsenal weren't flagged – more booing for the lino.

The much-vaunted Turkish-German Meszut Ozil, short-haired and sleepy-eyed, signed for £42 million from Real Madrid and he's finding it hard to make an impact in this intensely fought, incident-packed contest – but now he prompts Wilshere – Jack Wilshere, the Hertfordshire bull terrier, chain-smoking seventies throwback, he won't be shirking a tackle – but he's narked to find Zabaleta robustly holding him off.

Arsenal send the long ball down the City left again – their old chum Gael Clichy has been in poor form lately and they figure they can exploit this – but Giroud overruns the ball – he seems offside but once again the lino didn't flag – and a storm of booing erupts, next time he gets one wrong they might score.

On twenty minutes, a stupendous burst from Vincent Kompany, pouncing on Ramsey's incipient short pass to release Giroud on a fast-paced counter, he intervenes dramatically – he jolts Giroud with the intensity of his shoulder charge –Giroud appeals to the ref in vain-Kompany stumbling, off balance, he recovers at once, pinging the ball from his right foot to his left as he swerves past Ramsey, leaving the lion of Caerphilly staggering – then he perfectly prompts Alvaro Negredo to close in on goal – but Koscielny's late challenge is just enough to make the big Spaniard angle his shot wide. Negredo ruefully applauds his captain – and well he might salute a bravura compendium of power and skill, a flashback to the attacking centre- halves of yesteryear.

A minute later, Kompany features in more orthodox style, heading Ramsey's cross away from goal, in doing so he finds Clichy wide – Clichy merely pumps the ball upfield parallel with the touchline – but Silva deftly keeps it in play – he dances inside – and sends Negredo away chasing a diagonal ball – huge Gooner roars as Polish keeper Wojtech Szczesny beats the bearded Spaniard to the ball
Silva purses his lips and swipes his arm across his chest in vexation.

Moment of comedy after Yaya's rugged challenge sends Ramsey staggering on the touchline – Mr Atkinson sounds his whistle against City – Yaya, thinks he's been called for a foul, throws his hands behind his head, "SHOUDDEN, EET WASS SHOULDAIR!" – Ramsey smiles, "IT'S FOR A THROW-IN" – And it is, Arsenal's way – Yaya laughs.

Negredo – Silva – Yaya – and Yaya's lightning reverse flick inside Flamini - though the City strikers can't get on it – is absolutely superb, a living flame.

From the sublime to the banal for the mighty Ivorian – Silva shoots – it's blocked by Koscielny – it rebounds to Negredo – he pulls the ball back to Yaya on the edge of the box – but he balloons his shot high over the bar.

Arsenal respond by sending Monréal away with good passes up the left flank – Negredo tracking back brings his compatriot down with a lunging tackle – Martin Atkinson speaks to Negredo at some length and the Beast nods dutifully – credit to Mr Atkinson for grizzled sagacity, not wanting easy early bookings to mar the tone of this enthralling game

Walcott takes the kick – Pantilimon's punch is a weak one, more of a push really – the ball drops to Ozil just inside the box – but his first touch is surprisingly clumsy – Yaya boots it clear.

Just turned the half hour, so much has happened, most of it high class stuff from City but now a succession of defensive errors gifts Arsenal the equaliser, Yaya a touch languid in the centre circle and Ramsey robs him – groans of YA-YA! – City caught clean on the hop – Ozil to Walcott on the edge of the box – Walcott's mishit shot – that's not going anywhere – but yes it is – Demichelis stoops to head it clear – did he need to? – the ball skims his long hair – and a motionless Pantilimon watches as it sails past him into the net, 1-1 – scarcely a deflection but there was no call, a persistent frailty in the Sky Blues' defence regardless of who's keeping goal – Pantilimon is the main culprit, Demichelis' error can't be overlooked – but, further upfield, Yaya wipes his nose and sniffs disgustedly as if he'd just smelled garbage– "FERQ!", he punches his fist, he knows full well the initial error was his.

Walcott's doubly infantile cradle- rocking celebration, he smirks with glee– his missus is expecting, it seems.

THEO ! THEO!

David Silva, his visage as rigid as a mask, sets City back on the attack, intent on regaining the lead as soon as possible – Fernandinho – Yaya – Yaya sets Silva free in the centre circle – a measured pass to Negredo – he gets on it, his angled shot will surely find the net – but no, he rolls it the wrong side of the post – he sinks to his knees and grinds his teeth – on the touchline, Pellegrini cups his nose in his hand, he'd been ready to shout in acclaim.

City back on the attack, Silva at the heart of it – but Arsenal's splendid centre back pair, Koscielny and Mertesacker, are the frontline of the resistance, the Gooners pipe up

Arse-naw ! Arse-naw !! ARSE-NAW!!!

Ironic Citizen cheers as the lino flags Monréal offside this time – all the more so as it looked like he was on.

38 and City seize the lead back, 2-1 with a Negredo goal, it stems from a sumptuous Yaya pass with the outside of the foot – Zabaleta splendidly kills it at once – and plants it into the six yard box for Negredo to chase – Koscielny's full -blooded attempt to pull off a last-ditch tackle – but he can't – the ball's in the back of the Arsenal net, with Alf dinking it neatly over Szczesny
Beast Beast Beast!!!
Zabaleta leaps to hug the big man Negredo, the two Spanish speakers exult in English ' EEYESS!

Shock upon shock for the Gooners behind the goal as they see Koscielny rise from his unavailing challenge – then collapse in the six yard box, his knee buckling under him, looks dreadful, could be a cruciate job
Play's held up for a full four minutes with an ambulance crew on– but what happened exactly?
Finally, Koscielny's stretchered off to devoted applause from the Gooners and respectful clapping from the Citizens, the French stopper with the Polish name, he's hard but fair, a worthy opponent
Thomas Vermaelen, Arsenal's demoted ex-captain takes the place of the stricken Koscielny.

Play resumes, Fernandinho tackles Walcott – loose ball, Silva tackles out Ozil both ex-stars of La Liga but David Silva's a killer in the Prem and Ozil isn't – a perfect pass from Silva to Nasri – Nasri a bit slow to take full advantage – but he forces a corner.

Arsenal with their backs to the wall during stoppage time, City win another corner, Nasri takes it – Demichelis, battered and bandannaed, aged thirty-two, he looks forty – he attacks it, no doubt about it, City've been practising set pieces on the training ground – but his powerful effort flies over the angle.

Half time.

Scarcely has the second half started than Sergio Aguero goes down injured – he hadn't been challenged, just looking for a pass – Nasri has a laugh with Flamini, he doesn't yet realise the seriousness of his teammate's injury – but he does now as the trainer and physio come on – Kompany and Yaya run over, looking concerned at their prone comrade – he shakes his head, can't continue, no stretcher needed, he'll go off under his own steam, but he's limping, looks like a calf injury.

Better news for the Gooners via TV, Koscielny's injury's just a deeply lacerated knee.

Pellegrini tells Jesus Navas to warm up, there'll be no like-for-like substitution, say Dzeko coming on – instead Navas'll bolster the mid-field – and provide an outlet to cause trouble for the faltering left back Monréal-this may be a key move.

Mertesacker looking to start a counter –he's spotted that City have left a gap – he finds Ramsey – but Silva's alert and ruthless, he scampers in to bring Ramsey down, rattling his shins for good measure – Mr Atkinson books Silva, the Spanish maestro wasn't bothered, he made sure a dangerous counter-attack was stymied at source.

Arsenal look to counter but pay the price for a slack Ozil pass in the City half – it puts Giroud under pressure – he tries a hurried back pass to Flamini in the centre circle – but Fernandinho robs Flamini – he darts into space – he passes to Negredo and Negredo sets off – but he's tackled – Fernandinho picks up the loose ball – he drives into the penalty box – he pauses for a moment, stern -faced and concentrated – he curls a glorious shot wide of the full-length dive of Szczesny – this is the Brazilian dynamo's first goal for City – LEGAOW ! rapturous applause from behind the North Stand goal – he reciprocates with a blown kiss, his face wreathed in smiles – his teammates surround and hug him,

3-2, 50 minutes, Blue Moon! Pellegrini applauds the brusqueness and beauty of Fernandinho's strike.

From the restart Arsenal look for a riposte, in all -out attack mode, Ozil with a much better pass, he plays Wilshere through in the box – Wilshere tussles for the ball with Clichy – Clichy concedes a corner – he complains to Mr Atkinson, "HEY, LOOK, REF!" he mimics a flailing elbow – Mr Atkinson ignores him – Wilshere paces menacingly after Clichy, giving him a hard stare – Zabaleta seeks to pacify Wilshere – but Wilshere merely curls his lip and pushes Zabaleta away – Zabaleta frowns and shakes his head, susses Wilshere for a hopeless case– it's a high-intensity physical contest all right as well as one of high skill – but Wilshere's reaction is playground stuff, a boy among men.

Arsenal attacking ceaselessly, Ramsey – Ozil – wide for Sagna – the curiously coiffured Frenchman curls in a cracking cross – Giroud's got a free header from the edge of the six yard box – but he heads wide

Wenger on the touchline, etching further furrows into his wrinkled brow as he frowns and swivels in despair – "WHATZEFERCK !"

Giroud lies prone, eyes averted from the scene of his gaffe.

City look to respond, Nasri – Silva – Silva neatly bisects Mertesacker and Flamini – and finds Negredo – Negredo passes the ball beyond Vermaelen right into the path of Nasri – but Szczesny reacts quickly to snatch the ball off Nasri 's boots.

Giroud and Zabaleta fight for the ball on the touchline, shoulder to shoulder, but Giroud's shoving – Mr Atkinson gives Arsenal the kick – Zabaleta "'E- push ME ! – ferk!".

Zaba's right in the thick of it as half the Arsenal team appeal to Mr Atkinson for a penalty for handball with the serried ranks of Gooners braying biliously against Mr Atkinson when he doesn't give it – gaunt and grizzled though he's only forty-two, the whistler from Leeds has been reffing since he was sixteen – veteran of countless controversial decisions, abuse doesn't faze him -this was the way of it, Wilshere chipped a pass through a crowded City box, looking for Walcott – Zabaleta thwarted the move, via thigh, armpit and the inside of his motionless arm – the ball went out of play over the goal line

A huge concerted Arsenal appeal, Wilshere dashes towards Mr Atkinson, all jutting neck and curled lip – Mr Atkinson "SHUT UP!" Walcott's incensed, his eyeballs popping- "HAND, HAND!!" he bawls, touching his own heavily tattooed arm under his pristine white sleeve as if Mr Atkinson was a foreigner unversed in the English terms for body parts – Giroud yells at close range "TWIZE – 'E DO EET TWIZE !" – but Mr Atkinson's unmoved though half a dozen Gunners are breathing down his neck, he awards a corner

Arsenal corner – Pantilimon fumbles – Kompany heads it clear.

Further Arsenal pressure – they've stuck it to City for ten minutes solid after conceding the third, a virtual siege on the sky blue goal.

On sixty-two minutes Arsenal score their third, it's Walcott again, Ozil – Ramsey – Ramsey deftly chips the ball over the heads of Kompany and Zabaleta – then Walcott improvises an abrupt and brilliant lob – it soars even over the wingspan of the 6 foot 8 inch Pantilimon and finds the top right-hand corner – an instant, throaty roar of acclaim from the Gooners – FACKINAOWYAIR ! they're hellbent on the Premiership title after ten years of gutwrenching failure – they see City as pretenders to the throne who must be done down, overthrown in their own backyard.

Walcott's strike was the climax of an eleven pass move, classical Wenger Arsenal – and the grey-haired Frenchman rises like a wraith from the bench, clenching and shaking his bony fists, 3 -2!

Arsenal attacking again, looking for the equaliser, Giroud and Zabaleta tussling for the ball again – Mr Atkinson gives Arsenal a free-kick – Zaba chokes on the verge of a sweary outburst, buttons his lip – "that's – NOT !

Sixty-six minutes, City re-establish their two-goal lead, anything you can do we can do better, another multi-pass move, thirteen this time, in the last stanza Kompany steers a long pass to Yaya – he toe-flicks the ball to Nasri – he plays it wide to Navas– and suddenly La Liga is come to the Etihad as Navas, ex- Sevilla steals half a yard on Monréal, ex- Malaga – Navas sends a hard low cross to the near post – and there's David Silva, sometime wizard of Valencia, quicker to react than Vermaelen and Mertesacker, he pounces – he opens his slight frame and fires the ball into the roof of the net before Szczesny can move a muscle – small and lean as Silva is, his timing imparts the force, his boot whipped through the ball like a golf club in the hands of Sergio Garcia
Silva and Navas in a leaping hug, VIVA ESPANA ! VIVA EL CITY!
Citizens rise up in a roar behind the North Stand goal – and then the roar resounds, all over the Etihad, 4-2
Manuel Pellegrini, aesthete and tactician, applauds the beauty of the goal.

Arsenal stunned but still looking to respond – Wilshere a cross to Giroud – Giroud and Zabaleta go up for it – Giroud slips and appeals – but Mr Atkinson gives City the kick – Giroud "'E WASS FOWLEEN' ME DOWN" – Zaba, imperturbable, glances coldly at him.

Arsenal still pressing hard and Wilshere delivers a fierce 25 yard drive – it's creeping under the bar – but no, Costel Pantilimon with his two metre plus reach leaps up and, at full stretch, tips it over left-handed, a tremendous save.

Arsenal's corner – Fernandinho and Wilshere scrapping for the ball on the goal-line – it goes over – Mr Atkinson awards a goalkick –

Wilshere doesn't like it, he bawls "WHAAI? WHY?", looks like he's close to snapping

Shouts from the East Stand right next to the ranks of the Gooners, aimed to push him over the edge " yer wanker, Wilshere ! " yer little chav !"– Wilshere looks up, curls his lip and unleashes a one- fingered gesture at the Citizens – Mr Atkinson doesn't notice – jeers of Citizen derision.

Wilshere misplaces passes, knows he's been a fool, worried about it, ref never seen it buh I'll git dan wivver vid, shoulden leh um git to me, norvern baarsteds !

Seventy-one minutes and David Silva goes off, well applauded – he's replaced by James Milner

Will Wenger respond by taking off Wilshere ?, no he doesn't, strangely, it's Flamini he removes – he sends on the Stuttgart sprinter, Gnabry.

Dangerous City move after Navas robs a floundering Monréal on the touchline – he feeds Nasri – Nasri drives on goal – he sends the ball back to Navas at full speed, Navas so fast he once wrecked a treadmill – Szczesny's forced to come out wide – and Navas rounds him– he fires from an acute angle but can only hit the side netting – Navas lies prone, gutted he wasted his moment of glory

Monréal's pissed off with the lino – he raises two closed fingers, indicating two fouls against him, as he saw it

Wenger fuming to the fourth official," IT WAS A FOUL, I TELL YOU!"

Fifteen minutes left and Wenger takes off Giroud who's been labouring in vain all afternoon – he sends on the eccentric Dane, Nicklas Bendtner- Bendtner, he mixes in royal circles, was shacked up with Baroness Caroline Luel- Brockdorff , a grim and lanky figure, he sports a stunted ponytail.

Citizens roar with delight as Zabaleta robs Wilshere on the halfway line – he spies Yaya clear and gives him the ball – Yaya surges to the D – and unleashes a shot – but it's just wide.

Yaya sets off on a 40 yard run through midfield – brushing aside first Wilshere then Monréal – he passes wide to Nasri – Nasri beats Mertasacker and Vermaelen but he can't get past Sagna – Yaya rebukes his greed.

Last five minutes and Arsenal look knackered – Yaya – Nasri – Nasri dances round Sagna then skips past Vermaelen – but Mertesacker dispossesses him with a fine last ditch challenge – Nasri shuts his eyes, sinks to his knees and beats the turf– he realises he's gone too far in his urge for an individual goal.

Clichy wins the ball – lays it off to Fernandinho – what lungs the Brazilian's got to unleash a 25 yard run at this stage of a fully committed stint !– more than that, he uncorks a fizzing, spinning shot – Szczesny pulls off a fine save, knocking it up with both fists over the bar.

City attack relentlessly, Demichelis – Nasri – Navas – Nasri – Navas – he crosses to Nasri who's unmarked – but he fires over – the Frenchman blames a bobble, he petulantly kicks the air – " DAM BALL, SHEET!"

Yet another City attack, Arsenal being overrun, this time Nasri contents himself with a quick pass to a teammate, that's after robbing Wilshere who falls down – to Fernandinho who's embarked on another 25 yard run – he's in the D– he returns the ball to Nasri – and it's Nasri back to Fernandinho – he rounds Mertesacker– and dinks the ball over Szczesny for his second goal, 5-2
Fernandinho's delighted, LEGAOW! he snaps a mock pic of himself to the photographers behind the goal, send that back to Brazil, don't forget, let Scolari see it then he'll choose me for the Mundial

Some Citizens chanting EASY EASY EASY !!! which it certainly wasn't, anything but, Arsene Wenger sullenly wipes his mouth.

But there's life in Arsenal yet, as City relax – a cross is fired over – and Bendtner leaps to head it in – goal, no, the lino flags for offside – Bendtner glares at him icily but doesn't contest it.

Five minutes stoppage time announced-Nasri goes off to a standing ovation, Arsenal find a last burst of energy, a perfectly flighted cross from Sagna catches the City centrebacks off guard – and Mertesacker heads home, 5-3, a minute left, certainly a surer reflection of the balance of play no Arsenal celebration – though the Gooners roar behind the goal but – before they've even time to sing about their BFG, City've scored yet again.

An unwise back pass from Gnabry – and there's the indefatigable Fernandinho pouncing – and going off on yet another 25 yard run – right into the box – he jinks past Mertesacker – he slips the ball wide to Milner, on as sub – Milner's in the six yard box – he rounds Szczesny – he's bound to score – but no, the Pole trips him before he can pull the trigger – Citizens roar for Szczesny's dismissal – but, according to the laws, Mr Atkinson can't go beyond a yellow, the keeper was of course the last man but Milner was facing away from goal when he was brought down.

Yaya will take the penalty – Szczesny, clad in black and looking bleak, tries some dodging antics- useless, Yaya cracks it past him, shrugs his shoulders, BEN' LORS QUOI ? 6-3 congratulations all round, Fernandinho playfully punching Yaya's arm.

Mr Atkinson sounds the final whistle – Arsenal players go over to salute their loyal fans – except Ozil doesn't – and Mertesacker reprimands his fellow-countryman, towering over him and wagging an admonishing finger, scheisskerl !– Ozil looks chastened but still can't bring himself to do his duty.

Arsene Wenger brusquely extends a hand to the victorious Manuel Pellegrini – then he strides grim- faced down the tunnel – he'd hoped to put City nine points adrift of Arsenal – but the Sky Blues have reduced the lead to a mere three- so intense a clash, full of fury but full of football too, a great match, it might've been for the title-maybe! whatever, the Gunners have been spiked !

Graham Gordon

5. Riding Out the Storm of Rage

Newcastle United 0   City 2

St. James Park, January 12   2014

Under leaden skies in the great barn of St James Park City take on a Newcastle now more pragmatic since consigning Ben Arfa to the bench whilst Loic Remy's more dangerous than Papiss Cisse- Yohan Cabaye, the thin, short-haired, stubble-bearded Frenchman, they kept him away from the Emirates, he's the brains of their otherwise obvious attacking play

City field a very strong team with Demichelis and Kolarov replacing Lescott and Clichy

Seven minutes and City score with a goal of perfect simplicity, Silva in possession, he turns a circle to throw off Anita – he delivers a perfectly weighted ball inside Gouffran- it's rolling to a stop right into Kolarov's stride – Kolarov's instant lateral low ball – Dzeko steaming in at the near post – he beats Taylor to the ball – and stretches to poke it into the roof of the net- Dzeko and Kolarov in a bounding Balkan celebration
Pellegrini on the touchline "that's GOOD !" And it is !

Sissokho – Remy – he angles a cross – Kompany's skewed clearance launches an instant counter – Nasri – Silva, deep in the centre circle – he lays it off to Kolarov – Silva's flattened by Williamson straight afterwards – but Kolarov delivers a dangerous through ball across the goalmouth behind Taylor – Negredo's onto it – no, sliding in, his bright brown boots miss contact by a couple of inches only

Mark Jones doesn't seem to have seen the off the ball foul on Silva, a Magpie statement of intent

Taylor's crude foul on Dzeko – Silva freekick – it finds Negredo unmarked – but he puts his header onto the roof of the net – he holds his face in his hands ruefully and purses his lips

the French/ Central African defender Yanga- Mbiwa hoists a deep, high cross – Zabaleta miscues his header – loose ball on the byline – Cabaye pounces on it and whips a high shot from an extreme angle – and Joe Hart leaps to turn it brilliantly, one –handed, behind for a corner

From the corner, taken on 33 minutes, comes extreme controversy – which will dominate the rest of the match

City clear the ball but it finds Tiote 20 yards out – the Mohican-tonsured Ivorian opts to blast it on goal even through a packed goalmouth – he connects perfectly with a left foot half volley – it flies through the goalmouth, brushes Silva's boot – the slightest nick off Demichelis – Gouffran's the furthest forward standing in an offside position – he swerves out of the way – it rockets into the net just inside the far post

St James erupts with delight at the velocity of the strike – Tiote runs crazily to the bench – he's hugged by Newcastle assistant manager, little, grim- faced John Carver – the Newcastle bench are jubilant-Pardew, the long-term controversy freak, he's racing around with a smirk on his lips, chortling smugly.

don't speak too soon, Newcastle – Joe Hart protests – "HOW AM I S'POSED TO SAVE IT WHEN I CAN'T EVEN SEE IT?" He points out Gouffran as his impediment, truth to tell there were three Magpies who were standing offside as Tiote launched the strike.

Massive moment for Mr Jones – Kompany has a quiet word, prosecuting his case, –the ref goes over to consult his linesman Ron

Ganfield – Kompany goes over too and so does Cabaye – the officials confer – and Mr Jones signals that he's disallowed the goal for offside

Roars of rage reverberate round St James's Park "INTAHFEERUN??? intahfeerun' with the furcan pleer?? thee nevah furcan tootched 'Art !"

Pardew's laughter has turned cynical now, he wags a forefinger towards the ref and sneers "YEAH! YEAH! YEAH! YEAH!"

The game resumes to an incessant storm of booing, City win a freekick after the Italian Santon trips Nasri on the Newcastle byline – but the Newcastle players are more interested in besieging Mr Jones, Cabaye, Tiote, Gouffran even the goalkeeper Tim Krul has raced the whole length of the pitch to berate the official about the disallowed goal – Mr Jones stands his ground, face twitching – "MOVE AWAY!" – and they do, grudgingly

With Pardew bellowing furiously on the touchline, Newcastle turn their anger into dirt – Mr Jones books Sissokho for a trip – and Cabaye for dissent – then there's ironic cheers as he also books Fernandinho for a trip.

The fourth official, the gaunt Martin Atkinson, with a woolllen cap pulled right down to his eyebrows, speaks to Pardew, urging calm – continued howls of anger from the Barcode crowd – they're even boo-ing a throw in which wasn't given in their favour– Pardew's making it ten times worse by loudly contesting every decision.

Sissokho brings down Kolarov, he was booked earlier and should be seeing red – but no, Mr Jones takes no action.

in stoppage time a major touchline incident with Pardew blasting Manuel Pellegrini, Pellegrini's objected to Mr Atkinson that Pardew's trying to referee the match – Pardew comes over, tightlipped, finger raised – "I'LL SAY WHA' I FACKIN' LIKE !!"

as he retreats, Pardew very slowly and vehemently to Pellegrini "SHAT YOUR NOISE, YOU FACKIN' OL' KANT!!!! Fackin' 'ell !"

Pellegrini doesn't retaliate – Mr Atkinson speaks to Pardew, counselling restraint.

As the teams go off at half time, Pardew confronts Mr Jones, careful this time to avoid expletives - Mr Jones ignores him and Pardew shouts after him "the linesman's right and you're wrong, the linesman's RIGHT and you're WRONG, it's not offside, there's no savin' it and YOU SHOULD BE EXPERIENCED ENOUGH TO KNOW THAT!"

The half-time interval has done nothing to quell the Geordie crowd's rage "cheats – cheats – cheats"

Tiote's booked for fouling his compatriot Yaya, who's had a quiet game.

Dzeko's withdrawn – Navas comes on – Dzeko receiving ice treatment on the bench, someone's booted his shins.

Negredo's flattened out wide by Williamson – Mr Jones doesn't book Williamson and Pardew's bile appears to be intimidating the ref – Silva takes the freekick – Negredo's powerful header, holding off the burly Taylor – Krul somehow gets a knee on it at point-blank range

Yaya retaliates against Tiote – freekick – it's headed out by Kompany – it reaches Tiote – Cabaye – Cabaye makes ground in a trice – and drives a tremendous shot from 25 yards – Joe Hart brings off a great save, diving full length and turning it round the post corner – Santon and Zabaleta tussle for the ball – Zabaleta swings a boot, kicks empty air – but Santon goes down just the same– Zaba stands over him angrily "you BAS-TAR!" Santon shrugs, he'd like to have got Zabaleta sent off but Mr Jones didn't oblige.

Yaya's done nowt and he's taken off, Garcia's sent on

More rough stuff from Newcastle – Cabaye brutally bundles Navas over the touchline – but Mr Jones refrains from action, he should've produced a second yellow and sent the Frenchman off.

a third outstanding save from Hart – a quick Newcastle move – Remy slips two defenders and gets through – he aims his shot on the angle – but Hart saves it with his outstretched left boot

and, as Newcastle's furious efforts begin to run out of steam, their play plumbs new depths with an appalling foul which takes Nasri out of the game
Nasri working hard in defence and eager to start a counter is assailed from behind by Yanga- Mbiwa– he hacks and kicks at Nasri in a failed attempt to bring him down – finally he scythes him down with a vicious chop across the knee
Nasri lies on the turf in agony, receiving treatment from the City medical team
It's fully five minutes before he can be stretchered off
Yanga – Mbiwa offers to shake his hand but Nasri refuses, ENFANT D'UNE SALOPE!
James Milner is sent on to replace Nasri.

City gaining the upper hand as a tired Newcastle get even dirtier– then Pardew sends on Hatem Ben Arfa hoping for a belated touch of class

A bad tackle by Santon on Kolarov – Kolarov gets up and shrugs it off.

City surging into attack – a fine Navas cross – Kompany shoots – it's blocked – it loops up – a wonderful back header from all of ten yards by Fernandinho – but it hits the bar.

Mr Atkinson indicates seven minutes of injury time.

A scramble in the City goalmouth – Taylor's dangerously free – but he's stopped by a tremendous block tackle from Kolarov

Ninety-five minutes, 0-2 and City get the goal which clinches victory, it comes from a counter-attack, Garcia – Milner – Milner delays, spies Negredo breaking – and flicks the ball through for him – Negredo's in the clear but he's 40 yards out – he surges on – he's s one-on-one with Krul – he shoots – but he fails to get his shot round the keeper – a lucky rebound – yes but he 's right behind the bouncing ball – and coolly plants it in the net.

pandemonium on the City bench, Dzeko "yes!" Manuel Pellegrini "so GOOD!" – Kiddo's bouncing about – but it 'll be Ruben who's the celebration master, arms upraised, looking to the skies – "GOL-GOL-GOL-GOL-GOL -GOL – GOOOOOOOOL !!!!!!"

The final whistle sounds, the Geordie crowds move sullenly off, this is a vital City victory and no mistake, achieved bravely in the face of constant intimidation roared on by an infuriated crowd.

6. Driving the Lamborghini to White Hart Lane

Tottenham Hotspur 1   City 5

January 29 2014

Within a month of Spurs being thrashed 6-0 at the Etihad in November, Andre Villas Boas was sacked and replaced by his assistant Tim Sherwood – a young British tracksuit manager being bigged up by the media – they've won five out of six games since he took over, he restores Danish playmaker, Eriksen, whom he previously implied was lazy, also Dembele but he still has Sandro, Paulinho and Vertonghen injured.

City select Clichy at left back, possibly to counter the speed of Lennon and Walker, Negredo still feeling the effects of his shoulder injury, he's on the bench and Dzeko partners Aguero upfront.

Torrential rain bucketing down over White Hart Lane.

City moving well from the off, only five minutes gone and Aguero narrowly fails to score a superb goal, a good pass from Fernandinho puts him through – he drives Dawson across the D – he turns abruptly, veers past the Romanian Chiriches – and explodes a ferocious shot past keeper Lloris' outstretched right hand – it cannons off the shivering far post, rebounding all of 20 yards – Dawson, he already knew what Aguero can do, still he looks stunned.

Then the first sign of dodgy refereeing, Dzeko and Walker tussling for the ball, Andre Marriner calls Dzeko for a foul, Dzeko indignant, mutters "ferkoff!"

Ten minutes, a fine one two between Dzeko and Aguero – but Dzeko spoils his good work by unwisely opting to shoot – and ballooning – Aguero gestures, why no ball to feet ??– Yaya rebukes Dzeko too.

City open the scoring on the quarter hour, a nine pass sequence, Hart-Demichelis-taken out of defence via Clichy-Dzeko- Fernandinho-Yaya-Kompany-he steers a fine pass to Silva – Silva immediately and precisely feeds Aguero – Dawson can't react in time – and Kun instantly pots the ball past Lloris, struck with sidespin, as precise as a Selby snooker shot with stun – it creeps in neatly on the fourth bounce.

Pellegrini "That' SO GOOD!" damn right, it is! Cleverly constructed buildup involving almost the entire team and superbly finished.

A minute later, Aguero dropping back – Navas – Navas' lightning dart across midfield - to Dzeko – Dzeko takes it well – then he slashes the ball wide.

Sherwood stubble -bearded, wild- eyed and tightlipped, he looks distraught – his sidekick Les Ferdinand's gesticulating frantically, they know full well they're in trouble, that City 'll overrun them if it goes on like this.

Not till eighteen minutes do Spurs mount a significant move, Yaya loses the ball – Adebayor strides down the inside left channel – he sidefoots a shot – but it's deflected for a corner

Eriksen takes the corner – he really whips it – Joe Hart's nonplussed – a dangerous moment of hesitation – it rebounds off Vincent Kompany – and Hart grasps it just ahead of Adebayor – the lanky Togolese gestures, look here, you lot, see, I was almost in there!

Citizens " City reject, City reject!"

On twenty minutes a sparkling City attack is denied a second goal only by a stupendous save from Hugo Lloris, that's Lloris from Nice, the scion of an upper middle-class family, mother a lawyer, father a Monaco banker it went like this, Fernandinho jabbing a pass to Silva –he prompts Clichy – Clichy beats the gormless Kyle Walker with ease – he hoists a cross high above Dzeko's head – Danny Rose, the Doncaster lad, ex-Leeds – he leaps to head it clear but is well and truly outjumped by Aguero – springing up, Kun meets it perfectly, muscles in his neck bulging as he makes contact – a certain goal – Pellegrini acclaims it – no, at the last split second Lloris plucks the ball out of the air, the Tottenham crowd roar in relieved acclaim – Aguero holds his head in disbelief, he'll praise Lloris later but right now he hates him – in the technical zone, Pellegrini cups his nose with his hand at a brilliantly abrupt strike incredibly denied – for Hugo Lloris, skinny, gaunt, bemoustached this is the moment he's dreamt of all his life, the boy from Nice, all he wanted was football, now as proud as his old man would've been if he'd broken the bank at Monte Carlo.

ominously for Spurs, David Silva is pulling the strings, he describes one of his menacing circles – Yaya – Navas – a dangerous cross to the far post – Dawson staggering as he heads it away for a corner
Navas takes the corner – Kompany heads on goal – Rose has to kick it off the line – but his clearance is shallow and high – Silva loses his balance as he heads it strongly for Aguero – but Kun shoots well wide agitated at his miss, "God!" Then he mutters testily in Spanish.

Zabaleta dispossesses Sigurdsson – but he's fouled and sent sprawling by Chiriches– no foul given, another error by Mr Marriner.

City are giving Spurs a total shellacking and the men in white are resorting to desperate measures, Sherwood screaming at his players.

Yaya shoots – it deflects off Eriksen – Navas pounces – to Zabaleta, he's free on the edge of the box – he unleashes a powerful left foot shot – with Lloris beaten all ends up, it swings over the far angle.

Zaba scarcely reacts to his near miss– but, as Mr Marriner runs into earshot, he gives off about the refusal to deal with Chiriches' foul in the earlier incident – Mr Marriner is not having his authority questioned, he ostentatiously summons Zabaleta, of course there's previous between those two because Mr Marriner sent off Zaba at Wembley

Zaba "WHO, ME?" Mr Marriner's staring eyeballs are popping out of his skull – "YES, YOU!" he snarls – "LESS OF IT! GOT IT?" Zabaleta curls his lip but decides it's better to let it go.

Almost the first half-hour gone already and City are interpassing majestically and driving forward with tremendous verve

Silva shoots, it's deflected over the byline, Mr Marriner hesitates – Silva glares, that samurai look, he's sussed Mr Marriner's not up to the job thus virtually a foe -Silva points to the corner flag – from the corner, Rose throws himself down, making out Zabaleta's fouled him – Mr Marriner falls for it.

City press relentlessly in search of the second goal their play deserves, Navas wins a corner – Dzeko shoots – and there's a white shirt with # 42 on it and both hands all over the ball, he's virtually caught it, it's the nineteen-year-old French lad Nabib Bentaleb, Sherwood's encouraging new blood and he's given him his chance but Bentaleb's lost his cool – City attackers appeal for hands – Mr Marriner rejects it.

After half an hour of intense attacking with only one goal to show for it, foiled by Lloris and Mr Marriner, City's energy levels inevitably drop and Tottenham finally get in the game, their crowd, till now stunned into silence, starts to make noise.

Yaya's booked for a foul – Mr Marriner's got it right this time, Yaya's raked his studs down Dembele's calf, fearing he'd start a counter – Yaya protests to Mr Marriner, one finger raised, signifying it's his first foul – Mr Marriner rightly brushes this aside

Dembele, Malian-Belgian, Yaya to Dembele in French, nothing personal, pal, you understand?

Rose beats Yaya – he launches a fine long through ball, meant for Adebayor – who's striding through the City defence – till Vince Kompany gets there first– he passes to Yaya– but Yaya loses the ball – Rose surges onto it – just outside the box, Yaya challenges him – so does Zabaleta and they tussle for the ball – Rose goes to ground, appealing to Mr Marriner who gives him the freekick

Yaya strides towards Mr Marriner looking to confront him - but Kompany, fearing a red, pushes him away, Yaya flinching and staggering, how powerful is Kompany to do that!

Zabaleta getting in on the act, teeth gritted, seething with resentment towards Mr Marriner – " FECKIN' ELL !"

But he defers to Captain Kompany, Vincent the diplomat, master of language, arm on Mr Marriner's shoulder, discussing the situation, but pointing to Rose as the culprit,- Mr Marriner's sickly smile, my decision is final and all that – Kompany's politeness is tinged with sarcasm "OH YES, OF COURSE!" Still he's made the point to the West Midlands whistler, it will remain in his mind for the next decision he has to make.

And it's decision time right now because, from the freekick, Spurs have the ball in the net but it's disallowed, Eriksen takes the corner, whips it in, fires it like a shot behind City's rearguard – Joe Hart can't get near it – but Dawson's at the far post –and he volleys it into the roof of the net

City appeal at once for offside – and yes, there's the linesman, good on you, Mr Ledger, his flag's raised -Mr Marriner does not overrule – a storm of boos round White Hart Lane – Sherwood's on his feet yelling and bawling furiously on the touchline.

There's an incident immediately afterwards, Aguero and Dawson challenge for a high ball – and Aguero's down on the ground, prone and kicking the turf- Yaya, he's not had his best game and his temper's ready to snap, he's in Dawson's face – Dawson flinches slightly even as he snarls a rebuff -"FUCK OFF !– NEVER USED ME ELBOW!"

that's true enough but he caught Kun a right clout on the side of the head with his shoulder.

Spurs' already physical approach intensified because they reckon they were robbed of a goal.

Adebayor attacking, Citizens chanting 'City reject, City reject! – Demichelis tackles him firmly but fairly, at a 90 degree angle – as he's jolted by the impact, Adebayor stamps on Demichelis' knee, looking to distract Mr Marriner by an exaggerated head over heels tumble – Demichelis gets up- he limps for a few seconds – then he turns and confronts Adebayor – who's still seated on the turf in victim pose – Demichelis, fluent in German, doesn't speak much English yet and no French with which to let the big Togolese have a piece of his mind, he mimes the stamp, his bootstuds millimetres from Adebayor's knee – but Mr Marriner books Demichelis for the challenge – Aguero, furious, gives off in Spanish about the mistreatment of his fellow- countryman,- Mr Marriner get the drift of it and books him for dissent

The Spurriers are loving this!

Pellegrini firmly expressing his dissatisfaction to the fourth official

Demichelis speaking to Mr Marriner and showing the blood on his knee, Mr Marriner should insist that he go off and be treated for this but he doesn't.

Play resumes, Aguero chases the ball with Dawson – sprinting, he suddenly grimaces, stops, sits down – Mr Marriner summons the City doc – looks like hamstring, a real shame the way he was playing– Aguero limps off a minute before half time, Pellegrini sends on Jovetic.

Jovetic in the thick of it straight away, looking to dribble on the touchline, he's fouled, Adebayor pushes him over the line – as he falls,

Mr Marriner indicates a City freekick – Rose, following up, blasts the ball at Jovetic – it misses but the intent was there.

Jovetic gets up, so this is the Premiership, red in tooth and claw, huh? If Sherwood sussed him for a softie, he's mistaken

Navas takes the freekick- Demichelis storms in on it-but heads it high over.

As they troop off for half-time, Demichelis approaches Mr Marriner and points to his bloodstained knee – Mr Marriner looks the other way, ridiculous that City have only one goal to show for their dominance.

Second-half, Dembele, said to have an ankle knock, is replaced by the burly Frenchman Capoue, signed from Toulouse

Seems like Capoue has clearly had certain instructions from Sherwood, he badly fouls Silva, stamping on his foot. Mr Marriner takes no action

Pellegrini complains to the fourth official.

Now, around the fiftieth minute, comes a dramatic twist, a penalty for City and a red card for Spurs, Fernandinho driving through midfield – he plays Dzeko right through in the box – Rose comes in with a last-ditch corner -conceding tackle– Dzeko falls – City players all appeal – Mr Marriner doesn't look like he'll give it – till he looks to Mr Ledger who's raised his flag at once, well done that man again!

Spurs furious, all of them except Rose himself, strangely quiet, seems like he knows full well that, though he got the ball, he brought down Dzeko with his trailing leg

City demand Rose's dismissal, he was the last man, Navas waves an imaginary card, Silva, eyes blazing, " REF, FOR FACKIN' ELL, YEAH, THASS OFF!" Captain Kompany gives Silva the eyes, like a headmaster warning off an over-zealous prefect who's got above himself, he makes his case to Mr Marriner, explaining carefully – "he's- BROUGHT him down!"

Dawson leads the counterclaim "NO! – e's took the BALL !" then 'E'S FELL !" (pointing to Dzeko)

Mr Marriner brandishes red to a storm of boos – and Rose slinks off, head down.

Yaya prepares to take the spot kick

Dawson still arguing the toss with Mr. Marriner, gesticulating, "fuckin' bad call! YOU'VE RUINED IT, YOU 'AVE!" -an accurate assessment – from a Spurs point of view!

Mr Marriner has heard something that sounded distinctly unseemly from Walker over by the touchline, he races after him, finger wagging – Walker "I JUS' SAID 'NO', ALL AS UH SAID WAS 'NO'!" Mr Marriner has made his point, he leaves it at that

Yaya takes the spot kick – he coolly sends Lloris the wrong way and nets in the opposite corner, 0-2

a jubilant Dzeko leaps on Yaya's back and knocks him to the ground – the smaller men, Silva, Navas, Fernandinho stoop over the fallen hero patting his mighty chest

Tim Sherwood agitated, eyes wild with fury and the whole crowd turn on Mr Marriner

" Ooze the wenker, ooze the wenker, ooze the wenker in the bleck!"

Three minutes later City score a third goal, with David Silva at the heart of a fine team effort, Navas at pace on the edge of the box – he prompts the overlapping Zabaleta – who pulls the ball neatly back to Silva in the centre of the goalmouth – Silva in his pomp, a change óf feet leaves Dawson on the deck, a feint and a jump lead acceleration leaves Eriksen running the wrong way – Silva shoots hard, left footed – it strikes the post with Lloris helplessly sprawled – Jovetic's challenge, he harries the balding Rumanian Chiriches into an aimless clearance – Dzeko's straight on it, he half -volleys it high into the back of the net

Dzeko exultant – his teammates converge.

But within a few minutes, Spurs scramble a goal back, from a corner – taken by Lennon who's got nowhere all game against Clichy – Zabaleta falls, leaving a gap, a lucky bounce – and Capoue jabs a boot on it – Fernandinho on the goal-line instinctively uses a hand – but deflects it down and in, 1-3

doubtless if he'd kept it out that way, Mr Marriner would've been able to even the score, one penalty after another and a second red card but the Spurriers are cheering lustily, "cam on you whaaites!"

Just turned the hour, Pellegrini begins removing his key players with the upcoming clash against Chelsea in mind, Yaya walks off with his usual rolling gait -Adebayor, interpreting it as time -wasting, pushes Yaya – Yaya shakes him off, gives him a look of contempt, and departs
Nastasic comes on and Demichelis is sent into midfield.

Naughton, Spurs substitute, soon gets into the swing of things, tripping Navas after being nutmegged – Mr Marriner books him.

Silva – Jovetic – Clichy – an excellent long high ball into the box for Dzeko – he chests it down – but slams it high over, what would the score be by now if Dzeko's radar was functioning?
Dzeko closes his eyes in vexation at yet another error.

Silva is the master of events – he dances past Capoue– to Jovetic – then Silva darts along the touchline, expecting a return pass – which Jovetic fails to execute, it goes out of play – Silva rebukes Jovetic, eyes blazing " BETTER BALL!!" – Jovetic immediately raises his hand in humble apology.

Twenty minutes left and Pellegrini instigates a keepball session, to torture ten- man Tottenham and tire them out, Silva will orchestrate.

Adebayor still in sullen mood – he loses a tussle for the ball with Zabaleta – but Mr Marriner calls it a freekick for Spurs – Zabaleta kicks the ball away in anger – Mr Marriner books Zabaleta, that one's been in the pipeline all night.

Twelve minutes to go, 1-4, Dzeko traps a long ball – he lays it off promptly to Fernandinho – who glides between Capoue and Dawson – a good pass to Jovetic in space wide left – Jovetic cuts in and shoots – it's on target and Lloris might well've saved it – but it deflects off Chiriches' knee, leaving the keeper utterly helpless, it's in the bottom corner, just inside the far post

Jovetic's first Premiership goal, he deserves the luck after his injury tribulations – his teammates converge, chuffed for him – then he celebrates looking towards the Citizens, making a heart sign with his fingers, showbiz touch that, leave it out.

With the game well and truly won, Pellegrini takes off Silva and sends Kolarov on.

Three minutes left, close to being 1-5, a good move. Dzeko's fine pass inside a defender to Navas – Navas tears away – a low cross for Jovetic in the six yard box, he anticipates it well, – but Chiriches gets a leg on it, taking the weight off the pass– that means Jovetic arrives too soon and falls – just behind that, Kolarov pounces on the loose ball – and slams it goalwards – a good save by Lloris with his boot.

One minute left and it IS 1-5, a City corner – Dzeko in the middle of the box, he shoots, careful to keep it low this time – but it rebounds off Bentaleb – Kompany jabs in the goal from close range – he's delighted and a bit amused- a bellringing celebration- " one five, ONE FIVE AGAIN!"- same score here as it was the year City won the title, an omen maybe.

White Hart Lane was and would remain the zenith of Pellegrini's attacking football in 2013-14, both beautiful to watch and devastatingly effective. It was grounded in skilful ball retention, in transitioning from defence to attack with speed and accuracy and in intelligent interpassing. Spurs' hectic, boisterous play could not match it. Sherwood's team rarely mounted significant moves and Hart was little more than a spectator whilst Hugo Lloris needed to bring off an incredible save to deny Aguero's powerful point blank header.

All City defenders played with poise. Demichelis seemed far more at ease and Clichy looked back to his best. In midfield Fernandinho worked with tireless accuracy and Navas showed flashes of high skill. The team was not dependent on fantastic individual bursts by Yaya – he was, on this occasion, no more than adequate.

David Silva was an absolute master of space, generating wave after wave of attacks which opened up Tottenham time and again. Refusing to be intimidated by abrasive tackling, he showed a streetwise appreciation of the match situation. He was the first to demand Rose's dismissal. With Spurs only one goal down despite City's first half dominance, Kun off the field, the Beast not there and Dzeko's radar malfunctioning, he realised he needed to be right at the centre of events and it was he who set up the crucial third goal, the one which broke Spurs' hearts. Finally, he orchestrated Pellegrini's instructions for keepball in order to tire Tottenham out and thus add two more goals to the tally.

Sergio Aguero's performance was also world-class till injury forced him out. He was only narrowly foiled of a hat-trick. He showed all the attributes of a top striker: anticipation, speed, strength on the ball, the ability to strike both low with little backlift and delicately with real finesse and to deliver bold headers which were remarkably powerful for a small man.

Jovetic did his best to make up for Aguero's absence and, though Dzeko was off target with the shooting, he did a lot of very good work just the same.

Aguero's goal encapsulated all that was best about City, Pellegrini style, not just the striker's finish but the way in which no less than nine members of the team had contributed to the passing sequence which set it up.

By now the fans 'Sheikh Mansour'song had really caught on. It praises Manuel Pellegrini in a surreal lyric about the Sheikh going to Spain in a Lamborghini. By reference to the luxury sports car, a vehicle which combines immense power with elegant appearance, this struck exactly the right note. The football City played as White Hart Lane was absolute Lamborghini style!

7. Deeper Than the Studmarks on the Wall

Hull City 0   Manchester City 2

The KC Stadium March 15 2014

To the KC Stadium in Kingston-upon-Hull, Saturday lunchtime, returning to the Premiership after three weeks away in the Cup competitions. Nine points behind Chelsea with three matches in hand, and needing to make a statement of intent.

With Aguero out injured and Negredo sadly off form, Pellegrini opts for Dzeko as the sole striker, returning Garcia to midfield. Demichelis, suspended for the game at the Camp Nou, returns.

Hull City have reached the semi-final of the FA Cup but are languishing in the lower reaches of the Premiership. Since the early season visit to the Etihad, they've added two new strikers in the January transfer window, the Irishman Shane Long, ex- West Bromwich Albion, and the Croatian Jelavic who failed at Everton

First minute, Kompany, who stated he "had nothing left in the tank" after the match in Barcelona, looks stressed as he brings down Long on the left
Huddleston, shorn of his hirsute locks, whips a dangerous free-kick across the goalmouth but both Long and Jelavic have wandered offside. Their boss, Steve Bruce, portly and rubicund, bawls them out.

Citizens in good voice with Blue Moon, the Lamborghini Song and the Pablo Zabaleta Song. Hull supporters respond with generic chanting.

Yaya starting further forward than usual, looking to complement Dzeko.

Dangerous Hull action, Figueroa whacks a ball down the left touchline – it goes past Kompany who's moved over – Jelavic gets on it and goes to the byline – he gets past Demichelis and puts the ball into the goalmouth – but Clichy boots it clear.

Nine minutes, potential disaster for City as Vincent Kompany is sent off by Lee Mason, Kompany picks up a back pass from Garcia and dawdles on the ball, looking to pass it back to Joe Hart – Jelavic rushes over and challenges – as they tussle, Jelavic levers Kompany down – but Mr Mason doesn't blow for a foul – Kompany gets up slowly – seeing Jelavic getting past him, he pulls his shirt and wrestles him to the ground – Mr Mason purses his lips as he jogs straight over and, before the Hull players even appeal, he reaches into his top pocket and brandishes a red card, glaring at Kompany and pointing the way for him to depart a vast roar from the Tigers' supporters - "YES!"

Kompany gets up, enraged and incredulous, his hands covering his face – "NO!" – He advances on Mr Mason as Joe Hart and Yaya converge plus Jelavic and Rosenior- " ref, REF! -it was HIM who fouled ME– you missed a foul! – There was a foul, a FOUL!!" Kompany points to his eyes and then turns into Buster Bloodvessel mode, Joe Hart counsels restraint, "LET IT GO" – Kompany ignores him, Yaya points to the precise spot where Jelavic committed the initial offence – but Mr Mason, baldheaded and bull-headed, his arm still raised in the gesture of dismissal, remains unmoved

Kompany hands his armband to Yaya and, with a face like thunder, walks off, as he leaves the field, Kolarov runs from the subs' bench to make a gesture of consolation – but Kompany walks on before making a closed thumb gesture, spied by the BT cameras hounding him even as he reaches the tunnel, where, still indignant, he kicks a wall, leaving stud marks on the masonry.

Hull's freekick, delayed by a minute and a half, is an anti -climactic thump into the City wall.

Pellegrini responds, not doing the obvious thing- sending on Joleon Lescott and sacrificing a attacker. Instead he pushes Garcia back into central defence, alongside Demichelis.

A mere four minutes later, City seize the lead with a wonder goal from David Silva, a reverse pass from Yaya – Silva's quick trap and shift to his left – he looks up and picks his spot – and, from all of 25 yards, veering his body away from the line of strike, he sends the ball hurtling goalwards, seeming to obey his orders as if on a piece of elastic tied to his boot, it swings in from wide of the post half a yard just inside the upright, Scottish international keeper Allan McGregor is helpless as it accelerates into the back of the net
Silva wags a finger as he runs round in celebration, his teammates acclaim him shoulder to shoulder, their joy mixed with relief, VAMOS!
it's only Silva's fifth goal of the season, he'd truly be on the Messi level if only his marksmanship equalled his generalship!

On the touchline, Manuel Pellegrini's anxious to curb the celebrations, fearing the transition from despair to elation might result in a loss of concentration.

No such problem for the Citizens, an ultra-loud version of ' Hey Jude'.

Hull appear nonplussed by the turn of events and, minute by minute, City, boosted by their one goal cushion, nullify their opponents' one-man advantage by superior ball retention and far more intelligent movement, opting for short passes to preserve energy.

It takes half a dozen minutes before Hull muster a response, a half chance for Jelavic as the Egyptian winger Elmohamady loops a cross for him yet, with Garcia and Zabaleta in close attendance, he can't get on the end of it.

Briefly Hull succeed in asserting their numerical advantage – often dependent on crosses, they vary the action with a real move, Figueroa – Long – back to the Irishman Meyler – forward for Long again –his low cross seeks Jelavic – yet Demichelis gets there first with a last-ditch tackle – and Hart picks up.

Yaya has moved further back, looking to compensate for Kompany's enforced departure.

Demichelis prominent again, winning a fierce tackle and promptly finding Silva, lying deep.

City's defence looking good, Demichelis staying very tight on Long, Clichy weighing in with a good tackle, Gael greatly improved since his early season gaffes, looks like he's adjusted to the high line.

Demichelis with a fierce tackle on Long, the Irishman's laughing in embarrassment at his own discomfiture.

City with ten men behind the ball, Dzeko falling back in midfield, Joe Hart with very little to do.

Suddenly Yaya frees Silva in space with the thinnest of flicks – Silva moves into the D, the defenders back away – he lays it off wide to the overlapping Zabaleta – a cross aimed for Dzeko – but it's wide.

Just round the half-hour, and only the narrowest of margins foils City of a second goal, at the climax of a ten man, slow passing move, Zabaleta, the ball bouncing nicely up for him – he launches a fulminating shot, an inswinging volley from 20 yards which shocks McGregor, reacting late – the ball crashes down off the underside of the bar, lands on the goal-line, bounces up – and is headed behind for a corner by Curtis Davies last season, City would doubtless have appealed for a goal and far better refs than Mr Mason might well've been in two minds – but, now, with Goal Decision System, BT can quickly demonstrate the same pictures Mr Mason would've seen on his wristwatch, most but not all of the ball had actually crossed the line

Zabaleta flabbergasted, "JESU-MARIA!"

Further close passing, almost Barcelona style, Demichelis and Garcia joining in as to the manner born.

Ten minutes before half-time and there should be a second sending-off, this time for a Hull City player, an exasperated Elmohamady challenges Silva late – and viciously kicks his shin as he was raising a leg to trap the ball – Silva's in pain on the ground but, happily, he's all right – Mr Mason produces yellow, it should be straight red for a totally unprovoked foul and a potential leg breaker.

A couple of minutes later in this incident -packed game, Hull get the ball in the net but it's already been flagged offside with three Tigers in an offside position, (including Meyler before he nipped back onside) -it was a simple cement -mixer cross yet he fired a fierce angled cross shot right through Joe Hart, it would've been a fine strike had it been legitimate,

the linesman at least is doing his job- which involves repeated flag raising as Demichelis perfectly marshals the back four into an unbreacheable offside trap into which yellow and back shirts continually run, Shane Long in particular is the culprit.

The free kicks which Hull are constantly conceding through being caught offside are nicely taking up the time, Blue Moon!

Demichelis and Garcia look assured as they win the long, high balls which are coming their way.

suddenly Huddlestone, hitherto lethargic, lob-volleys a ball down the City middle – Demichelis might be caught on the hop but he's not caught out and he heads it powerfully away, just as well, because Long, onside for once, was behind him with a clear run on goal.

Following suit, Livermore, till now almost as ineffective as Huddlestone, springs to life with a well struck daisycutter – Joe Hart has to go full length to cover it, he exhales in relief as he sees it fly past the post.

Just before half-time, Martin Demichelis, full of confidence, starts a move –   Silva, then Merlin's back flick – but no other City player picks it up.

Second half and Steve Bruce has taken off Figueroa and sent on Sone Aluko.

Only three minutes in and already Shane Long has run offside yet again while muffing a header – Bruce remonstrates with him, doubtless he spent half time telling him how to measure his runs.

The City offside trap, marshalled by Demichelis, catches four yellow and black shirts simultaneously offside !

Zabaleta mistimes a tackle on Meiler – he's booked – he acknowledges a fair cop.

Long's game intelligence is surely very low, Jelavic unmarked, calls for the ball down the middle – and Long promptly passes to Elmohamady out on the wing instead – the Egyptian shoots wide – Jelavic furious, gesturing wildly at Long.

After nearly an hour Bruce opts for invention, taking off Meiler and replacing him with George Boyd, Boyd the lanky, skinny, bandanna -wearing wildcard, brought up in the Medway towns, Scottish qualification via the grandparent rule.

The Tigers are increasing the pressure but continuing to rely on high crosses, Huddlestone, Livermore and now Aluko seem unable to affect the outcome but, fom one cross, Dzeko does vital work, diverting a freekick behind just as Chester was about to get in a close range header.

Free kick City after Livermore's sly foul on Silva – Silva grounded but laughing contemptuously, they've been fouling him like this ever since he was a little lad in the alleys of the Canary Islands and the only way the older boys could get the ball off him was to kick him
Nasri takes the freekick – Garcia – he hooks it back to Demichelis – who cracks the ball over.

Dzeko called for a slight aerial touch on Curtis Davies, much milder than Jelavic's foul on Kompany which Mr Mason chose to overlook.

Boyd shows his skill beating Zabaleta with ease on the touchline – Garcia does well to force the ball out for a corner – nothing from it, Hart grinning at the Hull players, evidently not impressed with their challenges.

suddenly there's yet another major incident, Boyd spots an opportunity – and he races diagonally beyond Yaya to claim a pass from Rosenior – he's in on goal – Joe Hart comes out and spreads his frame – Boyd takes the ball deftly round him – but opts for a dying swan dive – the ball runs out of play – on the turf, with Zabaleta standing over him rebuking him, Boyd claims a penalty, so does Rosenior – Mr Mason looks hard but ignores the claim – Joe Hart, incensed that Boyd ever thought he'd get away with it, gets up and advances menacingly on the diver, towering over him, features contorted with rage – "you FUCKIN'

WANKER! – SHIT'OUSE –" Boyd "shi'aows yerself !" Hart then goes head to head with Boyd, barely restraining himself from a headbutt

Boyd backs off, looks scared, does he spit at Hart?

By this time Martin Demichelis has acted far more promptly than the lurking Mr Mason, fearing that his young teammate may be sent off, he calmly stands between him and Boyd, gently restraining the Hull player – Mr Mason produces yellow against Joe Hart for threatening conduct but he takes no action against Boyd for simulation. Demichelis ever the peacemaker, streetwise but safe.

Boyd falls in the penalty area and claims Fernandinho has pushed him off the ball in an aerial challenge – yet the contact was too slight to bring him down – Boyd appeals to Mr Mason but he disregards him – with the Citizens loudly booing Boyd.

City almost score, Silva very clever footwork – his low cross is deflected off a defender perfectly into the path of Fernandinho who's read it in a flash – he's right through with only McGregor to beat – but he scuffs his shot.

on the touchline, Pellegrini raises his arms in despair and Rubin, on the bench, looks very agitated

Citizens showing loyalty in song "OH, OH, FER-NAN –DEEN - EE-OH!"

City slowly running the clock down with keepball.

Hull gormlessly trying crosses to the very end, Elmohamadiy sends one over for Jelavic – but he puts it wide.

A fine City counter, one of the few they've tried in the circumstances, almost leads to a goal – Clichy adroitly beats Jelavic- then Elmohamady – Silva – Clichy – Clichy delivers a fine long pass to Dzeko– he's one-on-one with the keeper but all of 30 yards out – he looks to chip MacGregor but the Scottish keeper spreads himself in front of Dzeko's feet and smothers the attempt.

Right at the end of normal time, City finally score a second, Silva at the heart of it – he chest-traps a high ball, he puts Davies on his back with a feint – and moves off – Dzeko strides ahead, looking back and calling for the ball – and Silva sends a perfect 15 yard pass rolling to a stop at his feet- Dzeko takes it instinctively first time and slots it, 0-2, game over

Dzeko's first strike in eight games, he grits his teeth as his team-mates converge- " YES!"

Pellegrini almost jubilant on the touchline, hugged by a frantic Kiddo" YE-YE-YE-YE-YEAAAAAH!"

Blue Moon, this game's in the bag

This was one of the crucial matches of the season. Inside ten minutes City were down to ten men and without their charismatic skipper. All the odds were against them even gaining a draw. Yet Martin Demichelis rose to the occasion in splendid style, marshalling the defence in the captain's absence, looking twice the player.

Given that City were rejoining the Premiership title race at a critical juncture, just after having been eliminated from two other competitions, this was a really significant victory, built on a foundation of solid defence, and resolute team spirit yet illuminated by David Silva's masterly skill.

BT cameras and commentary had begun inauspiciously with Manuel Pellegrini having to brush aside foolish questions in the pre-match interview. Then there was the way in which Vincent Kompany was hounded almost to the dressing room after his controversial sending-off, not to mention endless replays of the incident between Joe Hart and George Boyd - concentrating on whether or not the Hull forward had spat at the City keeper- which plumbed the depths of cheap sensationalism.

At the end of the day, however, City's triumph against the odds left an indelible impression – far deeper than Vincent Kompany's stud-marks on the wall of the KC Stadium.

8. The Door's Open, Let's March Right Through !

Crystal Palace 0   City 2

Selhurst Park

April 27 2014

Citizens buoyed by the news from Anfield (with goals shown on the big screen), Liverpool beaten 0-2 by Chelsea thus leaving the destination of the title back in City's hands.

City without Silva, he has a knock, Garcia preferred in midfield to the slightly below form Fernandinho, Milner preferred to Navas and Yaya returning.

Palace and Pulis, Tony Pulis widely saluted for his work in bailing out Palace from relegation danger and lifting them to mid-table, five wins on the trot including away to Everton.

Amicable greetings between Pulis and Pellegrini – who's recently praised him – but signs of unpleasantness from the Selhurst Park crowd, Ultra flags and a banner with 'you have the money, we have the soul' emblazoned, signs of showbiz too with American-style cheerleaders
Citizens respond with the Zabaleta song.

Yaya launches City's first attack, chipping the ball into the goal-mouth for a lively looking Aguero to chase, he tries to shoot while on the turn but can't quite connect.

Four minutes and City score, an expertly created, ruthlessly fin-ished goal, Yaya and Aguero shuttle the ball between them – then Yaya's delicate, precise ball into the box – Dzeko was calling for it and he moves off smart between the centre backs, the Scouser Dann and the masked man, Mariappa – he rises high and sideways on – he powerfully heads the ball down into the back of the neck from eight yards

Manuel Pellegrini smiles and shakes his fists, Dzeko races over to the Citizens, inciting their support and shouting "COME ON!"

EDDIN ZHEKKO-OH OH EDDIN ZHEKKO-OH OH

The Irishman, Delaney, his slow backpass is seized on by Aguero, moving at high speed – yet Speroni, the sad- looking, bearded Argentinian keeper, comes out promptly and blocks for a corner.

City imposing control, excellent move, Milner on the right, pulls the ball back – it's cleared – but only to Yaya – he chips the ball through for Zabaleta who's making a fine run – Zaba looking to head it on goal but muffs the chance sideways – and covers his face.

Palace unable to fathom City high line/offside, well marshalled by Demichelis, Jerome lucky not to be booked by Howard Webb for barging Demichelis.

Another good City move, Zabaleta (already booked by Howard Webb) – Aguero, his skill on the ball – then he passes to Yaya – who shoots – Delaney's in the way of it, his hands across his chest and Mr. Webb turns down Yaya's appeal for hands.

Two minutes before half-time and Yaya scores a magnificent goal, climaxing a 50 yard run from deep within his own half, Zabaleta heads clear – Yaya on the ball, outmuscles the Frenchman Bolassie who loses his balance – Yaya promptly lays it off ten yards to Dzeko – and bursts past a stupefied Ledley to take the return – he outruns Ward – he lays it off ten yards again, this time to Nasri – then he outsprints Delaney to take the return from Nasri – at the edge of the box, Delaney comes back at him desperately trying to get in a tackle yet losing his balance in the process – the ball bobbles up off the Irishman's leg – yet Yaya gets it immediately under control – he weaves inside past Dann – and curls a beautiful shot between Mariappa and Dann, leaving Speroni helpless, it finishes high in the far corner of the net.

Yaya, ably assisted by Dzeko and Nasri has defeated no less than seven Palace players, he's shown the speed and stride of a fine quarter-miler, the balance of a bend runner, great finesse in dribbling and great precision and despatch with the shot he runs towards the delighted Citizens, executes a clumsy knee slide, rises, points to his chest and, with an edge of anger, snarls and then flings an arm back over his shoulder his teammates converge, they stand around him, touching his head, crowning his football genius -Manuel Pellegrini utterly delighted, his usually impassive visage wreathed in smiles "YE-E-E-ES! COME ON!"

Immediately afterwards Pellegrini chides his men when, seeming to relax after Yaya's masterstroke, they allow a ball to fly across the box only just out of reach of Jerome, it was flagged offside, even so Pellegrini was not happy, understandably so.

Second-half and Palace briefly enjoy some possession with heavy hitter Puncheon swiping a drive goalwards, it may have been going wide yet Joe Hart gets down to it and palms it round for a corner – from which he powerfully punches so hard the ball goes upfield into touch – Palace try a long throw in but Yaya blocks the run of the attacker.

Palace come into the game for a while, painstakingly constructing some neat moves with City playing within themselves.

Just before the hour another fantastic Yaya burst, some 40 yards, this time down the right touchline but this time foiled by Palace, Yaya pounces on a loose clearance, doesn't control the ball first time yet, as Ledley hesitates, Yaya accelerates past him, instantly passing forward to Dzeko – Dzeko aims his return into Yaya's stride path but well ahead of him – and Yaya sprints down the touchline to leave Delaney and Ward in his wake, one on the line, the other five yards inside, – he lengthens his stride like a quarter-miler – leaves Delaney adrift as he gets on the ball and takes it to the byline – even as Ward slides into a tackle, Yaya glides the ball back past him, looking for Aguero – yet Dann gets there first with Yaya looking to rest after another phenomenal burst and squatting on the byline, breathing heavily in front of snickering Palace supporters, " E'S KNECKERED, look ah 'im, fackin' kneckered!" - the wily Dann senses the chance of a break, he passes to Chamakh, the ex-Arsenal Moroccan, lying deep – Chamakh's scarcely been in the game till now – yet he skips out of Dzeko's tackle – runs ahead, far too fast for Garcia – catches Zabaleta too far up field and passes beyond him, looking for Jerome down the flank– Kompany half slips and lets Jerome through, the Selhurst Park crowd excited for the first time in the match – yet Kompany recovers brilliantly and closes Jerome down at speed before he has a chance to pass back to Puncheon who was yelling for the ball, this was a vital block for City, striving to maintain their superior goal difference. "Here's to you, VINCENT KOMPANY, CITY LOVESYA more than you will know! "

Yaya – Nasri – Aguero – Kolarov, a good move – Garcia – Yaya, he's at walking pace this time, he sidles past Mariappa – he curls a shot from 20 yards but it's over the bar – suddenly he does look very tired and, preserved for the clashes which lie ahead, he's taken off in favour of Fernandinho.

Milner plays Aguero in – as he does so, he's flattened by Ward off the ball – Aguero shimmies then cracks the ball goalwards with the outside of his foot – yet straight at Speroni who clutches the ball to his midriff and Mr Webb books Ward.

Ten to go, Pellegrini takes Aguero off, keeping him for future battles.and sends Jovetic on.

At the end of normal time, City might've added a third goal, admittedly from a mishit cross from Fernandinho which catches Speroni out with a ball which lands on the roof of the net.

Final whistle, amiable handshake between Pulis and Pellegrini – Pulis, gone are the days when he used to whine about City, crafty Pelle, his praise has taken the wind out of the Welshman's sails.The team walk over and applaud the travelling Citizens whose support's been loud and long.

This was an absolutely vital victory for City. With Lamborghini football temporarily shelved, due not of course to ideology but to the succession of injuries – Aguero, Negredo, Silva, this was almost a classic case of the 'grinding out a result ' beloved by the pundits.

But such a verdict would reckon without Yaya's massive contribution. His fantastic bursts evidenced athletic gifts reminiscent of Usain Bolt over 200 metres and Michael Johnson over 400. The truly astonishing thing was the way he blended his lung -bursting running with astute and delicate passes and imperious shooting. Even before that, it was his delicate chip which set up Dzeko for the first goal.

Edin Dzeko himself continued to do vital work, not only with his headed goal but with the short passes where he was Yaya's main adjutant during the Ivorian's long runs.

Behind Yaya and Dzeko was a defence which stayed firm and closed the door on Palace's strong -running attackers. Martin Demichelis had another excellent game. His calm, astute marshalling of defence was proving a really significant factor in City's challenge for the title. What's more, he'd now established a good understanding with Vincent Kompany with both centre backs nicely complementing each other's work. As for Kompany himself, his superb recovery and block when Palace were counter-attacking at high speed and threatening a goal was crucial in maintaining City's goal difference.

Liverpool's slip-up against Chelsea immediately before this game had opened a door which many Citizens had feared was closed after the loss at Anfield. Without doubt City had seen their chance for redemption and had boldly taken it. Those loyal Citizens who'd made the trip to South London recalled the run-in to the 2012 title, notably the game in Newcastle in which Yaya also made a tremendous contribution. Both team and supporters departed Selhurst Park in high spirits.

Graham Gordon

9. Junking the Jinx

Everton 2   City 3

Goodison Park

May 3 2014

Goodison Park on the last but one weekend of the season. Evertonians, usually found aggressively supporting their team, look strangely apathetic.The weather's overcast, the atmosphere's as downbeat as the gloomy old stadium itself.

For the Sky Blues themselves, everything's clear cut but far from easy. Liverpool's stumble against Chelsea and City's win at Selhurst Park means they can clinch the title if they win all their remaining games. But their record at Goodison is one of almost unbroken failure. It's been the graveyard of their hopes over the years.

Everton, for their part, have lost ground in the struggle with Arsenal for Champions League qualification but they're not yet out of the picture. For most of their supporters, however, the prospect of Liverpool winning the title is an unpleasant one -many of them openly tell the Citizens "we hope yous do us today to STOP THEM !". The atmosphere inside the stadium, except for the Citizens in the Bullens pocket, is subdued with many Toffees studying their mobiles even at kick-off. The ad boards include one for the movie ' Bad Neighbours' which is what Liverpudlians, watching on TV and for once hoping for an Everton victory, will fear is an omen.

Everton cannot play Gareth Barry, on loan from City, and former Sky Blue Sylvain Distin, out with an injury lately, is only on the bench.

But skipper Jagielka has recovered and will take his place alongside the Paraguayan, Alcaraz and youngster John Stones in a three centre back formation similar to the one with which boss Roberto Martinez thwarted Mancini's City in last year's Cup Final.

City, today in white shirts with blue stripes, continue with Garcia rather than Fernandinho in midfield. Pellegrini has stated that Silva's ankle doesn't permit him to play matches every three days- so he' s on the bench.

A couple of minutes gone and whatever anyone may have thought, Everton are going for it-their attitude's positive unlike their fans.

Ross Barkley, Everton's prodigious twenty-year-old, looks to start an attack but Kompany intercepts.

Stones – Osman – Lukaku– Baines – a good Everton move but Baines' cutback to Naismith is behind him and the blond, close-cropped Scot can only dig out a shot and put it wide.

Martinez is on the touchline, scowling and bellowing orders, what- ever the fans think, he'll make sure City have to sweat for victory today. Meanwhile, Citizens sing a derisive song about Steve Gerrard inviting amused Evertonians to join in.

Osman's chip looking for Lukaku, now shorn of his flowing locks, he proved a handful at the Etihad in October but the City skipper reads it and heads it away.

Yaya and Nasri loitering and swapping passes – Nasri chip, Jagielka has to put it behind for a corner, Nasri takes it –Garcia gets up well but heads it straight into Howard's arms – Jagielka rallies the troops.

Nasri – Aguero – he accelerates laterally away from Stones – Stones recovers and tackles – but Aguero escapes and passes inside the next man to Zabaleta, a good chance but Zaba balloons it high and wide, he covers his face.

Now Naismith gives a good pass to Barkley – Barkley turns Zabaleta in an instant – crowd gasps there – but Zabaleta gets back at him, shields the ball and fends off Barkley – who appeals for a foul but Lee Probert simply jogs away.

Citizens strike up the Zabaleta song.

Then, on ten minutes, a bolt from the blue, a stunning Ross Barkley goal, which some will soon compare with the teenaged Wayne Rooney's famous effort against Arsenal ten years ago, this one's relished by the neutrals and it's bound to delight the Red Scousers watching on Sky!

It started with Baines on the touchline – inside to Naismith – his instant layoff no apparent danger, Barkley's 20 yards out, the goal-mouth's packed – but Barkley strikes it first time, blowing out his cheeks with effort, he delivers the ball high, looping, accelerating fast, swirling then dipping, flying feet over Hart's leap – no goalkeeper could stop this one as it crashes low into the back of the far corner. That's roused the Evertonians from their apathy," WHARRABOUT THA, PHUKKHIN 'ELL, EH!!! EZEGRREATIM, INNIE !!! "

Demichelis can't believe his eyes, his hands raised in horror, yet Kompany impassively blows his nose then claps his hands for a positive reaction,

Barkley's celebration is modest, just a boyish jump in front of the pumped-up Park End but Martinez clenches his fists and, high in the directors' box, Bill Kenwright savours the strike, open –mouthed, if we have to sell him to United, that's another ten million on the fee! – no doubt about it, the Wavertree lad has scored a goal worthy of Yaya Toure!

Citizens responding in song, "we're Manchester City, WE'LL FIGHT TO THE END!"

Naismith finds Barkley, he beats the first man and jumps past Zabaleta, full of menace, yet Kompany, who seems to be over his knee injury, calmly intercepts.

City passing sequence, Dzeko – Clichy – Nasri – Yaya, instant control and he shrugs off Osman – Osman comes back at him with a tackle – Yaya unleashes a curler, right-footed, it flies just over, Yaya "ferqeet, ferq!"

Everton mount a lengthy sequence, sitting on the lead, defying City to get the ball off them, thirty passes – and City can do nothing – some Toffees hurray each pass, most silently taking it in, worried looks on the City bench, Kiddo glum, arms folded, still he's seen it all before, it'll improve.

Ruben seems to have aged years, wrapped in an overcoat, wearing a black scarf

Manuel Pellegrini, anxious looking, he rises and moves to the touchline, shouting " COME ON!", City must take a risk.

Twenty and Barkley, buoyed up by his wonder strike, he bursts away in midfield, he beats Garcia all ends up – he sidesteps Demichelis – he drives into the box, full of menace – yet Kompany gets in a perfect tackle, just lands his heel on the ball – and, Clichy just gets a toe on it as Barkley loses his balance – City force the ball away, vital City defensive work this, Barkley's the only one in blue to appeal for a penalty – Mr Probert takes no interest and runs off.

Twenty-two minutes and suddenly City are level, Nasri good pass to Yaya – Yaya jumps out of Osman's tackle – he passes inside Alcaraz to Aguero, wide right – the Paraguayan tries to tackle him out but can't – Aguero scuttles in on goal and with little backlift, as usual, he lunges into the ball low and hammers his bullet shot inside Howard's near post. ARRIBA!

his strike reminds him of his title-clincher against QPR but he doesn't want Mr Probert to book him so he contents himself with raising his shirt a couple of inches delight on the City bench, Pellegrini, arms pumping – Kidd jumps up shouting "Yeah!", 1-1.

but there's a bitter taste in the cup of celebration, like vinegar in the wine, even as Everton prepare to kick off again, Aguero alerts the bench and points to his groin, Kun is clearly hors de combat – Pellegrini gestures to him to go down – he does so, in the centre circle, this irritates the Evertonians and Mr Probert stops play, the City physio's on, so is Ruben, talking in Spanish to Kun, treatment for a couple of minutes.

Aguero has to go off, he trudges away down the tunnel, Fernandinho will replace him, neither of the attacking substitutes, Negredo and Jovetic will be entrusted with this job, Pellegrini signals to Yaya, you go up just back of Dzeko, Garcia and Fernandinho will hold the midfield

On the half-hour mark, City create danger through Yaya, the passing picks up speed, Yaya – Zabaleta – Milner – through to Yaya – he drives to the byline – Barkley, defending now, tries to halt him but Yaya's strength and shimmy's too strong – Yaya steers a low cross through the six yard box – Stones unwisely flicks a boot at it, lucky not to connect or it would've been an own goal – and Jagielka gets ahead of Dzeko – and clears.

Something of a lull, both City wingers are watching the Everton fullbacks, Milner, working hard as always, is coping well with Baines – Nasri is putting in an unusually hard stint and nullifying Coleman

City's main problem is in the heart of midfield where Garcia's failing to deal with Barkley, it's no easy task, of course.

Nasri tries a shot from the edge of the box – it flies over, he grimaces – " CA' LORS, CA-NON !" – next Manuel Pellegrini's calling instructions on the sidelines.

Mr Probert annoying both teams, Osman accosts him insisting Fernandinho should be booked for fouling him – Dzeko about the award of a goal kick instead of a corner, Mr Probert, eyes closed, "go away".

now he does take action, he books Garcia for shorts -pulling on Lukaku, Garcia's badly exposed for pace at times, Kompany complains to Mr Probert about the booking, futile, the black-haired Wiltshire whistler's rowed with Wenger, Fat Sam and even SAF, he'll pay it no heed.

Naismith, as dangerous as anyone in blue except Barkley – he gets past Garcia who crazily raises his hands but thinks better of it – Naismith shoots from 30 yards, well wide.

Citizens uptight, a draw's no good then, at a crucial time, two minutes before half-time, City take the lead with a great Dzeko header, excellent teamwork in the buildup, 1-2

Kompany's long forward pass to Fernandinho – Fernandinho, he gets past his man with a swift turn – and plays Dzeko in – Dzeko moves to the byline, he tries to steer the ball across the six yard box but Howard, diving, kicks it clear-

Milner races after the loose ball – Baines slow to contest – Dzeko drifts back onside, almost casually, disarmingly – yet now he calls for the ball – and Milner delivers a fine, even sumptuous, slow dropping cross – and Dzeko, from over ten yards out, he's got clear of Jagielka and Stones – he soars to meet it and headbutts it with immense force, thumping it first bounce on the goal-line with Howard well beaten just inside the post

Dzeko races to the wildly celebrating Citizens, teeth bared, veins bulging in his neck,"YES!" he names himself "YES, DZEKO YES!" –

His teammates converge shouting "GREAT GOAL !" – "Yeah!" "Hey hey hey !!!"

And on the very turf where Dixie Dean, the greatest of Everton legends, once reigned supreme, Dean, they're opening a Wall of Fame tribute to him in two days time and right here the Bosnian Diamond's headed a stupendous goal worthy of the black-haired Birkenhead boy, scowling under his centre parting, the one who scored sixty in a season all those years ago!

second half, a breathtaking opening, only a superb Joe Hart save stops an Everton equaliser – then Dzeko puts City further ahead

Martinez redeploys, he shifts Stones to right back-City attacking, Fernandinho a backheel pass to Milner – but his shot's weak – it's cleared and the break is on, instigated by Barkley from the edge of the Everton box – he races 40 yards right through the middle of the park with Toffees roars of "GO ON, LA!" ringing out – Garcia's too slow to hold him and can't risk tripping him – Barkley, he bisects Kompany and Zabaleta to play Naismith through – Zabaleta can't catch the Scotsman – he's one on one with Hart – he hits his shot low down and fast to the keeper's left – but Hart dives full-length and just gets the tips of his left glove on it, diverting it for a corner

Martinez arm raised ready to salute the goal but has to choke his celebration, the corner's cleared.

And straight afterwards Everton are caught out as a consequence of Martinez' tactical change, Stones drifts back into the centre, force of habit-Nasri darts into the empty space and calls for the ball – Fernandinho obliges – Stones belatedly goes back – but Nasri's ball skill's too much for him, Nasri swerves away and places the ball across the six yard box – Dzeko, who called for it, connects and it goes in – simple goal really,

Everton caught with their pants down, Stones, the big Barnsley boy, still got a lot to learn but he knows he's goofed –"AW NOR, AW SHIT!"

Eddin Dzeko-oh

Pellegrini raises his arms – Kiddo leaps up "YEAH!"

Citizens "we shall not be moved!" 1-3.

good Everton move, Baines – Barkley Lukaku – Baines – Lukaku – Zabaleta nips it in the bud with a fine tackle.

Slight Kompany error but Garcia's dropped back to deal with it.

Everton's charge subsiding, Martinez clapping his hands, urging them forward

Then a long stalemate s ended on sixty-four minutes by an Everton goal which may well've been offside.

Baines, loosely marked by Zabaleta, delivers a sumptuous cross – Osman can't quite get on it –or has he? Whatever, Lukaku, unmarked, makes a diving header which strikes the inside of the near post with Hart not moving – it creeps over the line

City players surround Mr Probert protesting the goal on the grounds of offside, Demichelis wagging a finger, he's not having his marshalling of the line challenged like this, Kompany glowering, gesticulating, indicating comparative positions, Nasri speaks slowly and deliberately as if to someone in a foreign language "OS-MAN was OFF-SIDE !" but Mr Probert will have none of it, insisting that Osman didn't touch the ball, -2-3.

Meanwhile Yaya has gone off for reasons unclear and Kolarov is on-Everton take off Jagielka and bring on Gerard Delofeu, the Barcelona loanee.

Osman held back by Fernandinho – but he gets away – and goes past Kompany but Zabaleta stops him with a fine tackle, Osman's narked by Fernandinho's challenge, screening the ball – to Mr Probert "that was a foul!" But Mr. Probert disagrees.

City reassert themselves with a good move, Milner – Nasri – Zabaleta, he takes the ball in his stride and shoots – yet Howard just gets his studs on it – City win the ball back – they interpass– Kolarov, he shoots but it's immediately deflected for a corner, from the corner, Kompany heads the ball but it's blocked -then Demichelis shoots and that's blocked too

Zabaleta yelling "come on!"

Nasri, grimacing as if he's had a knock, comes off, David Silva finally comes on

Fernandinho screens the ball from Naismith – Naismith claims to Mr Probert that Fernandinho barged him and he actually mimics the barge on Mr Probert himself, Mr Probert has a quiet word about that one.

Twelve to go and a bizarre incident, Dzeko slips, falls awkwardly and lies prone, face down, but Mr Probert doesn't stop play – then City call for a stretcher but Mr Probert won't allow one on, nor will he allow the physios – Kompany intervenes, firmly requesting a stretcher, Mr Probert – "I ASKED HIM if he needed one but but he didn't want one"

five minutes' hiatus, boos from the crowd, the players on both sides nonplussed, finally Mr Probert relents and the stretcher comes on – Dzeko goes off on it – he's roundly booed

City have used all their substitutes now and so Dzeko will return after treatment from the physios.

With five minutes officially left (actually more due to the Dzeko delay) Everton come close to the equaliser, once again Barkley's at the back of it, a weaving run, he beats Silva – and gets past Clichy – but

Demichelis races across decisively and delivers a great sliding tackle on the byline – he can't get it behind for a corner but he forces the ball firmly away – but Delofeu, the highly skilful young Catalan, sets off on a great solo run, he bustles plus Kolarov – he moves away from Silva – he swerves past Garcia who's trying to grab his shirt, thankfully he didn't succeed – Delofeu shoots on the angle from six yards out – yet Joe Hart gets his body on it and deflects it into the side netting, another fine piece of work from the City keeper, crucial really

Everton corner and there's Dzeko defending it.

Next Delofeu beats Clichy – yet Kolarov's challenge is successful.

Two minutes left, Fernandinho robs McCreadie – he moves past two men – he looks for Dzeko but overhits it – and Howard collects.

Six minutes of injury time indicated, Pellegrini orders everyone back, Martinez tries to crank up the pressure, Citizens desperate for the final whistle.

City win a corner but opt against a shot – the name of their game is keepball and they carry it out to the letter, Everton can scarcely get a touch on the ball.

Yet, with half a minute left, there's a moment of danger for City, Naismith gets the ball past Demichelis looking for Alcaraz – the ball bounces just before the byline inside the box – Hart coolly opts to let it go rather than run the risk of a collision with Alcaraz – who tumbles, no real appeals – Mr Probert correctly gives a goal kick.

Mr Probert finally blows up, huge hugs all round from the City players – Zabaleta shouting "YEAH YEAH YEAH!!!" Never mind The Beatles, what about Status Quo, the Zabman's favourite band- I like it, I like it, I like it, I like it, I la-la-la like it, I la-la-la-like it -here we go-o, ROCKIN' ALL OVER THE WORLD !!!

This was a crucial and splendid win for City. At a venue long regarded as their bogey ground, and facing a combative Everton side who, regardless of their fans' apathy, made a real fight of it. Going one down to Ross Barkley's bolt from the blue, they needed top-quality goals from Aguero and Dzeko to put themselves ahead.

Another stalwart defensive performance was key to the victory. Two men stood out - Vincent Kompany who, for the most part, contained the livewire Barkley and Joe Hart who produced two excellent saves. Hart's role was vital. This was probably his finest display in a City shirt.

City had well and truly junked the Goodison jinx and placed themselves in pole position to regain the title. Within ten days, they would do just that!

ABOUT THE AUTHOR

G raham Gordon is a sports historian. He is also the author of 'Master of the Ring' (Milo Books), the critically acclaimed bi-ography of Jem Mace, First Heavyweight Champion of the World and Father of Boxing.

Passen; —
webber
Monocouche

Chalk colour

15105117R00182

Printed in Poland
by Amazon Fulfillment
Poland Sp. z o.o., Wrocław